MELVIN HARRIS

Study Questions
for Daily Bible Readings

Part 2

Study Questions for Daily Bible Readings, Part 2
Copyright 2021 by Melvin Harris.

Published by Torch Runner Publications
An Imprint of Harris House Publishing
Harrishousepublishing.com
Colleyville, Texas, USA

Cover Design by Gentry Fisher

ISBN: 978-1-946369-06-2
Subject heading: RELIGIOUS / BIBLE STUDY

Dedication

I dedicate this book of Study Questions to my children, grandchildren, and great grandchildren. My desire is that they will come to love the Word of God as I do.

I appreciate the encouragement that I have received through the years. Our Sunday School Class (later became our Engage Group) has been a great help in birthing this collection of "Questions & Answers". They have been faithful in answering questions each week and correcting many of the mistakes that were in the original documents. Their excitement when answering these questions has certainly been a great encouragement to me. Friends and family have also encouraged me. Harris House Publishing has been awesome in getting these documents in printable form. Last but-not-least, my wife and best friend, Charlotte, has always been with me, always encouraging when I am discouraged.

Note from the Author

This book of *Study Questions for Daily Bible Readings* is meant to be used in conjunction with the *One Year® Bible*, New International Version, by Tyndale House Publishers, or oneyearbibleonline.com.

Answers can be downloaded at harrishousepublishing.com/melvin.

The purpose for these questions is to slow readers down a little and cause them to think about what they are reading. (It is easy when doing Bible reading to just read fast and, at the end of the reading, have a difficult time remembering a word that has been read.)

The idea of study questions and answers was born out of our Sunday School class using the *One Year® Bible* to read through the Bible each year. Each Sunday we would do our study on the date of that Sunday. As a teacher, I found out that the students could better contribute to class discussion if they answered some questions before getting to class. Therefore I started writing questions for the class and handed them out the previous Sunday. I would then take the written questions and, like the students, I would write the answers with pencil or pen and then go over the answers with the class on Sunday. Soon I realized that it would be good to compile the answers on the computer as well as the questions. I also thought that this could help teachers who might want to use this concept for their Sunday School lessons. The plan worked well except for leap years because Sunday came on a different date every year.

Over a period of about eight years, the "questions and answers" have been completed for the entire *One Year® Bible* NIV version. It is my desire that this tool be used to help people become more familiar and have a greater love for God's Word.

NB: I have tried to stick to questions that can be answered directly from the text of the "New International Version" and stay away from doctrinal questions so that this tool could be used by many denominations. As teachers go through this study, they can emphasize their own doctrines. Also, realizing that there were several writers of the Psalms, I have used the word "Psalmist" to include any writer of a Psalm instead of trying to determine which person wrote that particular Psalm and use the author's name in the question.

STUDY QUESTIONS FOR JULY 1

1.   II Kings 18:13-19

    a.   In what year of King Hezekiah's reign did Sennacherib king of Asssyria attack the cities of Judah?

    b.   What message did Hezekiah send to the king of Assyria?

    c.   What did the king of Assyria require of Hezekiah?

    d.   Was the king of Assyria satisfied with what Hezekiah sent? What did the Assyrian king do next?

    e.   Who did the king of Assyria say that Judah was depending on for their deliverance? What did he say about that country?

    f.   What did Eliakim and Shibna request from the field commander? Did the field commander agree?

    g.   What did the field commander say in Hebrew to the people on the wall?

    h.   Did the people on the wall answer? Why?

    i.   What did Hezekiah do when he heard the report that Eliakim and Hilkiah brought?

    j.   What did the Lord say through his prophet Isaiah?

    k.   What did Hezekiah do when he received the letter from the messengers of Sennacherib?

    l.   What message did Isaiah send to Hezekiah?

    m.   What did the Lord say concerning the king of Assyria?

    n.   What did the Lord say he would do for the city and for whose sake would he do this?

    o.   What happened that night?

    p.   What did Sennacherib do?

    q.   What happened to him one day while he was worshiping?

2.   Acts 21:1-16

      a.   What group of people did Luke, Paul and companions tear themselves away from in chapter twenty one, verse one? (See Acts chapter twenty verse seventeen)

      b.   What six locations are mentioned in their trip from Miletus to Tyre?

      c.   What were they planning to do with the ship's cargo?

      d.   What did they do when they found disciples in Tyre?

      e.   What did the disciples encourage Paul not to do?

      f.   What did they do with the disciples and their wives on the beach?

      g.   What did Agabus predict would happen to Paul?

      h.   How did Paul answer when the people pleaded with Paul not to go up to Jerusalem?

      i.   Who was Mnason?

3.   Psalms 149:1-9

      a.   We have noticed that there are a number of Psalms that start and end with the same words. What are these words that also occur in this psalm?

      b.   To whom were the people to sing?

      c.   Where were they to give God's praise?

      d.   How were they to give God's praise?

      e.   In what does the Lord take delight?

      f.   Where was the praise of God to be?

      g.   What was to be in their hands?

4.   Proverbs 18:8

      a.   What are words of gossip like?

      b.   Where do words of gossip go?

1. II Kings 20:1-22:2
   a. Who became ill to death?

   b. What did the prophet Isaiah, say to Hezekiah?

   c. How did Hezekiah respond to this news?

   d. What did Hezekiah remind God in his prayer?

   e. Did God hear his prayer? What was God going to do?

   f. What did Isaiah tell them to do with the figs?

   g. What was the sign going to be that the Lord was going to heal Hezekiah?

   h. What did Hezekiah do for the messengers that the king of Babylon sent with his letters and gifts?

   i. Why was the prophet Isaiah concerned with these actions? What did the prophet say was going to happen to everything in Hezekiah's palace?

   j. Who succeeded Hezekiah as king? How old was the new king?

   k. Did the new king follow the Lord?

   l. What did the king do to his own son?

   m. What promise did God make to Israel if they would follow everything that he commanded them?

   n. What was God going to do to Jerusalem because the people did not follow God?

   o. When Manasseh died, where did they bury him?

   p. How old was Ammon when he became king?

   q. Who succeeded Ammon as king? How old was he when he became king? Did he do the right thing?

2. Acts 21:17-36
   a. Look at Acts chapter twenty-one verse one, whom was the "we" referring?

   b. How were they received?

c.   What did Paul do when he meet with James and the elders?

d.   What did they do when they heard this?

e.   What rumor had been passed around about Paul?

f.   What did the brothers tell Paul to do? Did Paul do it?

g.   What did the Jews from the province of Asia do when they saw Paul in the temple? What did they say about Paul that was not true?

h.   How did the city react to these charges?

i.   What did the commander of the Roman troops do to restore order to the city of Jerusalem?

j.   What did the commander ask about Paul?

k.   What did the commander order his troops to do with Paul?

l.   What did the crowd keep shouting?

3.   Psalms 150:1-6
   a.   Where should God be praised?

   b.   For what should God be praised?

   c.   How should God be praised?

   d.   Who should praise the Lord?

   e.   How does this Psalm start and how does it end?

4.   Proverbs 18:9-10
   a.   Who is brother to slacker?

   b.   Where do the righteous run to be safe?

STUDY QUESTIONS FOR JULY 3

1.   II Kings 22:3-23:30

    a.   What did Josiah have his secretary do in the eighteenth year of his reign?

    b.   Who was to keep track of the money collected by the doorkeepers?

    c.   What did Hilkiah find in the temple of the Lord?

    d.   What did Shaphan do with the book that was given to him by Hilkiah?

    e.   What was the king's reaction when he heard the words of the book?

    f.   What word did the prophetess Huldah, give to the men that Josiah sent to inquire of the Lord?

    g.   What promise did God give to Josiah because he humbled himself?

    h.   What covenant did Josiah enter into with God? Did the people agree to keep the covenant as well?

    i.   What did the king order Hilkiah, the high priest to remove from the temple? What did they do with these items?

    j.   What did the king do with the quarters of the male prostitutes that were in the temple of the Lord?

    k.   Why did the king desecrate Topheth?

    l.   What did the king remove from the entrance to the temple of the Lord?

    m.   What did Josiah do with the altars the kings of Judah had erected on the roof and the altars that Manasseh had built in the two courts of the temple of God?

    n.   What order did the king give in regard to the Passover?

    o.   Did Josiah's action stop God's anger toward Judah?

2.   Acts 21:37-22:16

    a.   What was Paul's request to the commander of the soldiers?

    b.   Did the commander grant Paul's request?

    c.   What language did Paul use to speak to the people? What language had he used to speak to the commander?

d. When did the crowd become quiet?

e. Who trained Paul in the law of his fathers?

f. What had Paul done to the followers of Jesus?

g. What changed the direction of Paul's life?

h. What answer came when Paul asked, "Who are you Lord"?

i. What did Jesus answer when Paul asked, "What shall I do Lord?

j. What promise was given to Paul?

3. Psalms 1:1-6
   a. What man is blessed?

   b. In what is this man's delight?

   c. What is this man like?

   d. What are the wicked like?

   e. Will the wicked stand in the day of judgement?

   f. What does God do over the way of the righteous?

   g. What happens to the way of the wicked?

4. Proverbs 18:11-12
   a. What do the rich think about their riches?

   b. What is said about the heart before a man's downfall?

   c. What comes before honor?

STUDY QUESTIONS FOR JULY 4

1.   II Kings 23:31-25:30
      a.   How old was Jehoahaz when he became king?

      b.   How long did he reign? How was Jehoahaz related to Jeremiah?

      c.   What did Pharaoh Neco do to Jehoahaz? What did he do to Judah?

      d.   How did Jehoiakim raise money to pay Pharaoh Neco?

      e.   Why did the Lord send Babylonian, Aramean, Moabite, and Ammonite raiders against Judah?

      f.   Who were Jehoahaz, Jehoiakim, and Jehoiachin?

      g.   What did Nebuchadnezzar do with all the treasures from the temple of the Lord and the royal palace?

      h.   How many craftsmen and artisans did Nebuchadnezzar carry away from Jerusalem?

      i.   How many fighting men did he deport to Babylon?

      j.   How long did Zedekiah reign?

      k.   Did he rule righteously?

      l.   What happened to Zedekiah's army?

      m.   What happened to the temple and the royal palace at Jerusalem?

      n.   How much did the bronze from the pillar, the sea and the movable stands that Solomon had made for the temple, weigh?

      o.   How tall was the capitol on top of one of the pillars?

      p.   Where did Judah go into captivity? How long was Jehoichin in exile?

      q.   How long did Jehoichin receive a regular allowance?

2.   Acts 22:17-23:10
      a.   What happened to Paul while he was praying in the temple?

      b.   What did the Lord tell him?

c. To whom was Paul to take his message?

d. At what point did the crowd raise their voices and shout "Rid the earth of him he is not fit to live"?

e. What did Paul ask the centurion?

f. How did Paul become a roman citizen?

g. What happened to the ones that were going to question Paul?

h. How was the commander going to find out why Paul was being accused by the Jews?

i. How did Paul divide his accusers?

j. What did the Sadducees believe? What did the Pharisees believe?

k. What was the commander afraid might happen to Paul?

l. What did he command his troops to do?

3. Psalms 2:1-12
   a. What is the Psalmist's first question?

   b. What is the Lord's reaction?

   c. Who installed the king of Zion?

   d. What did he instruct the kings of the earth to do?

   e. What promise is given to those that take refuge in the Lord?

4. Proverbs 18:13
   a. What is a person's folly and shame?

QUESTIONS FOR JULY 5

1. I Chronicles 1:1-2:17
   a. In this genealogy, what Bible character does it jump to with a very abbreviated list of names?

   b. What were the names of Noah's three sons?

   c. How many grandsons did Noah have? (Don't count great grandsons)

   d. In chapter one, verse twenty-nine, how many descendants are listed for Isaac and Ishmael?

   e. How many sons were born to Keturah, Abraham's concubine?

   f. How many kings reigned in Edom before any Israelite kings reigned?

   g. How many chiefs were there in Edom?

   h. How many sons did Israel have?

   i. Who was the most famous of Israel's sons?

   j. What happened to Er, Judah's firstborn?

   k. What two sons were born to Tamar, Judah's daughter-in-law?

   l. Who brought trouble on Israel by violating the ban on taking devoted things?

   m. How many sons did Jesse have?

   n. Who was his seventh son?

   o. How many daughters did he have?

   p. How many sons did Zeruiah, Jesse's daughter have?

   q. Who was the mother of Amasa?

   r. Who was Amasa's father?

2. Acts 23:11-35
   a. Where did the Lord say that Paul must testify about Jesus?

   b. What did the conspiracy of Jews bind themselves to do the next morning? How many were involved in the plot?

    c.   What did Paul do when he heard about the plot? What did the young man tell the commander?

    d.   What did the commander do?

    e.   What did the commander tell the young man?

    f.   What did the commander put in his letter to Claudius Lysias?

    g.   How far did the soldiers take Paul?

    h.   What did the calvary do when they arrived at Caesarea?

    i.   Did the governor agree to hear Paul's case?

3.   Psalms 3:1-8
    a.   What was the Psalmist telling the Lord about his foes? What were they saying about his God?

    b.   Who was the shield around the Psalmist?

    c.   What two things did the Lord do for him?

    d.   What did the Psalmist do because the Lord sustained him?

    e.   What would the Psalmist not fear?

    f.   What three things did he request for himself?

    g.   What did he request for God's people?

4.   Proverbs 18:14-15
    a.   What sustains a man in sickness?

    b.   What does the heart of the discerning acquire?

    c.   What does the ears of the wise seek?

STUDY QUESTIONS FOR JULY 6

1. I Chronicles 2:18-4:4

   a. How many sons of Caleb are listed in chapter two?

   b. Who married the daughter of Makir when he was sixty years old?

   c. How many children did Seled have?

   d. How many sons did Sheshan have? What did he do with his servant?

   e. How many sons were born to David while he reigned in Hebron?

   f. How long did David reign in Hebron?

   g. How long did David reign in Jerusalem? How many sons are listed here that he had while he was reigning in Jerusalem? Did he have more sons than the ones listed here?

   h. How many sons did Solomon have listed here?

   i. How many sons of Judah are listed here?

   j. To whom were the clans of the Zorathites related?

2. Acts 24:1-27

   a. Who brought charges against Paul?

   b. What happened when Paul was called in?

   c. What did Tertullus say in his introduction?

   d. Of what did he accuse Paul?

   e. Who joined in the accusations that Tertullus brought against Paul?

   f. What did Paul say in his introduction?

   g. What did Paul say in his defense?

   h. What did Paul admit?

   i. What did Paul say about the Jews from the province of Asia? What did Paul say he was on trial for that day?

j.   Then what did Felix do? What did Felix order the centurion to do?

k.   Several days later, what did Felix do with his wife Drusilla, who was a Jewess?

l.   Why did Felix leave Paul in prison?

3.   Psalms 4:1-8
   a.   What four requests does the Psalmist make in the first verse?

   b.   What two questions are asked of men?

   c.   What does the Psalmist say that men should know?

   d.   What does he say that the Lord will do when the Psalmist calls?

   e.   What should men not do in their anger?

   f.   What should they do in their beds?

   g.   What kind of sacrifices should they offer?

   h.   What were many asking?

   i.   With what did the Lord fill the Psalmists heart? What was it greater than?

   j.   Why was the Psalmist going to be able to lie down and sleep in peace?

4.   Proverbs 18:16-18
   a.   What does a gift do for a giver?

   b.   Who seems right? When does that change?

   c.   What does casting the lot do?

STUDY QUESTIONS FOR JULY 7

1.   I Chronicles 4:5-5:17
      a.   How many wives did Ashur have?

      b.   In this passage, how was Jabez described?

      c.   What was Jabez's prayer?

      d.   Did God answer Jabez's prayer?

      e.   Name the seven men of Recah.

      f.   What three fathers are mentioned here that were craftsmen?

      g.   What kind of workers are mentioned in chapter four verse twenty-one?

      h.   In chapter four verse twenty-two, from where did these records come?

      i.   What kind of workers are mentioned in chapter four verse twenty-three? Who did
            they work for?

      j.   How many children did Shimei have? How many were sons and how many were
            daughters? What was said about the number of children that his brothers had?

      k.   What did five hundred Simeonites, led by Pelatiah, Neariah, Pephaiah and Uzziel
            do to the remaining Amalekites who had escaped?

      l.   Why were Reuben's rights as firstborn given to the sons of Joseph?

      m.   Who was the strongest of Reuben and all his brothers?

      n.   Who was a leader of the Reubenites?

      o.   Where did the Gadites live?

      p.   When were all these entered into the genealogical records?

2.   Acts 25:1-27
      a.   Where did Festus go from Caesarea? Who appeared before Festus? Against
            whom were they presenting their charges?

      b.   Why were these people urging Festus to transfer Paul to Jerusalem? How did
            Festus answer them?

c.   When did Festus go back down to Caesarea? When did he convene court?

d.   When Paul appeared before Festus, who stood around him bringing many serious charges against him? Could they prove these charges?

e.   What did Paul say in his defense? What did Festus ask Paul if he was willing to do? How did Paul answer?

f.   How did Festus rule on Paul's appeal?

g.   Who arrived a few days later? What did Festus discuss with them?

h.   Did Paul's accusers bring the type of charges that Festus expected? What kind of charges did they bring?

i.   How did the king and queen enter the audience room?

j.   For Festus, what was unreasonable to do to a prisoner?

3.   Psalms 5:1-12
      a.   What did the Psalmist do in the morning?

      b.   Does God take pleasure in evil?

      c.   Where did the Palmist want God to lead him?

      d.   What was the Psalmist's request about his enemies?

      e.   Who does the Lord bless? How does he surround them?

4.   Proverbs 18:19
      a.   What is more unyielding than a fortified city?

      b.   What is like the barred gates of a citadel?

1. I Chronicles 5:18-6:81
   a. How many men did the Reubenites, the Gadites and half-tribe of Manasseh have ready for military service?

   b. Who did they wage war against? Who helped them in their fighting?

   c. Why did God answer their prayers?

   d. How many camels, sheep, donkeys and people did they capture?

   e. How long did they occupy the land?

   f. Where did the half-tribe of Manasseh settle?

   g. Why did God stir up the spirit of Pul king of Assyria against the Reubenites, the Gadites and half-tribe of Manasseh?

   h. What did David put the men listed in chapter six verses thirty-three through forty-seven in charge of?

   i. Of what were their fellow Levites in charge?

   j. Who was in charge of the offerings?

   k. What locations were allotted to the descendants of Aaron?

   l. Who was given the fields and villages around the city?

2. Acts 26:1-32
   a. What did Agrippa give Paul permission to do?

   b. Why did Paul consider himself fortunate to stand before King Agrippa?

   c. What did Paul beg king Agrippa to do?

   d. Who knew how Paul lived since he was a child?
   e. Why did Paul say he was on trial that day?

   f. Why were the Jews accusing Paul?

   g. What was Paul convinced that he should do about the name of Jesus?

   h. What did Paul do in Jerusalem?

i.   What did Paul say that he tried to force the people that believed in Jesus to do?

j.   What happened when Paul went to Damascus?

k.   What did Jesus tell Paul to do?

l.   Was Paul obedient to the vision from heaven?

m.   What did Festus say about Paul?

n.   What did King Agrippa say to Paul?

o.   What did Agrippa say to Festus?

3.   Psalms 6:1-10

a.   What four things does the Psalmist request of the Lord in verses one and two?

b.   What two things does the Psalmist say about one that is dead?

c.   From what was the Psalmist worn out?

d.   How was the bed flooded and his couch drenched?

e.   Did the Lord hear the Psalmist's cry?

f.   What was going to happen to all the Psalmist's enemies?

4.   Proverbs 18:20-21

a.   How is a man's stomach filled?

b.   How are his lips satisfied?

c.   What kind of power does the tongue have?

STUDY QUESTIONS FOR JULY 9

1. I Chronicles 7:1-8:40
    a. In that day why was it important to know how many fighting men you had in your nation?

    b. How many fighting men did Tolah have during the reign of David?

    c. Why did the sons of Izrahiah have so many men ready for battle?

    d. How many sons did Zelophehad have?

    e.   Who killed Ezer and Elead?

    f. How many sons did Azel have?

2. Acts 27:1-20
    a. To whom were Paul and some of the other prisoners handed? What was his occupation? To what regiment did he belong?

    b. From where did the ship come that they boarded? Where was it going?

    c. Where did they land the next day?

    d. Who allowed Paul to go to his friends?

    e. What did it mean when it said that they passed to the lee of Cyprus?

    f. Where did they land after they sailed across the open sea off the coast of Cilicia and Pamphylia?

    g. What kind of a ship did the centurion find there that was headed for Italy?

    h. What does the scripture say about the headway they were making?

    i. How did they move along the coast and to what place did they come?

    j. What did Paul warn them about?

    k. Whose advice did the centurion listen to?

    l. In what port were they hoping to winter?

    m. What made them think they had made the right choice?

n.   How long did it take for the storm to hit?

o.   Why did the sailors put ropes under the ship?

p.   What did they do the next day? What did they do on the third day?

3.   Psalms 7:1-17
        a.   Where does the Psalmist find refuge?

        b.   From whom did the Psalmist ask God to deliver him? What would happen to the Psalmist if God did not deliver him?

        c.   What did the Psalmist ask God to allow if the Psalmist was guilty?

        d.   How did he want the Lord to arise? What did he want God to awake and do?

        e.   How did he want the Lord to judge him?

        f.   What did he ask the righteous God to search?

        g.   What should he bring to an end? What should he do to the righteous?

        h.   Who was the Psalmist's shield?

        i.   What happens to the one that digs a hole and scoops it out? What happens to the trouble he causes?

        j.   Why was the Psalmist going to give thanks to Lord?

        k.   To who was he going to give praise?

4.   Proverbs 18:22
        a.   What does he that finds a wife find?

1.   I Chronicles 9:1-10:14

        a.   In what book were the genealogies of Israel recorded?

        b.   Why were the people of Judah taken captive?

        c.   Who were the first to resettle on their own property?

        d.   Who had assigned the gatekeeper their positions of trust?

        e.   When did the gatekeepers count the articles used in the temple service?

        f.   Who was entrusted with the responsibility for baking the offering bread?

        g.   Who was in charge of the bread set out on the table every Sabbath?

        h.   Where did the musicians stay and why were they exempt from other duties?

        i.   Who was Saul's father?

        j.   What happened when the Philistines fought against Israel?

        k.   What happened to Saul's sons?

        l.   What did Saul ask his armor-bearer to do? Did he do it?

        m.   What did the armor-bearer do when he saw that Saul was dead?

        n.   When did the Philistines find out Saul was dead?

        o.   What did they do with the head of Saul?

        p.   What did the inhabitants of Jabesh Gilead do when they heard everything that the Philistines did to Saul?

        q.   Where were the bones of Saul and his sons buried?

        r.   Why did Saul die?

2.   Acts 27:21-44

        a.   Where is this story taking place?

        b.   What did Paul say the men should have done?

c.   What did he urge the men to do?

d.   What did the angel say to Paul?

e.   Where did Paul place his faith?

f.   On which night were they still being driven across the Adriatic sea? About what time did they realize that they were approaching land?

g.   What did they do to avoid running aground?

h.   What did the sailors do? What did the soldiers do so the sailors wouldn't escape?

i.   What did they decide to do when daylight came?

j.   Did Paul's prediction of everyone being safe come true?

3.   Psalms 8:1-9
    a.   Write Psalms chapter eight verse one.

    b.   Where did God set his glory?

    c.   What was the Psalmist's question when he considered God's heavens, the moon and the stars?

    d.   God made man a little lower than what?

    e.   With what did God crown man?

    f.   What work did God give to man?

    g.   What praise did the Psalmist give to God in verse nine?

4.   Proverbs 8:1-9
    a.   What does a poor man do? What does a rich man do?

    b.   Who is the friend that sticks closer than a brother?

STUDY QUESTIONS FOR JULY 11

1. I Chronicles 11:112-18
   a. Why did Israel come together to David at Hebron?

   b. What had the Lord said to David?

   c. What did the Jebusites say to David?

   d. What did David do?

   e. What did David promise to the one that lead the attack on the Jebusites?

   f. Who lead the attack?

   g. Why was Jerusalem called the city of David?

   h. Why did David become more and more powerful?

   i. What did David long for?

   j. What did David do with the water that his men brought him?

   k. How many mighty men are listed in I Chronicles chapter eleven verses twenty-six through forty-seven?

   l. How were these men armed?

   m. With which hand did they shoot?

   n. How were the Gadite warriors described?

   o. Who was the chief Gadite?

   p. How many men did it take to be a match for the least Gadite army commander?

   q. How many men did it take to be a match for the greatest Gadite army commander?

   r. What did Amasai, the chief of the thirty say under the influence of the spirit?

   s. What was David's response?

2. Acts 28:1-31
   a. How did they arrive at this island called Malta? Were the islanders friendly?

b. What was the first reaction of the islanders to Paul and the snake? How did the reaction change when Paul didn't die?

c. Who was Publius? What was wrong with his father?

d. What happened to the father when Paul prayed for him?

e. How long did they stay at Malta?

f. What ship did they use to leave Malta?

g. When they got to Rome was Paul put in prison?

h. Why did Paul appeal to Caesar?

i. How long did Paul stay in his own rented house?

j. What did Paul do to the people that came to see him?

3. Psalms 9:1-12
    a. What two things are requested from God in verse thirteen?

b. What two reasons did he give that he needed those requests?

c. What happened to the nations? What happened to their feet?

d. How is the Lord known? How are the wicked ensnared?

e. Where do the wicked return?

f. What does the Psalmist request of the Lord for the nations?

4. Proverbs 19:1-3
    a. How is the poor man and the fool compared?

b. What does one need with zeal?

1. I Chronicles 12:19-14:17

    a. When did some of the men of Manasseh defect to David?

    b. How did these men help David? What was said about these men as warriors?

    c. Why did the Philistines refuse to let David and his men go to battle with them against Saul?

    d. What happened to David's army day by day? What did this army become like?

    e. How many of Saul's kinsmen showed up? How long did they remain loyal to Saul's house?

    f. What did the men of Zebulun bring with them? How many men did they have?

    g. What kind of weapons did the tribes from east of Jordan have?

    h. What was this volunteer army determined to do? What did David say to the whole assembly after he had conferred with each of his officers?

    i. How did the assembly respond?

    j. How did they move the ark from Abinadab's house?

    k. What two men were guiding the ark? What happened when Uzzah reached out to steady the ark? What was David's reaction?

    l. Where did they take the ark? What happened to the house where the ark was left?

    m. What did the Philistines do when they heard that David had been anointed king of all Israel?

    n. What did David do? How did the Lord answer him?

    o. What happened the second time the Philistines attacked? What had God told David to do differently?

2. Romans 1:1-17

    a. What does Paul call himself?

    b. What did Paul say he was called to be?

    c. Who was Paul talking about that as to his human nature was a descendant of

David?

    d.   What did Paul say that they had received from this person?

    e.   To whom did Paul address this letter?

    f.   For what did Paul thank God first?

    g.   Why did Paul long to see them?

    h.   To whom was Paul obligated?

    i.   Was Paul ashamed of the gospel? Why?

3.   Psalms 9:13-20
    a.   What two things are requested from God in verse thirteen?

    b.   What two reasons did he give that he needed those requests?

    c.   What happened to the nations? What happened to their feet?

    d.   How is the Lord known? How are the wicked ensnared?

    e.   Where do the wicked return?

    f.   What does the Psalmist request of the Lord for the nations?

4.   Proverbs 19:4-5
    a.   What does wealth bring? What happens to a poor man's friends?

    b.   What is said about a false witness?

    c.   What is said about the man that pours out lies?

STUDY QUESTIONS FOR JULY 13

1. I Chronicles 15:1-16:36
    a. What did David do after he constructed buildings for himself?

    b. Who did the Lord choose to carry the ark of the covenant?

    c. Who did David assemble to bring the ark of the Lord to the place he had prepared for it?

    d. How many relatives did Kohath have with him?

    e. What did David tell the priests and the Levites to do?

    f. Why did God's anger break out on the people the first time David tried to bring back the ark?

    g. How did the Levites carry the ark?

    h. How many men were to sound the bronze cymbals?

    i. How many were to play the lyres?

    j. Who were to be doorkeepers for the ark?

    k. Who were to blow trumpets before the ark of God?

    l. How was David and the Levites clothed?

    m. What was Michal daughter of Saul doing as the ark of the covenant was entering the city of David? What was her reaction when she saw this spectacle?

    n. What did they do after they brought the ark and set it inside the tent?

    o. According to the Psalm that David submitted to Asaph and his associates, to whom were they to give thanks and what were they to make known?

    p. In verse thirty-four, why were they to give thanks to the Lord?

2. Romans 1:18-32
    a. Against what was the wrath of God being revealed?

    b. Who made the truth about God plain to man?

    c. What two invisible qualities of God have been clearly seen, leaving man without excuse?

   d.   Although men knew God, what did they not do? What happened to man's thinking and his heart?

   e.   To what did God give men over?

   f.   What did men receive because they committed indecent acts?

   g.   What did men do even though they knew God's righteous decree?

3.   Psalms 10:1-15
     a.   What two questions are asked in verse one?

     b.   What does a wicked man do in his arrogance?

     c.   What does the wicked man do to the greedy and what does he do to the Lord?

     d.   What two things does the wicked man say to himself?

     e.   What does the wicked man do near the villages?

     f.   What does he say about God?

     g.   In verse twelve, what does the Psalmist ask the Lord to do?

     h.   In verse fifteen what two things does the Psalmist ask the Lord to do?

4.   Proverbs 19:6-7
     a.   What do many people do?

     b.   Who is a friend of everyone?

     c.   What happens to a poor man?

STUDY QUESTIONS FOR JULY 14

1.   I Chronicles 16:37-18:17
      a.   Who did David leave before the ark of the covenant to minister there regularly,
            according to each day's requirement? Who did he give to minister with them?

      b.   What was the job of Zadok and his fellow priests?

      c.   After David was settled in his palace, what concern did he communicate to
            Nathan? How did Nathan reply? What did God tell Nathan in the night that
            David should not do?

      d.   In chapter seventeen verses nine and ten, what four promises does the Lord make
            to his people Israel?

      e.   Who would God use to build his house? What four promises does God make to
            this person?

      f.   What did Nathan do with this word from the Lord?

      g.   Then what did King David do?

      h.   How did David say that God had looked on him? What did David say about God
            in verse twenty of chapter seventeen?

      i.   What will men say when the promise that the Lord made concerning David and
            his house is established?

      j.   What did David do to the Philistines? What about the Moabites?

      k.   How many chariots, charioteers, and foot soldiers did David capture?

      l.   Where did David get some gold shields? What kind of metal did David get that
            Solomon used in making the sea?

      m.   What did David do with the articles of gold and silver and bronze that Hadoram
            brought him?

      n.   Where did the Lord give David victory?

      o.   In what capacity did David's sons serve?

2.   Romans 2:1-24
      a.   Who did Paul say had no excuse? Why did he say that they had no excuse?

27

b.   On what is God's judgement against those who do such things based?

c.   To what does God's kindness lead?

d.   What were they storing up for themselves because of their stubbornness and their unrepentant heart?

e.   What will God give to those who by persistence in doing good seek glory, honor and immortality?

f.   Does God show favoritism? What happens to the ones that sin apart from the law? What happens to the one that sin under the law?

g.   In verses twenty-one through twenty-three, what five questions does Paul ask if they think one thing and do another?

h.   What's written about the results of this kind of action?

3.   Psalms 10:16-18
    a.   How long is the Lord king?

    b.   What will happen to the nations?

    c.   According to verse seventeen, what does the Lord hear?

    d.   What else does the Lord do for them?

    e.   What does the Lord do for the fatherless?

    f.   What does this prevent man from doing?

4.   Proverbs 19:8-9
    a.   What does he who gets wisdom love? What happens to the one that cherishes understanding.

    b.   What happens to a false witness?

    c.   What happens to the one that pours out lies?

STUDY QUESTIONS FOR JULY 15

1. I Chronicles 19:1-21:30

    a. To whom did David want to show kindness? Why did he want to show him kindness?

    b. What did the Ammonite nobles say to Hanun?

    c. What did Hanun do to the delegation that David sent to Him?

    d. What did David tell his delegation to do?

    e. What did Hanun do with his thousand talents of silver?

    f. What did David do when he heard what Hanun did?

    g. How many charioteers and foot soldiers did David kill?

    h. What did David and his entire army do after they had plundered the ammonite towns?

    i. Who incited David to take a census of Israel?

    j. What did Joab think about this census?

    k. Why did Joab leave Levi and Benjamin out of the numbering?

    l. What did David say to God?

    m. What did God say to Gad, David's seer?

    n. Which option did David chose? Why?

    o. What did David say to Arunah'?

    p. When Araunah offered to give David the property, the oxen and the threshing sledges, how did David respond?

    q. How much did David pay Araunah?

    r. Then what did David do?

    s. Why didn't David inquire of the Lord in the tabernacle?

2. Romans 2:25-3:8

a. When does circumcision have value?

b. What happened to the people if they were circumcised but broke the law?

c. How will a person be regarded that is not circumcised but keep the law's requirements?

d. What did Paul say about a man that is only a Jew outwardly?

e. From where does a man's praise come that is a Jew inwardly; and circumcision is circumcision of the heart, by the Spirit?

f. What is the first advantage of being a Jew?

g. What phrase does Paul use about God being true?

h. What is Paul's comment about those that say, "Let us do evil that good may result"?

3. Psalms 11:1-7
a. Where does the Psalmist take his refuge?

b. What do the wicked do? Who do they shoot at?

c. What does the Psalmist ask about the foundations?

d. Where is the Lord?

e. Who observes the sons of men?

f. What is said about the righteous and the wicked?

g. Who is righteous? Who loves justice? Who will see the Lord's face?

4. Proverbs 19:10-12
a. What is not fitting for a fool to do? What is worse?

b. What does a man's wisdom give him?

c. What is a king's rage like? What is a king's favor like?

STUDY QUESTIONS FOR JULY 16

1.   II Chronicles 22:1-23:32

    a.   What did David say about the house of the Lord God and the altar of burnt offerings?

    b.   What order did David give concerning the aliens living in Israel?

    c.   How was the iron used that David supplied?

    d.   How much brass and cedar logs did David supply?

    e.   Why was David gathering all these things together even though God said Solomon was to build the temple?

    f.   Why did God choose Solomon instead of David to build the temple?

    g.   What was God going to grant to Israel during the reign of Solomon?

    h.   What did David tell Solomon would be the key to his success?

    i.   What did David tell Solomon that he had provided for the temple?

    j.   What did David do when he was old and full of years?

    k.   How many Levites were there that were over thirty years old?

    l.   What was the duty of the Levites in regard to the descendants of Aaron?

    m.   What two things are listed here of which the Levites were to be in charge?

    n.   What were the Levites to do every morning, and every evening, and whenever burnt offerings were presented to the Lord?

    o.   Did the Levites do their job?

2.   Romans 3:9-31

    a.   What is Paul talking about in this section of scripture? (Look back to the first part of chapter three)

    b.   Were Jews better than the Gentiles?

    c.   Who is under sin? Who is righteous? Who seeks God?

    d.   How many do good?

e.   To what does Paul liken the throat of mankind? Of what are their mouths full?

f.   How does Paul describe the unregenerated man in verses fifteen through eighteen?

g.   In verse twenty, what does Paul say is the reason for the law?

h.   Where can man obtain righteousness? How do the law and prophets relate to this righteousness?

i.   Is there a difference between a Jew and a Gentile that have faith in Jesus Christ? Why?

j.   Is God the God of the Jews only?

3.   Psalms 12:1-8
   a.   What did the Psalmist say about the Godly?

   b.   What about the faithful?

   c.   What did the Psalmist ask the Lord to do about flattering lips and boastful tongue?

   d.   For what reason was the Lord going to arise and protect the people?

   e.   What happens when what is vile is honored among men?

4.   Proverbs 19:13-14
   a.   What does a foolish son do to his father?

   b.   To what is a quarrelsome wife likened?

   c.   From where does a prudent wife come?

1.   I Chronicles 24:1-26:11

      a.   How many sons did Aaron have?

      b.   What happened to Nadab and Abihu, two of Aaron's sons?

      c.   Of the sons that were left, which family had the most leaders?

      d.   How many heads of family were in each division? How were they divided?

      e.   Who was the scribe that recorded the names in the presence of the king and of the officials?

      f.   When they started casting lots, which family did they start with?

      g.   On whom did the first lot fall?

      h.   On whom did the twelfth lot fall?

      i.   On whom did the twenty-fourth lot fall?

      j.   In chapter twenty-four verse nineteen, what did the forgoing list show? Who had prescribed the regulations for entering the temple of the Lord?

      k.   The rest of chapter twenty-four talks about the non-priestly Levites, how did they determine the order of service for these families? In whose presence did they do this?

      l.   Was there any discrimination between the young and the old of these families?

      m.   In chapter twenty-five, who set apart some of the sons of Asaph, Herman, and Jeduthun for the ministry of prophesying, accompanied by harps, lyres and cymbals?

      n.   Under whose supervision were these men? Under whose supervision were Asaph, Jeduthun and Herman?

      o.   How many musicians were there?

2.   Romans 4:1-12

      a.   What did Paul say would be true if Abraham was justified by works?

      b.   What did the scripture say about Abraham's belief?

c. How are the wages of a man that works credited?

d. How is the faith of a man that doesn't work but trusts God, credited?

e. What did David say about this?

f. What question does Paul ask in verse nine?

g. What two questions does Paul ask in verse ten? How does he answer his second question?

h. What sign did Abraham receive as a seal of righteousness?

i. Of what two groups of people was Abraham the father?

3. Psalms 13:1-6
   a. What two questions does the Psalmist ask in verse one?

   b. What two questions does he ask in verse two?

   c. What three requests does he make in verse three?

   d. What were his enemies going to say?

   e. What were his foes going to do when he fell?

   f. In whom was he going to trust?

   g. In what was he going to rejoice?

   h. To whom was he going to sing? Why?

4. Proverbs 19:15-16
   a. What does laziness bring?

   b. What happens to the shiftless man?

   c. What happens to the man that obeys instructions?

1. I Chronicles 26:12-27:34
    a. How were the gates assigned to the gatekeepers?

    b. Who was to be in charge of the east gate? The north gate? The south gate? The west gate and the Shalleketh gate?

    c. Whose descendants were the gatekeepers?

    d. Who was in charge of the treasuries?

    e. How many men were in a division?

    f. How many division were there?

    g. What extra comments were made about Benaiah, the third army commander?

    h. How many officers were over the tribes of Israel?

    i. Why didn't David count the men that were less than twenty years old?

    j. Who began to count the men but did not finish?

    k. Why did wrath come on Israel? Why was the number not entered into the annals of King David?

    l. Who was in charge of the royal storehouses?

    m. Who was in charge of the storehouse in the outlying districts, in the towns, the villages, and the watchtowers?

    n. Who was in charge of the supplies of olive oil?

    o. Who was Jonathan?

    p. Who was the king's counselor?

    q. Who was the king's friend?

    r. Who was commander of the royal army?

2. Romans 4:13-5:5
    a. How did Abraham and his offspring receive the promise that he would be heir of the world?

b.   What does the law bring? What happens when there is no law?

c.   Against all hope, what did Abraham do? What two things made it so hard to believe God's promise?

d.   Did Abraham waver in his faith? Of what was Abraham fully persuaded?

e.   Why was Jesus delivered over to death?

f.   What do people have that have been justified through faith?

g.   In what do we rejoice? In what else do we rejoice? Why would we rejoice in that?

h.   Why does hope not disappoint us?

3.   Psalms 14:1-7
        a.   What does the fool say in his heart?

        b.   How many do good?

        c.   With what are evildoers overwhelmed?

        d.   Where is God present?

        e.   What do evildoers do to the plans of the poor?

        f.   Who is the refuge of the poor?

        g.   From where would the salvation of Israel come?

        h.   What happens to Jacob and Israel when the Lord restores the fortunes of his people?

4.   Proverbs 19:17
        a.   Who lends to the Lord?

        b.   What will the Lord do for the one who is kind to the poor?

STUDY QUESTIONS FOR JULY 19

1.   I Chronicles 28:1-29:30
   a.   Who did David summon to assemble at Jerusalem?

   b.   What did David tell them was in his heart to do? What did God tell David?

   c.   Which son of David did God choose to sit on the throne of the kingdom of the Lord of Israel?

   d.   Who did God say would be the one that would build his house?

   e.   What charge did David give to his son Solomon?

   f.   What would happen if Solomon forsook God?

   g.   Where did David get all these instructions that he was passing on to Solomon?

   h.   In chapter twenty-eight verse twenty, what did David say to encourage his son. What promise did he pass on to Solomon?

   i.   What eight building products had David supplied for the building of the temple?

   j.   What did the group that Solomon called together give toward the work of the temple? How did David respond to this?

   k.   What did David say about the Lord when he praised the Lord in the presence of the whole assembly?

   l.   What did David say about our days on earth?

   m.   What did David request from God for his son in chapter twenty-nine, verse nineteen?

   n.   How many bulls, rams, and male lambs did they sacrifice the next day?

   o.   How long was David king over all Israel? Who was king next?

2.   Romans 5:6-21
   a.   What did Christ do for the ungodly?

   b.   How did Christ demonstrate his love for us? Through whom did we receive reconciliation?

   c.   How did sin enter the world?   How did sin come to all men?

d. Through what man did God's abundant provision of grace and of the gift of righteousness reign?

e. Finish Romans chapter five verse nineteen, "For just as through the disobedience of the one man the many were made sinners, so also through the

_____."

f. Why was the law added? What happened when sin increased? How does the reign of grace bring life?

3. Psalms 15:1-5
    a. What two questions does the Psalmist ask?

    b. The Psalmist suggests that there are ten things that are true of the man that is the answer to his questions, what is said about each?
        i.   Walk
        ii.   Does
        iii.   Speaks
        iv.   Tongue
        v.   Treats neighbor
        vi.   Slur
        vii.   Despises
        viii.   Honors
        ix.   Oath
        x.   Money
        xi.   Bribe

    c. What is the promise to the one that does these things?

4. Proverbs 19:18-19
    a. Why should a man discipline his son?

    b. What must a hot-tempered man pay?

    c. What happens if you rescue him?

STUDY QUESTIONS FOR JULY 20

1. II Chronicles 1:1-3:17
    a. How was Solomon able to establish himself firmly over the kingdom of Israel?

    b. Where did Solomon and the whole assembly go?

    c. How many burnt offerings did David offer to the Lord?

    d. What did God offer to Solomon? What did Solomon choose?

    e. Was God pleased with Solomon's choice? What extra things was God going to give to Solomon because of his choice?

    f. How many chariots did Solomon have? How many horses did he have?

    g. What did Solomon do with silver and gold and cedar?

    h. What two things did Solomon give orders to build? How many did he have on his work crew?

    i. Who did Solomon contact to send him cedar? What else did Solomon ask him to send?

    j. What was Solomon going to send for payment?

    k. How did the man answer Solomon?

    l. When Solomon took a census, how many aliens were there?

    m. When did Solomon start building the temple?

    n. What was the size of the foundation?

    o. What did Solomon use to overlay the panels?

    p. What was the size of the Holy Place?

    q. How did Solomon make the curtain? How many pillars did he make in front of the temple?

2. Romans 6:1-23
    a. What question does Paul ask to start off this chapter?

    b. How does he answer his own question?

c. If we are united with Christ in death what will happen in his resurrection?

d. Why should one be crucified with Christ?

e. What did Paul believe would happen if a believer died with Christ?

f. To what should a believer be dead? To what should a believer be alive?

g. What should a believer offer instead of offering part of his body to sin?

h. Why would sin not be the master of a believer?

i. Why did Paul put this in human terms?

j. What is the wages of sin? What is the gift of God?

3. Psalms 16:1-11
   a. What does he ask for in verse one? Where does he take refuge?

   b. What good thing does the Psalmist own apart from God?

   c. What happens to the ones that run after other gods?

   d. What does the Psalmist's heart do at night?

   e. With what will the Psalmist be filled in God's presence? What will he receive at God's right hand?

4. Proverbs 19:20-21
   a. What should a person listen to and what should they accept?

   b. What is said about the plans of man's heart?

   c. What prevails?

1. II Chronicles 4:1-6:11

    a.   How long of a line did it take to measure around the cast metal sea?

    b.   On what did the sea stand? How many were there? What way were they facing?

    c.   How many basins were made? For what were these basins used? For what was the sea used?

    d.   How many lampstands were made? Where were they positioned?

    e.   In the courtyard of the priests, with what did he overlay the doors? Where was the sea placed?

    f.   How many pounds of bronze was used in Solomon's temple?

    g.   What thirteen items are mentioned here that were either made of gold or overlaid with gold?

    h.   What did Solomon bring in when the work on the temple was completed?

    i.   What did Solomon summon the elders of Israel, all the heads of the tribes and the chiefs of the Israelite families, to do?

    j.   Where was the ark of the Lord's covenant placed?

    k.   What was the only thing in the ark of the Lord's covenant?

    l.   How many priests were sounding trumpets? What did the trumpeters and singers do? What accompanied them? What did they sing?

    m.   What did the king do while the whole assembly of Israel was standing there?

    n.   What did Solomon say about his father in chapter six verses seven through nine? What did Solomon say about God's promise in verse ten?

2. Romans 7:1-13

    a.   What question does Paul ask the brothers if they knew about the law?

    b.   How long is a married woman bound to her husband? What happens if the husband dies?

    c.   What is a woman called if she marries another man while her husband is still alive? After her husband dies, if she marries another man, is she called the same thing?

d. Why did the brothers die to the law? To whom would they belong?

e. Is the law sin? What would Paul not have known if the law had not said, "Do not covet"? What does verse twelve say?

f. What was the answer to Paul's question, "Did that which was good, then become death to me?"

g. What happened so that sin could be shown to be sin?

3. Psalms 17:1-15
    a. For what three things does the Psalmist start out asking God in this Psalm?

    b. What does the Psalmist say that the Lord will find when the Lord probes his heart?

    c. What did the Psalmist resolve about his mouth? What did the Psalmist say about his steps?

    d. In verses eight through fourteen, the Psalmist talks about his enemies, what four things does the Psalmist request from the Lord?

    e. In verse fifteen what would happen to the Psalmist when he awoke?

4. Proverbs 19:22-23
    a. What does a man desire?

    b. What is better than being a liar?

    c. Where does the fear of the Lord lead?

STUDY QUESTIONS FOR JULY 22

1.　II Chronicles 6:12-8:10
    a.　What was the size of the platform that Solomon made out of bronze?

    b.　What did Solomon do before the whole assembly of Israel?

    c.　What promise that God made to David, did Solomon ask the Lord to keep?

    d.　What did Solomon ask the Lord for when God's people prayed toward the temple?

    e.　What did Solomon ask for when Israel has been defeated because of sin and then turned back and confessed God's name in the temple?

    f.　What does Solomon ask for when famine or plague comes to the land and people and they spread out their hands toward the temple?

    g.　What does he ask for when a foreigner comes and prays toward the temple?

    h.　In chapter six verse forty two, of what promise does David remind the Lord?

    i.　What happened when Solomon finished praying?

    j.　Why couldn't the priests enter the temple?

    k.　What was the reaction of the people when they saw fire coming down? What did they say?

    l.　How many sheep and cattle were sacrificed?

    m.　Did God answer Solomon's prayer?

    n.　In chapter seven verse seventeen and eighteen, what promise did God repeat?

    o.　Who did Solomon use for his slave labor? For what did Solomon use the Israelites?

2.　Romans 7:14-8:8
    a.　In describing the conflict inside himself, what did Paul say the law was? What did Paul say that he was?

    b.　What was Paul's conflict about what he wanted to do and what he did?

    c.　What did Paul say about the law.

d. How much good was dwelling in Paul?

e. How could Paul be rescued from his body of death?

f. For whom is there no condemnation? How is that possible?

g. On what does the person that lives according to the sinful nature have his mind set? What about the one that lives in accordance with the Spirit?

h. What does Paul say about the mind of a sinful man and a mind controlled by the Spirit?

3. Psalms 18:1-15
   a. Who does the Psalmist love?

   b. Who was the Psalmist's rock, fortress, and his deliverer? In whom did he take refuge?

   c. Who did the Psalmist call on? Who is worthy of praise?

   d. How did the Psalmist describe his contact with death? What did the Psalmist do when he had the struggles with death?

   e. What happened to the earth and the foundations of the mountains when God became angry?

   f. What was laid bare at the blast of the breath of God?

4. Proverbs 19:24-25
   a. What is said about the sluggard?

   b. What will happen if a mocker is flogged?

   c. What will happen if a discerning man is rebuked?

STUDY QUESTIONS FOR JULY 23

1.   II Chronicles 8:11-10:19
     a.   Why did Solomon say that he was bringing up his wife from the city of David?

     b.   Where did Solomon get his direction for sacrificing on the altar that he built in front of the portico?

     c.   Did Solomon follow what his father, David had ordained in regard to the priests and Levites?

     d.   What was the job of the Levites?

     e.   Where did Solomon go after he finished building the temple?

     f.   What did Hiram's ships bring back from Opher for Solomon?

     g.   Why did the queen of Sheba go to Jerusalem?

     h.   How did the queen react when she talked to Solomon and saw his kingdom? To whom did the queen give praise?

     i.   What did Solomon make with the wood that Hiram and Solomon's men brought from Ophir?

     j.   What was the weight of the gold that Solomon received yearly?

     k.   How was Solomon's throne described? Why weren't some of Solomon's goblets and household articles made of silver?

     l.   How many horses did Solomon have?

     m.   Who was Rehoboam?

     n.   What did the people of the kingdom ask of Rehoboam?

     o.   What two sets of advisors did Rehoboam consult? Which advice did he follow?

     p.   How did the people react?

2.   Romans 8:9-21
     a.   What does Romans chapter eight verse one say? Why was there no condemnation?

     b.   How is the Christian controlled?

c.   Where does the Spirit of God live?

d.   What does the scripture say about the body of one that has Christ in him? What about the Spirit?

e.   Did the brothers have an obligation to the sinful nature?

f.   What happens when by the Spirit, one puts to death the misdeeds of the body?

g.   What kind of Spirit does the Christian receive?

h.   If they were children, what were they?

i.   What does Paul say about their present sufferings?

j.   For what does the creation wait?

3.   Psalms 18:16-36
     a.   Who reached down and took hold of the Psalmist? What did he do about the deep waters? What about powerful enemies?

     b.   Who was the Psalmist's support?

     c.   Why was he rescued?

     d.   How did the Lord deal with the Psalmist?

     e.   In verses twenty through twenty-four, how does the Psalmist describe himself?

     f.   How does God show himself to the faithful? The blameless? The pure? The crooked?

     g.   What sustains the Psalmist? Why does God broaden the path beneath the Psalmist?

4.   Proverbs 19:26
     a.   What kind of a son brings shame and disgrace?

1. II Chronicles 11:1-13:22

    a. What did Rehoboam do when he arrived in Jerusalem?

    b. How many fighting men did he have?

    c. What did the word of God say through Shemaiah? Did they obey God's word?

    d. What did Rehoboam do to protect himself?

    e. Who did the priests and Levites side with? Why did they side with him?

    f. How many wives and how many concubines did Rehoboam have? How many sons and how many daughters did he have?

    g. What did Rehoboam and all Israel do with the law of the Lord?

    h. What was the reason that God allowed Shishank, king of Egypt attack Jerusalem?

    i. What did the Egyptians do to the fortified cities of Judah? How far did they come?

    j. What did the Lord do when the leaders and the king of Israel humbled themselves?

    k. What did Shishak, king of Judah do with the treasures of the temple?

    l. Did Rehoboam completely follow the Lord?

    m. How often was there warfare between Rehoboam and Jeroboam?

    n. Which group of people were following the Lord; Abijah king of Judah (southern kingdom)or Jeroboam king of Israel (northern kingdom)?

    o. Why were the men of Judah victorious?

2. Romans 8:22-39

    a. What has been groaning as in the pains of childbirth?

    b. What else groaned inwardly? What are they waiting for?

    c. Who helps us in our weakness?

    d. How is one helped when he don't know how he should pray?

e.   What things work together for the good of those who love God?

f.   What can separate one from the love of Christ?

g.   How can one be more than a conqueror?

3.   Psalms 18:37-50

a.   What had the Psalmist done with his enemies?

b.   Who armed the Psalmist for battle?

c.   What did God do to the Psalmist's enemies?

d.   What did the enemies do? Did anyone save them?

e.   Who delivered the Psalmist from the attacks of the people?

f.   What do the foreigners do before the Psalmist?

g.   Who is exalted?

h.   Who was the Psalmist going to praise?

i.   Who gives his king great victories? Who showed unfailing kindness to David and his descendants forever?

4.   Proverbs 19:27-29

a.   What happens if you stop listening to instruction?

b.   What does a corrupt witness do to justice?

c.   What is prepared for mockers?

STUDY QUESTIONS FOR JULY 25

1.	II Chronicles 14:1-16:14
	a.	Where was Abijah buried?

	b.	Who succeeded him as king?

	c.	Did Asa serve God?

	d.	What did Asa do about foreign religions?

	e.	What was Asa's command to Judah?

	f.	Who gave Asa rest?

	g.	How many men did Asa have from Judah? How many from Benjamin?

	h.	Which army had the big shields and spears and which had the small shields and the bows?

	i.	What happened to the vast Cushite army when Asa called out to the Lord?

	j.	What did the men of Judah do to the Cushites?

	k.	What was the warning and prophesy given to Asa by Azariah?

	l.	What did Asa do when he heard the words of the prophet?

	m.	Why had a large number of Israelites come over to Asa?

	n.	What happened in the thirty-sixth year of Asa's reign?

	o.	Why did Asa send gold & silver from the Lord's temple to Ben-Hadad king of Aram?

	p.	Did Ben-Hadad help Asa?

	q.	How did Asa get in trouble with God?

	r.	What punishment did Asa receive for not trusting in God? What did Asa do with the seer?

2.	Romans 9:1-21
	a.	Why did Paul have great sorrow and unceasing anguish in his heart?

b.   Had God's word failed?

c.   Is it Abraham's natural children who are God's children?

d.   How was the promise about Abraham's offspring stated?

e.   Is God unjust?

f.   Who decides what God is going to do?

g.   Why did God raise up Pharaoh?

h.   Do humans have the right to talk back to God?

i.   What illustration is used to show that God can do whatever he wants?

3.   Psalms 19:1-14
      a.   What do the heavens do?

      b.   What do the skies do?

      c.   How does the Psalmist describe the sun?

      d.   What does he say about the law of the Lord?

      e.   What do the precepts of the Lord give to the heart?

      f.   What is more precious than gold and sweeter than honey?

      g.   May the _____ of my _____ and the _____ of my _____ be _____ in your _____ O Lord, my _____ and my _____. Psalms chapter nineteen verse fourteen

4.   Proverbs 20:1
      a.   What is a mocker

      b.   What is a brawler?

      c.   What does the Proverbs say about the person that is drawn away by these drinks?

STUDY QUESTIONS FOR JULY 26

1. II Chronicles 17:1-18:34
   a. Jehosaphat was the king of what kingdom?

   b. What did he do to strengthen himself against Israel?

   c. Why was the Lord with Jehosaphat?

   d. Who established the kingdom under his control?

   e. What did Jehosaphat do in the third year of his reign? What book did these men take with them?

   f. What kept the kingdoms around of the land surrounding Judah from making war with Johosaphat?

   g. What did the Arabs bring Johosaphat?

   h. What did Ahab the king of Israel do when Johosaphat came to visit him? What did Ahab ask Johosaphat in chapter eighteen, verse three?

   i. What was Johosaphat's answer? What did he stipulate that they needed to do first?

   j. What did Micaiah say that he saw in chapter eighteen, verse sixteen?

   k. How was Ahab enticed to into attacking Ramoth Gilead?

   l. What did Zedekiah ask when he went up and slapped Micaiah? How Micaiah answer him?

   m. What did the king of Israel order to be done to Micaiah? What did Micaiah declare?

   n. Which king went into the battle in disguise?

   o. What did the king of Aram order his chariot commanders to do?

   p. What happened to the king of Judah?

   q. What happened to the king of Israel?

2. Romans 9:22-10:13
   a. Who was the object of the Lord's mercy? From whom were they called?

b. What did Hosea say that showed that the Gentiles would also be involved in the call of God?

c. What did Isaiah cry out about Israel?

d. How does Paul compare the Gentiles and Israel in chapter nine, verse thirty through verse thirty-two? What was the stumbling block?

e. What was Paul's prayer for the Israelites?

f. According to chapter ten, verse nine and ten, how can one be saved?

g. In regard to salvation , is there any difference between Jew or Gentile?

3. Psalms 20:1-9
   a. This Psalm is one that was repeated before going into battle. Nine things were desired for the king in this chapter, what are they?

   b. What two things were the people going to do when they were victorious?

   c. What two things did the Psalmist know about what the Lord does?

   d. What do some people believe in? What happens to them?

   e. What do the people of the Lord believe in? What happens to them? What is the last request for the king?

4. Proverbs 20:2-3
   a. What is a king's wrath like?

   b. What happens to the one that angers a king?

   c. What is a man's honor?

   d. What is every fool quick to do?

1.   II Chronicles 19:1-20:37
    a.   What did Jehu the seer, say to Jehoshaphat?

    b.   What did Jehoshaphat do after he heard this message?

    c.   What did he tell the judges to do?

    d.   Who did Jehoshaphat appoint to administer the law of the Lord and to settle disputes?

    e.   Who was to be over them in matters concerning the Lord? Who was to be over them in matters concerning the king?

    f.   Who came to make war on Jehoshaphat? What did Jehosaphat do when he heard about this?

    g.   Who stood before the Lord?

    h.   What did the spirit of the Lord say through Jahaziel?

    i.   What did Jehoshaphat do when he heard this word? What did all the people of Judah and Jerusalem do?

    j.   What did Jehoshaphat encourage the people to do?

    k.   What did the king appoint men to do as they went out?

    l.   Who set ambushes against the men of Ammon and Moab and Mount Seir?

    m.   What did the men of Judah see when they came to the place that overlooks the desert?

    n.   How long did it take to collect the plunder?

    o.   What did they do in the Valley of Beracah?

    p.   What did Jehoshaphat fail to do in his reign?

    q.   With whom did Jehoshaphat make an alliance in the later part of his reign? What was prophesied against the king because of this alliance?

2.   Romans 10:14-11:12
    a.   What four questions does Paul ask in chapter ten, verses fourteen and fifteen?

b.   Did all of the Israelites accept the good news?

c.   From where does faith come?

d.   What does Isaiah say in chapter ten verse twenty? What did he say concerning Israel?

e.   How does Paul answer the question, "Did God reject his people?" ?

f.   What was God's answer to Elijah's statement that he was the only one left?

g.   What does Paul say about his own present time?

h.   Did Israel stumble so as to fall beyond recovery?

i.   What made it possible for salvation to come to the Gentiles?

3.   Psalms 21:1-13
      a.   In whose strength did the king rejoice?

      b.   Where did the king get his joy?

      c.   Who blessed the king & placed a crown of pure gold on his head?

      d.   How did the king's glory become great?

      e.   In whom did the king trust?

      f.   Who is to be exalted?

4.   Proverbs 20:4-6
      a.   What does a sluggard find at harvest time?

      b.   What does a man of understanding do?

      c.   Is it easy to find a faithful man?

1. II Chronicles 21:21-23:21

    a. Where was Jehoshaphat, king of Judah, buried? Who succeeded Jehoshaphat as king? Why was this man chosen?

    b. What did this king do to his brothers along with some of the princes of Israel?

    c. How long did he reign as king? Why did the Lord allow this man to be king even though he did evil in the sight of the Lord?

    d. What did Edom do in the time of Jehoram? What did the Edomites do to Jehoram?

    e. Why did Libnah revolt against Judah?

    f. What was the Lord going to do to Jehoram, his people, his sons, his wives and everything that was his?

    g. What did the Philistines do against Judah and Jehoram?

    h. Who regretted the death of Jehoram? Where was he buried?

    i. Who became king next? Did he do right in the eyes of the Lord?

    j. What did the Lord bring about through Ahaziah's visit to Joram?

    k. Who was Athaliah? What did she do to the royal family of the house of Judah? Who was saved from that family?

    l. What did Jehoida, the priest say the Levites and the priests were to do? Did they obey what Jehoida said?

    m. What did Jehoida and his sons do regarding the king?

    n. What did Athaliah do when she heard the noise of the people running and cheering the king? What did Jehodiah have the commanders of a hundred do with Athaliah? Why was the city quiet?

2. Romans 11:13-36

    a. Who was Paul talking to?

    b. Who was the apostle to the Gentiles?

    c. What was Paul hoping for his own people?

d.   What happens if the part of the dough offered as first fruits is holy? If the root is holy, what about the branches?

e.   What should the Gentiles not do over the original branches?

f.   What does Paul say God will not do if he did not spare the natural branches?

g.   Of what does Paul not want the Gentile to be ignorant?

h.   In verse thirty-six, what does Paul say about God?

3.   Psalms 22: 1-18
a.   When was the phrase "My god, my god why have you forsaken me," repeated in the new testament?

b.   Who was enthroned as the holy one, the praise of Israel?

c.   In whom did the fathers put their trust? Did he deliver them?

d.   Who used the words of verse eight in the new testament?

e.   What request is made in verse eleven? What does the Psalmist say about the bulls and the lions?

f.   What kind of death seems to be described in verses fifteen, sixteen, and seventeen?

g.   Whose garments and clothing are spoken of in verse eighteen?

4.   Proverbs 20:7
a.   What kind of a life does a righteous man lead?

b.   Who are blessed?

STUDY QUESTIONS FOR JULY 29

1. II Chronicles 24:1-25:28
   a. How old was Joash when he became king? How long did he reign in Jerusalem? Since he died while he was still king, how old was he when he died?

   b. Who chose Joash's wives?

   c. What did Joash decide to do about the temple?

   d. What was done with the money collected in the chest that was placed outside the gate of the temple?

   e. What design was used to rebuild the temple?

   f. What did they do with the money that was left over from rebuilding the temple?

   g. How long were burnt offerings presented in the temple of the Lord continually?

   h. What did Joash do when the officials of Judah came and paid homage to him?

   i. Why did God's anger come upon Judah and Jerusalem?

   j. Who gave the order to stone Zechariah?

   k. Where was Joash when he died?

   l. Did Amaziah do what was right in the eyes of the Lord? What was said about his enthusiasm?

   m. Why didn't Amaziah execute the sons of the officials that murdered his father?

   n. How many men did Amaziah have that were ready for military service?

   o. Why did the man of God say that the troops from Israel should not march with Judah?

   p. Why did God hand over Judah to Israel?

2. Romans 12:1-21
   a. What does Paul urge the brothers to do with their bodies? What kind of a spiritual act did he call this?

   b. What did Paul say about conforming and transforming?

c. How were they to think about themselves?

d. What illustration does Paul use about the body?

e. What does Paul say about using the gifts given by God?

f. What should the believers do to the ones that persecute them?

g. What were they to do with the ones that rejoice and the ones that mourn?

h. What should be done when your enemy is hungry or thirsty?

i. How should one overcome evil?

3. Psalms 22:19-31
    a. Where does the Psalmist ask the Lord to be?

    b. What request does the Psalmist make about his life?

    c. To whom was he going to declare God's name?

    d. From where does the theme of the Psalmist's praise come?

    e. What does the Psalmist say about the poor?

    f. Who will bow down before the Lord?

    g. What will all the rich of the earth do?

    h. What is said about posterity and future generations?

4. Proverbs 20:8-10
    a. What does a king do when he sits on his throne to judge?

    b. What does the Lord detest?

1.   II Chronicles 26:1-28:27

       a.   Who did the people of Judah make king, in place of Amaziah?

       b.   How old was the new king when he became king? How long did he reign?

       c.   Did he do good or bad? Did he change in his lifetime?

       d.   Who helped him against the Philistines and the Arabs?

       e.   What did Uzziah build?

       f.   How many were in Uzziah's army?

       g.   What happened to Uzziah when he became powerful?

       h.   What did Azariah and eighty other priest tell Uzziah? What happened to Uzziah when he became angry?

       i.   Was Jotham a good king? Why did Jotham become powerful?

       j.   How old was Ahaz when he became king? Did Ahaz follow God?

       k.   What three things did Ahaz do to worship Baal? Whose ways was Ahaz following?

       l.   Why did God hand over Ahaz to the king of Aram and the king of Israel?

       m.   How many wives, sons and daughters did Israel take captive?

       n.   What did the prophet Oded say to the army of Israel? Did the army do what the prophet told them to do?

       o.   Why did the Lord humble Judah?

       p.   What happened to Ahaz in the time of his trouble?

       q.   Where was Ahaz buried when he died? Was he placed in the tombs of the kings of Israel?

2.   Romans 13:1-14

       a.   Should one be subject to governing authorities? Why?

       b.   Who is one that rebels against authority really rebelling against?

c.   For what type of people do rulers hold terror?

d.   Why should a person pay taxes?

e.   What does Paul say that a person should do about debt?

f.   What one rule sums up all the commandments?

g.   What fulfills the law?

h.   What is the Christian to put aside and what is he to put on?

i.   How were the Romans to clothe themselves?

j.   What were they to do about the desires of the sinful nature?

3.   Psalms 23:1-6
     a.   Who is the Psalmist's shepherd?

     b.   What does the shepherd make the Psalmist do?

     c.   Where was the Psalmist led?

     d.   Who guides his path?

     e.   Why did he fear no evil even while walking through the valley of the shadow of death?

     f.   What did the shepherd's rod and staff do for the Psalmist?

     g.   Where was the table prepared for him?

     h.   How long was he going to dwell in the house of the Lord?

4.   Proverbs 20:11
     a.   How is a child known?

1.   II Chronicles 29:1-36
     a.   How old was Hezekiah when he became king?

     b.   Did he do what was right in the eyes of the Lord?

     c.   What did Hezekiah do in the first month of the first year of his reign?

     d.   What did he say that their fathers had done?

     e.   What did Hezekiah intend to do?

     f.   How many family groups were represented by the Levites that set to work?

     g.   After the Levites assembled and consecrated themselves, what did they do to the temple of the Lord? Who ordered them to do this?

     h.   Who went in to purify the sanctuary of the Lord?

     i.   What did the priests bring out to the courtyard of the Lord's temple? What did the Levites do with these items?

     j.   For how many more days did they consecrate the temple of the Lord to purify it?

     k.   What did the priests and Levites report to the king?

     l.   What did king Hezekiah do early the next morning?

     m.   For what was the blood of the goats that were sacrificed used?

     n.   Where were the Levites stationed and what did they have with them?

     o.   What else began when Hezekiah gave the order to sacrifice the burnt offering on the altar?

     p.   What did Hezekiah tell the people to do after they had dedicated themselves to the Lord? Why did Hezekiah and all the people rejoice at what God had brought about for his people?

2.   Romans 14:1-23
     a.   What did Paul tell the Romans do for the one that is weak in faith?

     b.   Who accepted the man?

     c.   What does he ask about judging someone else's servant?

d.   Paul says one man considers one day more sacred than another, another man considers every day alike, who is each man doing this for?

e.   How about the man that eats and the man that abstains, who do they do it for?

f.   Who does one belong to whether they live or die?

g.   For what reason did Christ die and return to life?

h.   Who will stand before God's judgement seat?

i.   Who will give account of himself to God?

j.   What does Paul ask them to do in regard to passing judgement on one another?

k.   For the kingdom of God is not a matter of eating and drinking but what?

l.   What man is blessed?

3.   Psalms 24:1-10
     a.   To whom does the earth and everything in it belong?

     b.   Who may ascend the hill of the Lord? Who may stand in his Holy Place?

     c.   In verse eight, who is this king of glory?

     d.   In verse ten who is he, this king of glory?

4.   Proverbs 20:12
     a.   Who made ears that hear and eyes that see?

STUDY QUESTIONS FOR AUGUST 1

1. II Chronicles 30:1-31:21
   a. Who did Hezekiah invite to celebrate the Passover in Jerusalem?

   b. When were they going to celebrate the Passover?

   c. Why didn't they celebrate the Passover at the regular time?

   d. How did most of the people of Manasseh and Ephraim respond to the couriers ?

   e. What did they do with the incense altars?

   f. When did they slaughter the Passover lamb?

   g. What was the prayer of Hezekiah for the people that had not purified themselves?

   h. Initially how many days did they celebrate the Feast of Unleavened Bread?

   i. How many extra days did the assembly agree to celebrate?

   j. Did God hear the prayers of the priests and the Levites?

   k. What did the Israelites do to the sacred stones and Asherah poles in the towns of Judah?

   l. Why did Hezekiah command the people living in Jerusalem to give the portion due the priests?

   m. How did the people of Israel respond to this command?

   n. What did Azariah tell Hezekiah about the offerings brought by the people?

   o. What did Hezekiah decide to do to protect the offerings that the people brought?

   p. Who was in charge of the freewill offerings?

   q. What did Hezekiah do in everything he undertook? What was the result of this dedication?

2. Romans 15:1-22
   a. What should the strong do? How can one have hope?

   b. Who gives a spirit of unity? Who is one following when they receive the spirit of unity?

c.   Is the gospel only for the Jews?

d.   Where do the Gentiles need to place their hope?

e.   In what did Paul glory?

f.   What was Paul's ambition in regard to preaching the gospel?

g.   Why had Paul been hindered from coming to the Romans?

3.   Psalms 25:1-15
       a.   Who does the Psalmist trust?

       b.   How can one avoid being put to shame?

       c.   Who does he ask to show him his ways and teach his paths?

       d.   What does the Psalmist ask God to forget? How did he want to be remembered?

       e.   Why does the Lord instruct sinners in his ways?

       f.   What are the ways of the Lord for those that keep the demands of his covenant?

       g.   Who does the Lord confide in? To whom does the Lord make his covenant known?

       h.   Who releases the Psalmist from the snare?

4.   Proverbs 20:13-15
       a.   What happens to the one that loves sleep?

       b.   What is the boast of the buyer that complained about the quality of what he was buying?

       c.   What is the comment about lips that speak knowledge?

1. II Chronicles 32:1-33:13

    a. What did Sennacherib, king of Assyria do to Judah?

    b. What three things did Hezekiah do to prepare for the actions of Sennacherib?

    c. What five questions did Sennacherib ask to undermine the confidence of the people of Judah?

    d. Why did the officers of Assyria speak in Hebrew?

    e. What did king Hezekiah and Isaiah the prophet do?

    f. What did the angel do to the Assyrian army?

    g. What happened to the king of Assyria that had been bragging so loudly?

    h. Who saved Hezekiah and the people of Jerusalem?

    i. Why did the wrath of God not come upon Hezekiah and Judah and Jerusalem in Hezekiah's lifetime?

    j. What did Hezekiah do to house his great riches?

    k. Who succeeded Hezekiah as king?

    l. How many years did the next king reign? How did this king act before God?

    m. How did Judah under this king compare to the nations that the Lord had destroyed before the Israelites?

    n. What happened when the Lord spoke to this king and God's people?

    o. Who did God bring against the king and his people?

    p. What did the king of Judah do in his distress?

    q. What did God do when the king took these actions? What did the king know when he saw God work?

2. Romans 15:23-16:7

    a. Who was Paul talking about when he said, "I have been longing for many years to see you"?

b.	What was Paul's plan to be able to visit with them?

c.	Where was Paul headed right then?

d.	Who did Paul mention that were pleased to make a contribution for the poor at Jerusalem?

e.	Why did they owe it to the Jews?

f.	What two prayer requests did Paul voice to the Romans?

g.	Who did Paul commend to them?

h.	What five groups of people did Paul greet?

3.	Psalms 25:16-22
a.	What three things does the Psalmist request in the first three verses of this reading?

b.	What did he ask God to look upon?

c.	What did he ask about his life?

d.	What did he ask God to keep him from being?

e.	Where did he take refuge?

f.	What did he ask to protect him?

g.	Where was the Psalmist's hope?

h.	What does the Psalmist ask for Israel?

4.	Proverbs 20:16-18
a.	What is one to do with a garment that is put up for security if it is done for a wayward woman?

b.	How does food gained by fraud taste? What does he end up getting?

c.	What should one do if he is going to wage war?

STUDY QUESTIONS FOR AUGUST 3

1. II Chronicles 33:14-34:33
   a. To whom is "he" referring in chapter thirty-three, verse fourteen? (Look back to the first part of chapter thirty-three)

   b. What did he do to the height of the wall?

   c. What did he do about the foreign gods?

   d. To whom did the people continue to sacrifice at the high places?

   e. Where was Manasseh buried?

   f. How old was Amon when he became king? Did he live righteously?

   g. Who did Amon worship and offer sacrifices? How was he different than his father?

   h. How did Amon die? How did the people react?

   i. How old was Josiah when he became king? How long did he reign in Jerusalem?

   j. What did he do in the eyes of the Lord?

   k. What did Josiah do in the eighth year of his reign? What did he begin to do in the twelfth year of his reign?

   l. What did Josiah do in the eighteenth year of his reign?

   m. What was done with the money that had been brought into the temple of God?

   n. Who had charge of the laborers and supervised all the workers from job to job?

   o. Who found the book of the law that had been given to Moses?

   p. What did Josiah do about all the detestable idols from all the territory belonging to the Israelites?

2. Romans 16:8-27
   a. In this chapter Paul is closing his letter to the Romans, who were all these people that he is sending his greetings?

   b. In verse sixteen, how were they to greet one another?

c.   For whom did Paul urge them to watch out?

d.   Who are the ones that cause divisions, serving? How do they deceive the minds of naive people?

e.   Why was Paul full of joy over the people?

f.   About what did Paul want them to be wise? About what did he want them to be innocent?

g.   What was God, soon, going to do for them?

h.   How was Timothy related to Paul?

i.   What three relative of Paul sent their greetings?

j.   Who wrote down this letter for Paul? Whose hospitality did Paul enjoy? Who was the city's director of public works?

k.   How does Paul end this letter? (Romans sixteen verse twenty-seven)

3.   Psalms 26:1-12
    a.   What is David's first request of the Lord in this chapter?

    b.   In whom did David trust?

    c.   What did David ask for next?

    d.   What did David say he loved in this chapter and why did he love it?

    e.   Where did David stand and what was he going to do?

4.   Proverbs 20:19
    a.   What does a gossip do?

    b.   Who should a man avoid?

1.   II Chronicles 35:1-36:23
        a.   What did Josiah encourage the priests in? What did he tell the Levites to do? How were they to prepare themselves?

        b.   What were the Levites to do in the holy place?

        c.   Who provided for all the lay people? How many sheep and goats were provided for the Passover?

        d.   Who else contributed voluntarily?

        e.   What did the priest do with the blood? What did the Levites do?

        f.   What did they do with the Passover animals? What did they do with the holy offerings?

        g.   How long were the descendants of Aaron sacrificing the burnt offerings and the fat portions?

        h.   Where were the musicians, the descendants of Asaph?

        i.   For what was the entire service of the Lord carried out?

        j.   How long had it been since the Passover was observed like this in Israel? When was this Passover celebrated?

        k.   What happened to King Josiah when he went out to fight Neco king of Egypt? Who composed laments for Josiah?

        l.   Who became king in place of Josiah? How old was this man when he became king? How long did he reign as king?

        m.   Did Jehoiakim, the next king of Judah please the Lord?

        n.   How long did Jehoiachin reign in Jerusalem?

        o.   How many kings of Judah and Jerusalem, listed in chapter thirty-six, did evil in the eyes of the Lord?

        p.   In the last verse of this reading, what does Cyrus king of Persia say?

2.   I Corinthians 1:1-17
        a.   Who was writing this letter? To whom was it being written?

69

b. What does he send to them from God the Father and the Lord Jesus Christ?

c. For what does he always thank God? Why does he do that?

d. Who would keep them strong to the end?

e. What does he appeal to the Corinthians to do?

f. What three questions does Paul ask that illustrate that they should have no divisions?

3. Psalms 27:1-6
a. Who was the Psalmist's light and salvation?

b. What question does the Psalmist ask after he says, "The Lord is the stronghold of my life"?

c. What would happen to the Psalmist's enemies when they attack him?

d. What would his heart not do even though an army besieged him?

e. What one thing (broken into three parts) did the Psalmist ask of the Lord?

f. What three things will the Lord do in the day of trouble for the Psalmist?

g. What would happen to the Psalmist's head?

h. What was the Psalmist going to do at the Lord's tabernacle? What was he going to do to the Lord?

4. Proverbs 20:20-21
a. What happens to the man that curses his father or his mother?

b. What is said about an inheritance that is quickly gained?

STUDY QUESTIONS FOR AUGUST 5

1. Ezra 1:1-2:70
   a. When does this story of Ezra take place?

   b. Who moved the heart of Cyrus king of Persia?

   c. What did Cyrus do?

   d. What did the Lord, the God of heaven appoint Cyrus to do?

   e. What did Cyrus invite the people of Israel to do?

   f. Who was to provide the people of Israel with silver and gold , with goods and livestock and with freewill offerings?

   g. What did the family heads of Judah and Benjamin, and the priests and Levites do?

   h. Who assisted them with silver and gold, with goods and livestock, and with valuable gifts, in addition to all the freewill offerings?

   i. What did Cyrus send with the people of Israel?

   j. In all, how many articles of gold and silver were brought out?

   k. Why were the descendants of Hobaiah, Hakkoz and Barzillai excluded from the priesthood?

   l. How many people were in the company of people that returned to Jerusalem? How many more returned to Jerusalem with the Israelites?

   m. What is said about the priests, the Levites, the singers, the gate keepers and the temple servants?

2. I Corinthians 1:18-2:5
   a. What is the message of the cross to those that are perishing?

   b. What was written that is quoted here?

   c. What did God do with the wisdom of this world?

   d. What foolishness did God use to save those that believed?

   e. What did the Jews demand? What did the Greeks look for?

f. What did Paul preach? What did he say the message was to the Jews and to the Greeks?

g. How do man's wisdom and strength compare to God's?

h. What did God choose to shame the wise and the strong?

i. Who can boast before God? In whom should man boast?

j. On what should man's faith rest?

3. Psalms 27:7-14
   a. Who does the Psalmist want to hear his voice?

   b. What did the Psalmist's heart say of the Lord?

   c. What was the Psalmist going to seek?

   d. What did he say about God turning away?

   e. What did the Psalmist say about being forsaken by his father and his mother?

   f. What did the Psalmist want the Lord to teach him?

   g. What request did the Psalmist make in regard to his foes? What were the false witnesses doing to him?

   h. In what was the Psalmist confident?

   i. What did the Psalmist encourage his listeners to do in regard to the Lord?

4. Proverbs 20:20-23
   a. What is supposed to be done instead of saying, "I will pay you back for this wrong?"

   b. What does the Lord detest and what does not please him?

1. Ezra 3:1-4:24

    a. What happened when the seventh month came?

    b. What was their guide when they built the altar?

    c. What was the first feast that they celebrated? Of what event did this feast remind the people?

    d. Did they wait until the foundation of the Lord's temple was laid before they began to offer burnt offerings?

    e. What did they give to the people of Sidon and Tyre so they would bring cedar logs by sea from Lebanon to Joppa?

    f. Who were appointed to supervise the building of the house of the Lord? How old were the supervisors?

    g. Whose prescription did the priests and Levites follow carrying out their worship? What did they sing?

    h. What did many of the older priests and Levites and family heads, who had seen the former temple do?

    i. What did the people around Judah do to frustrate Judah's plans after Judah wouldn't let them help build the temple? How long did they persist in trying to frustrate Judah?

    j. Who wrote a letter to King Artaxerxes?

    k. In what language was the letter written?

    l. In essence, what did the letter say?

    m. What happened to the letter?

    n. What did the king find in his research?

    o. What order was issued?

    p. What did Rehum and Shimshai do when the letter from Artaxerxes was read? How long did the work on the house of the Lord come to a standstill?

2. I Corinthians 2:6-3:4

a. What kind of a message did Paul speak? Was it a message of wisdom of this age or of the rulers of this age?

b. Did the rulers of this age understand Paul's message?

c. Quote I Corinthians chapter two verses nine and ten.

d. Who searches all things?

e. Who knows the thoughts of man?

f. Who knows the thoughts of God?

g. What Spirit did Paul receive? Why had he received that Spirit?

h. What kind of words did Paul use?

i. Why does a man without the Spirit reject the things that come from the Spirit of God?

j. How did Paul address the Corinthians? What kind of food did Paul give the Corinthians? Why?

3. Psalms 28:1-9
a. To whom did the Psalmist call?

b. Who was the Psalmist going to be like if God remained silent?

c. What was the Psalmist going to lift his hands toward?

d. Why did the Psalmist say "Praise be to the Lord?

e. Who is the Psalmist's strength and shield?

f. Who does the Psalmist's heart trust?

g. What is the Psalmist's request for God's people?

4. Proverbs 20:24-25
a. How are a man's steps directed?

b. How should a man dedicate something?

STUDY QUESTIONS FOR AUGUST 7

1.   Ezra 5:1-6:22
     a.   Who set to work to rebuild the house of God in Jerusalem?

     b.   What two questions did the governor of Trans-Euphrates ask them?

     c.   Did this stop their construction?

     d.   To which king did they address their questioning letter?

     e.   Who did the Jews in Judah say they were?

     f.   Why had God handed their forefathers over to Nebuchadnezzar the Chaldean king of Babylon?

     g.   Which king gave them Sheshbazzar as governor and told him to rebuild the house of God on its site?

     h.   In this letter, what did they ask King Darius to do?

     i.   What did King Darius find?

     j.   How were the costs going to be paid for rebuilding the temple?

     k.   What were they to do with the gold and silver articles that had been taken from the temple?

     l.   What did Darius tell Tattenai and Shethar-Bozenai and their fellow officials to do?

     m.   What did king Darius reiterate about where the expenses were coming from?

     n.   What would happen to anyone that changed Darius' edict?

     o.   Did Tattenai, and Shethar-Bozenai and their associates carry out the decree of Darius?

     p.   How many days did the Israelites celebrate the Feast of Unleavened Bread? Why were they celebrating with joy?

2.   I Corinthians 3:5-23
     a.   What is Apollos and Paul?

     b.   Who makes the church grow?

c.   How is each man rewarded?

d.   What did Paul say was his part in building the church?

e.   What does the fire do to each man's work?

f.   What will happen to the worker if what he has built survives?

g.   What should one do if he thinks he is wise by the standards of this age?

h.   Should we boast about men?

3.   Psalms 29:1-11
a.   To whom should we ascribe glory and strength?

b.   What is over the waters? What thunders over the mighty waters?

c.   What does the Psalmist say about the voice of the Lord?

d.   What does God do to Lebanon and Sirion?

e.   What does the voice of the Lord do to the desert?

f.   What will all in the Lord's temple cry?

g.   Where is the Lord enthroned?

h.   Who gives strength to his people and blesses his people with peace?

4.   Proverbs 20:26-27
a.   What does a wise king do to the wicked?

b.   What does the lamp of the Lord search?

1.   Ezra 7:1-8:20
        a.   From what well known Old Testament character did Ezra descend?

        b.   Why did the king grant everything to Ezra that he asked for?

        c.   How many months did it take Ezra to travel from Babylon to Jerusalem?

        d.   To what three things did Ezra dedicate himself?

        e.   What was the king's purpose for sending Ezra and the group of Israelites to Jerusalem?

        f.   Who supplied the silver and the gold?

        g.   What did the king say they were to do first with the money? Then what?

        h.   What did King Artaxerxes order the treasuries of Trans-Euphrates to provide for Ezra the priest?

        i.   What six groups of people were to be tax free, tribute free, and duty free?

        j.   Who was Ezra to appoint?

        k.   Who was to teach the laws of God?

        l.   What did the king say was the penalty for not following God's law and the law of the king?

        m.   Who did Ezra praise because the king extended his good favor?

        n.   What did Ezra do?

        o.   How long did they stay at the canal that flows toward Ahava?

        p.   What group of people were missing? How did they take care of that?

2.   I Corinthians 4:1-21
        a.   How should men regard Paul, Apollos, or Cephas?

        b.   What is required of those that have been given a trust?

        c.   Who is to judge the servants of God?

d.   Paul says "Therefore judge nothing before the appointed time;" when will that be?

e.   In verse six Paul tells why he is teaching this principle, why is he?

f.   Give three contrasts that are made between the apostle and the Corinthians.

g.   List eight things the apostle suffered.

h.   Why did Paul send Timothy to Corinth?

3.   Psalms 30:1-12
       a.   Why was the Psalmist going to exalt the Lord?

       b.   What happened when he called on the Lord?

       c.   What did he call on the saints to do?

       d.   How long does God's anger last? How long does God's favor last?

       e.   When does rejoicing come?

       f.   How did God change his wailing?

       g.   How was he clothed instead of sackcloth?

       h.   How long was he going to give thanks?

4.   Proverbs 20:28-30
       a.   What keeps a king safe? How is his throne made secure?

       b.   What is the Solomon"s comment about young men? About old men?

       c.   How is evil cleansed?

STUDY QUESTIONS FOR AUGUST 9

1.   Ezra 8:21-9:15
   a.   Where were Ezra and the remnant that were with him? What did Ezra do?

   b.   Why was Ezra ashamed to ask the king for soldiers and horsemen to protect them?

   c.   What did Ezra do with the silver and gold that had been donated to the house of their God?

   d.   What weights and values are listed here of the donated items?

   e.   When did they set out? Where were they headed? What did they do when they arrived at their destination?

   f.   What did they do on the fourth day?

   g.   How was everything accounted for?

   h.   Then what did the exiles that had returned from captivity do?

   i.   How many bulls, rams, and lambs were sacrificed?

   j.   What disturbing news did Ezra hear from the leaders? How did Ezra react?

   k.   What did Ezra do at the evening sacrifice?

   l.   In chapter nine verse six, why did Ezra say that he could not lift his face to God?

   m.   Why had they, their kings and their priests been subjected to the sword and captivity, to pillage and humiliation at the hand of foreign kings?

   n.   How had the Lord been gracious to them?

   o.   How had the people disregarded the commands of the Lord?

   p.   How much had God punished them?

2.   I Corinthians 5:1-13
   a.   What report had Paul received about the church at Corinth?

   b.   What should the church have done?

   c.   What did Paul say about not being with them physically?

      d.   What did he say about their boasting?

      e.   What does Paul say about the yeast?

      f.   When Paul told them in a former letter not to associate with the sexually immoral people was he talking about the people of this world?

      g.   What other kinds of people does Paul lump with the sexually immoral?

3.   Psalms 31:1-8
      a.   Where did the Psalmist take refuge?

      b.   What five things does the Psalmist request in the first two verses?

      c.   What two things did he want God to do for him because God was his rock and fortress?

      d.   What did he want God to do because God was his refuge?

      e.   Where was the Psalmist going to commit his spirit?

      f.   What did the Psalmist hate?

      g.   In what was the Psalmist going to be glad and rejoice?

      h.   Where did the Lord set the feet of the Psalmist?

4.   Proverbs 21:1-44
      a.   Where is the king's heart? How is it directed?

      b.   What does man think about his ways? What does the Lord do?

1. Ezra 10:1-44
   a. Who gathered around him when Ezra was praying and confessing, weeping and throwing himself down before the house of the Lord?

   b. What did they also do?

   c. What did Shecaniah say to Ezra?

   d. According to what did he suggest that the king should do it?

   e. What did Ezra do when he rose up? Did the people do the things that Ezra suggested?

   f. To whose room did Ezra go? What did he do while he was there? Why did he do that?

   g. What proclamation was issued throughout Judah and Jerusalem?

   h. What would happen to anyone who failed to appear within three days?

   i. What did Ezra tell the people?

   j. How did the whole assembly respond?

   k. What were the problems mentioned here that would prevent the people from doing what Ezra told them to do?

   l. What plan was suggested to take care of the their obligations?

   m. Who opposed the plan?

   n. What did the exiles do?

   o. When did they sit down to investigate the cases?

   p. When did they finish investigating the cases?

2. I Corinthians 6:1-20
   a. What was Paul talking about to the believers at Corinth in verses one through verse seven?

   b. What did Paul say they were doing to their brothers? What should they have done?

c. What did Paul ask them if they knew about the wicked? Name the ten types of people that Paul lists here that will not inherit the kingdom of God, beside the wicked.

d. Paul said they used to be like that, what made them different now?

e. Paul said "everything is permissible to me" but what?

f. What promise is given to the believers in regard to the raising of the Lord from the dead?

g. What is said about two becoming one as regards the prostitute and the Lord?

h. What should they do about sexual immorality?

i. Why are believers not their own? Because of that what should they do with their bodies?

3. Psalms 31:9-18
   a. What was the first request of the Psalmist in this reading?

   b. How was the Psalmist's life consumed?

   c. What four things did the Psalmist say happened because of his enemies?

   d. In whom did the Psalmist trust? Who was his God?

   e. What was in God's hands?

   f. What is the Psalmist's prayer about the wicked in the last part of this Psalm?

4. Proverbs 21:3
   a. What is more acceptable to the Lord than sacrifice?

1.   Nehemiah 1:1-3:14
    a.   Who was Nehemiah's father?

    b.   What report did one of his brothers and some other men give about the Jewish remnant that survived the exile?

    c.   What did Nehemiah do when he heard this report?

    d.   What four things did Nehemiah request in his prayer?

    e.   What did he confess in this prayer?

    f.   What was Nehemiah to the king?

    g.   What question did the king ask Nehemiah? How did he answer the king?

    h.   What is the next question that the king asks? How did Nehemiah answer the king?

    i.   What two additional things did Nehemiah request from the king? What did Nehemiah say caused the king to grant his request?

    j.   Who else did the king send with Nehemiah?

    k.   What did Sanballat the Horonite and Tobiah the Ammonite think about the actions of the king and Nehemiah?

    l.   What did Nehemiah do after being in Jerusalem for three days?

    m.   What did Nehemiah tell the Jews, priests, nobles, officials and the others that would be doing the work? How did they respond?

    n.   What did Sanballet and Tobiah do?

    o.   Who rebuilt the sheep gate? The fish gate? The Jeshanah gate? The valley gate? The dung gate?

    p.   What was said about the men of Tekoa and their nobles?

2.   I Corinthians 7:1-24
    a.   In answer to the questions of the Corinthians, what did Paul say about a man marrying?

b.   Since there was so much immorality, what should each man have and each woman have?

c.   To whom does the wife's body belong? To whom does the husband's body belong?

d.   In verse five what does Paul say, the husband and the wife should not do? What was the exception?

e.   What did he say to the unmarried and the widow?

f.   What did he say about the brother that has a wife that is an unbeliever? What about the wife that has an unbelieving husband?

g.   In verse fourteen, why does he say that believers should follow the forgoing advice?

h.   What should they do if the unbeliever departs?

i.   What should one that is bought with a price not become?

3.   Psalms 31:19-24
a.   What does the Psalmist say about God's goodness? For whom was this goodness stored up?

b.   Where does God hide them?

c.   Where does he keep them safe from accusing tongues?

d.   Why did the Psalmist give praise to the Lord?

e.   What did the Psalmist say in his alarm?

f.   Who is to love the Lord? Who does the Lord preserve and who does he pay back in full?

g.   What does the Psalmist say to all who hope in the Lord?

4.   Proverbs 21:4
a.   What three things are sin?

1. Nehemiah 3:15-5:13

    a. Who repaired the fountain gate? What repairs did he make?

    b. What part of the wall did Nehemiah work on?

    c. Who worked next to Nehemiah?

    d. What did Sanballat say when he heard that the Jews were rebuilding the walls of Jerusalem?

    e. What did Tobiah say about the Jews wall building?

    f. What did the Jews pray?

    g. To what height had the walls been rebuilt at this point? What was said about the work of the people?

    h. How did Sanballet and friends react when they heard that the repairs to Jerusalem's walls had gone ahead and that the gaps were being closed?

    i. What did the Jews do to meet this threat?

    j. What kind of trouble was the rubble for the workers?

    k. In chapter four verse thirteen, what did Nehemiah do to protect the people from the invaders?

    l. What did Nehemiah tell the people?

    m. How did Nehemiah divide up his men?

    n. What did the ones that carried material do?

    o. What did the sound of the trumpet signal? Who did Nehemiah say would fight for them?

    p. Where were the men and their helpers to stay at night? Why were they to stay there?

    q. What did Nehemiah say when he shook out the folds in his robe?

2. I Corinthians 7:25-40

    a. What did Paul say about the virgins and marriage?

b.   Why was Paul saying these things?

c.   What did Paul tell them they should do if they were married? What did he tell them to do if they were unmarried?

d.   Was it a sin if a virgin married?

e.   Why did Paul say that Christians should not get engrossed in the things of this world?

f.   How long is a woman bound to her husband?

3.   Psalms 32:1-11
a.   Who is blessed?

b.   What happened when the Psalmist kept silent?

c.   When was God's hand heavy on the Psalmist? What happened to the Psalmist's strength?

d.   Then what did the Psalmist do?

e.   What should everyone do that is godly?

f.   Who was the Psalmist's hiding place and who protected him from trouble?

g.   What does the Psalmist say about the woes of the wicked? What does he say about the Lords's love?

h.   Who should rejoice and be glad in the Lord? Who should sing?

4.   Proverbs 21:5-7
a.   Where do the plans of the diligent lead? Where does haste lead?

b.   To what does the author liken a fortune made by a lying tongue?

c.   What did the violent refuse to do?

STUDY QUESTIONS FOR AUGUST 13

1. Nehemiah 5:13-7:60
    a. What is the time frame that Nehemiah is reporting in these chapters.

    b. Did he eat the food allotted to the governor?

    c. What had earlier governors done? How had their assistants acted?

    d. To what did Nehemiah devote himself?

    e. How much land did Nehemiah and his men acquire?

    f. How many Jews and officials ate at Nehemiah's table?

    g. What was prepared each day for Nehemiah and his crew? What happened every ten days?

    h. Why didn't Nehemiah demand the food allotted to governors?

    i. What message did Sanballat and Tobiah send to Nehemiah? Were their motives pure?

    j. What answer did Nehemiah send back to them?

    k. What did the letter say that Sanballat sent with his aide?

    l. What answer did Nehemiah send?

    m. What did Shemaiah suggest to Nehemiah? What was Nehemiah's answer?

    n. How did the enemies of Nehemiah react when they heard about the walls that were restored?

    o. Who did Nehemiah put in charge of Jerusalem? Why did he choose this man?

    p. When were the gates of Jerusalem to be opened? When were they to be closed?

    q. What did Nehemiah say about the city and the people?

2. I Corinthians 8:1-13
    a. What subject does Paul bring up in chapter eight?

    b. What did he say they all possessed?

       c.   What does knowledge do? What does love do?

       d.   What does he say about the man that loves God?

       e.   What did they know about an idol?

       f.   For them, how many gods were there? How many lords?

       g.   Did food bring them near God?

       h.   What warning did Paul give about exercising their freedom?

       i.   When they sinned against their brother and wounded their weak conscience, who were they really sinning against?

3.   Psalms 33:1-11
       a.   The Psalmist invited his listeners to sing, how were they to sing? To whom were they to sing?

       b.   How were they to praise the Lord?

       c.   What kind of a song were they to sing?

       d.   How were the heavens and the starry host made?

       e.   What did the Psalmist say that all the people of the world should do?

       f.   What does the Psalmist say about the plans of the Lord?

4.   Proverbs 21:8-10
       a.   What is the way of the guilty? What does he say about the conduct of the innocent?

       b.   What is better than to share a house with a quarrelsome wife?

       c.   What does an evil man crave?

STUDY QUESTIONS FOR AUGUST 14

1. Nehemiah 7:61-9:21
   a. In chapter seven verse sixty-four, why were some of the men excluded from the priesthood?

   b. When could they eat the most sacred food?

   c. What happened in the seventh month?

   d. Did the people listen to the book of the law as Ezra read it to them?

   e. Where did Ezra stand as he read the book of the law?

   f. How did the people respond to the reading of the law?

   g. What did the Levites do?

   h. What did Nehemiah, Ezra, the priests, scribes, and the Levites say to the people?

   i. What did Nehemiah say was the joy of the Lord for the people?

   j. On the second day of the month, what did the heads of all the families along with the priests and the Levites do?

   k. Why did the people go out and bring back branches and build themselves booths on their roofs and in their courtyards?

   l. What did Ezra do day after day from the first day to the last?

   m. Who chose Abram and brought him out of Ur of the Chaldeans and named him Abraham?

   n. How did God lead his people during the day? How did he lead them at night?

   o. What happened to the forefathers of these people? Did they obey God's commands?

   p. Did God abandon his people in the desert?

2. I Corinthians 9:1-18
   a. What four question does Paul ask the Corinthians in the first verse of chapter nine?

   b. What was the seal of Paul's apostleship in the Lord?

c.   What did Paul ask in his defense?

d.   What three examples does Paul use to show that a workers should be paid?

e.   What was written in the law about putting a muzzle on the ox while it is treading out the grain?

f.   If others had the right of support of the people, shouldn't Paul also have the right?

g.   What was Paul's reward?

3.   Psalms 33:12- 22
      a.   What nation is blessed?

      b.   What does the Lord see when he looks down from heaven?

      c.   Is a king saved by the size of his army?

      d.   Can a horse save?

      e.   On whom are the eyes of the Lord?

      f.   Who can deliver them from death and keep them alive in famine?

      g.   Who is our help and our shield?

      h.   What doers the Psalmist ask of God's unfailing love?

4.   Proverbs 21:11-12
      a.   What happens when a mocker is punished?

      b.   What does a wise man get when he is instructed?

      c.   What does the righteous one do to the house of the wicked?

1. Nehemiah 9:22-10:39
    a. Who gave kingdoms and nations to the Jewish people?

    b. What two kings and countries are listed here that God gave to them?

    c. How numerous were the Jewish sons?

    d. The word says "They ate to the full and were well-nourished; they reveled in your great goodness." But what five things did they do that disappointed God and caused God to turn them over to their enemies?

    e. What did the Jews do when they were oppressed by their enemies?

    f. What did God do for them?

    g. What cycle emerged?

    h. Why did God hand his people over to neighboring people?

    i. Why didn't God abandon and put an end to his people?

    j. Did the people serve God or turn from their evil ways?

    k. Because of the peoples sin, where did the abundant harvest go?

    l. What three groups of people affixed their seal to the binding agreement with God?

    m. To what eight things did the people bind themselves to do and not to do in chapter ten verses twenty-nine through thirty-two?

    n. How were the priests, the Levites and the people going to determine when each family would bring wood to burn on the altar of the Lord their God, as it was written in the law?

    o. What last thing did the people promise not to do in the last verse of chapter ten?

2. I Corinthians 9:19-10:13
    a. How did Paul use his freedom?

    b. What did Paul do so that he could share the blessings of the gospel?

    c. How many runners get the prize?

d.   Why did Paul beat his body and make it his slave?

e.   Who was the spiritual rock that accompanied the children of Israel through the wilderness?

f.   Why were the bodies of the Israelites scattered over the desert?

g.   "These things happened to them as _____ and were _____ as _____ for us, on whom the fulfillment of the age has come." I Corinthians chapter ten verse eleven.

h.   What does God do when one is tempted?

3.   Psalms 34:1-10
     a.   At what time does the Psalmist extol the Lord?

     b.   In what does his soul boast?

     c.   How can one make his face radiant and never covered with shame?

     d.   When the poor man called on the Lord, how many troubles did the Lord save him out of?

     e.   Who encamps around those that fear the Lord?

     f.   What man is blessed?

     g.   What does the man that fears God lack?

     h.   What good thing does the man that seeks God lack?

4.   Proverbs 21:13
     a.   What happens to the man that shuts his ears to the cry of the poor?

STUDY QUESTIONS FOR AUGUST 16

1.   Nehemiah 11:1-12:26
    a.   Where did the leaders of the people settle?

    b.   How did they decide what other people were to live in Jerusalem?

    c.   If they were not chosen to live in Jerusalem, where were they to settle?

    d.   What did the people say about the men that volunteered to live in Jerusalem?

    e.   Where did some Israelites, temple servants and descendants of Solomon's servants live? On whose property did they live?

    f.   What was the number of the descendant of Perez that lived in Jerusalem?

    g.   Who was the chief officer of the descendants of Benjamin? Who was over the second district of the city?

    h.   How many men were there from the priests that carried on the work of the temple?

    i.   Of what two things were the Levites in charge in regard to the temple?

    j.   Where did the temple servants live? Who was in charge of them?

    k.   Who were the singers under, that regulated their daily activity?

    l.   Who was in charge of the songs of thanksgiving?

    m.   Who were the leaders of the Levites? Where did their associates stand? How did they give praise and thanksgiving? Who prescribed this?

    n.   Who were the six gatekeepers? What did they guard? In what days did they serve?

2.   I Corinthians 10:14-11:2
    a.   From what did Paul ask the Corinthians to flee?

    b.   To what kind of people was Paul speaking? What were they to judge for themselves?

    c.   How did the many become one body?

    d.   To whom are the sacrifices of pagans offered?

e. What two things are said about the phrase "Everything is permissible"?

f. What were the Corinthians to do about food in the meat market? What were they to do if they were invited to eat at the house of an unbeliever? What if they were told that the meat was offered in sacrifice?

g. What restriction did Paul put on the Corinthians about following him?

3. Psalms 34:11-22
   a. What was the Psalmist going to teach the people?

   b. What three things does the Psalmist encourage the ones that love life and desire to see many good day, to do?

   c. On whom are the eyes of the Lord and his ears attentive to their cry?

   d. What happens to the righteous man that has many troubles?

   e. What promise is given to the one that takes refuge in the Lord?

4. Proverbs 21:14-16
   a. What does a gift given in secret do? What about a bribe concealed in a cloak?

   b. How does justice affect the righteous? How does it affect evildoers?

   c. What happens to the man that strays from the path of understanding?

1.   Nehemiah 12:27-13:31
      a.   From where were the Levites sought? Why were they brought to Jerusalem?

      b.   Where did the singers live?

      c.   What did the priests and Levites purify after they had purified themselves?

      d.   How many choirs did Nehemiah assign to give thanks?

      e.   Who led the procession?

      f.   With which choir did Nehemia go?

      g.   Under whose direction did the choirs sing? Why did they offer great sacrifices?

      h.   What did Eliashib the priest do with one of the large rooms that had been used to store the grain offerings and incense and temple articles?

      i.   What did Nehemiah do when he learned what evil thing Eliashib had done?

      j.   What did he learn about the portions assigned to the Levites? Where had the Levites and singers gone?

      k.   What three men did Nehemiah make responsible for distributing the supplies to their brothers?

      l.   What were the merchants doing on the Sabbath day? What did Nehemiah say they were doing by desecrating the Sabbath?

      m.   What did Nehemiah order them to do about the doors of the gates?

      n.   What did some of the merchants do the night before the Sabbath? What warning did Nehemiah give them?

      o.   What did Nehemiah see the men of Judah doing? What did Nehemiah do to the priests and Levites?

2.   I Corinthians 11:3-16
      a.   Who is the head of every man? Who is the head of the woman? Who is the head of Christ?

      b.   What does a man do that prophesies with his head covered? What about a woman?

c.   What is it like if a woman prays or prophesies with her head uncovered?

d.   What should a woman do if she does not cover her head?

e.   Should a man cover his head? Why?

f.   Who is the glory of man?

g.   From whom did woman come?

h.   Who was created for man?

i.   In the Lord is the woman independent of the man? Is the man independent of the woman?

j.   From where does everything come?

3.   Psalms 35:1-16
      a.   What did the Psalmist do about his enemies?

      b.   What was going to happen to the Psalmist's soul when God answered his prayer?

      c.   What would his whole being exclaim?

      d.   What does the Lord do for the poor and needy?

      e.   How did the Psalmist humble himself?

4.   Proverbs 21:17-18
      a.   What happens to the one who loves pleasure?

      b.   What is said about the one who loves wine and oil?

      c.   Who became the ransom for the righteous?

      d.   What about the unfaithful?

1.   Esther 1:1-3:15

    a.   When did this story take place?

    b.   How was the kingdom of Xerxes described?

    c.   In the third year of Xerxes, how long did he display the vast wealth of his kingdom and the splendor and glory of his majesty?

    d.   How long did the banquet that he gave at the end of those days, last? How was the wine served?

    e.   On the seventh day what did king Xerxes command his eunuchs to do? What was the result? How did the king react?

    f.   What punishment did the king mete out?

    g.   Who became the new queen? To whom was she related?

    h.   In chapter two verse eighteen, what three things did the king do in honor of the new queen?

    i.   What did Mordecai discover and report to the king, through the new queen, during the time he was sitting at the king's gate?

    j.   Who did king Xerxes honor after these events? Who knelt down and honored Haman? Who refused to bow down or pay honor to him?

    k.   How did Haman react when he heard that Mordecai would not bow down? What did Haman look for?

    l.   What did Haman say to the king? What did Haman offer to do to carry out this business?

    m.   What did the king do? What did he say about the money?

    n.   What did the royal secretaries do on the thirteenth day of the first month?

    o.   What did Haman and the king do? What about Susa?

2.   I Corinthians 11:17-34

    a.   What did Paul hear about them when they came together as a church? What were they doing at the Lord's Supper?

    b.   What four questions does Paul ask in verse twenty-two?

c. What did Paul receive from the Lord about the bread? What did he receive from the Lord about the cup?

d. What were the Corinthians doing every time they ate that bread or drank that cup?

e. What should a man do before he eats of the bread or drinks of the cup?

f. Why were many weak and sick among them and many fallen asleep?

g. What should one do if they are hungry? Why should they do that?

3. Psalms 35:17-28
a. What question does the Psalmist ask the Lord in verse seventeen?

b. What fourteen things does the Psalmist request of the Lord in verses seventeen, nineteen, and twenty-two through twenty-seven?

c. What does he promise the Lord in verse eighteen?

d. How does he describe his enemies in verse twenty?

e. In verse twenty-one, what did the Psalmist's enemies do to him?

f. In the last verse, what was his tongue going to do? What does he promise to do all day long?

4. Proverbs 21:19-20
a. It is better to live in a desert than to do what?

b. What is in the house of the wise?

c. What does the foolish man do?

STUDY QUESTIONS FOR AUGUST 19

1.   Ester 4:1-7:10
     a.   What was the family relationship between Queen Esther and Mordecai?

     b.   Why was Queen Esther in great distress about Mordecai?

     c.   What did Hathach find out that was wrong with Mordecai?

     d.   What did Mordecai ask queen Esther to do?

     e.   How did Queen Esther respond? How did Mordecai answer the queen?

     f.   What did Queen Esther ask Mordecai to do?

     g.   What did Esther do on the third day? Did the king accept the queen's visit? What was Esther's request?

     h.   What was Esther's request at the first banquet?

     i.   What happened when the king could not sleep after the first banquet?

     j.   Who did the king want to honor? Who did Haman think that the king wanted to honor?

     k.   Who did the king pick to carry out the honor of Mordecai?

     l.   What did Esther request at the second banquet?

     m.   Who did Queen Esther point out that dared to do such a thing?

     n.   Who did Haman beg for his life? What did the king see when he came back into the room?

     o.   What did the attendants do with Haman?

     p.   What did Harbono say to the king?

     q.   What did the king say to do with Haman?

2.   I Corinthians 12:1-26
     a.   Why was Paul giving the Corinthians this information?

     b.   What one thing does Paul point out here that one speaking by the Spirit of God, can not say?

c.   Are all gifts the same? Is the Spirit different?

d.   List the gifts mentioned here.

e.   How many Spirits are involved in these gifts?

f.   What illustration does Paul use to demonstrate many parts being one?

g.   If the ear should say, "Because I am not an eye, I do not belong to the body," would it cease to be part of the body?

h.   What happens to the rest of the body if one part suffers or one part is honored?

3.   Psalms 36:1-12

a.   What was in the heart of the Psalmist?

b.   What does the wicked man do in his own eyes?

c.   What does the wicked man do even on his bed? To what does he commit himself?

d.   What is the psalmist's comments on God's love, faithfulness, righteousness, and justice?

e.   Who finds refuge in the shadow of the Lord's wings?

f.   Who has the fountain of life?

g.   In verse eleven, what two requests does the Psalmist make?

4.   Proverbs 21:21-22

a.   What does the person find that pursues righteousness and love?

b.   What does a wise man do?

STUDY QUESTIONS FOR AUGUST 20

1.	Esther 8:1-10:3

	a.	What did King Xerxes give to Queen Esther?

	b.	What did the king do for Mordecai?

	c.	What did Queen Esther request of the king in chapter eight verse five?

	d.	How did the king respond?

	e.	In what language were the orders that were written by Mordecai, in the name of king Xerxex, given?

	f.	How were the orders sealed?

	g.	How were the orders distributed?

	h.	What rights did these orders give to the Jews?

	i.	What was Mordecai wearing when he left the king's presence?

	j.	What happened to the enemies of the Jews on the thirteenth day of the twelfth month of Adar? What had these enemies hoped for?

	k.	How many men did the Jews kill and destroy in the citadel of Susa?

	l.	In chapter nineteen verse thirteen, what further request did Queen Esther make?

	m.	What did the Jews do to celebrate the victory that God had given them? What did they call this celebration?

	n.	What did Mordecai send in his letters to all the Jews in the one hundred and twenty seven provinces.

	o.	Where did King Xerxes impose tribute?

	p.	What rank did Mordecai obtain in his life time?

	q.	Why was Mordecai held in high esteem by his many fellow Jews?

2.	I Corinthians 12:27-13:13

	a.	Who did Paul say was the body of Christ? Who all was a part of the body?

	b.	Who did God appoint in his church?

c.   What question did Paul ask the Corinthians in regard to the workers in the church.

d.   What is the subject of chapter thirteen?

e.   To what did he liken one that speaks extremely well but doesn't have love?

f.   How often does love fail?

g.   What happens when perfection comes?

h.   Of the three, faith, hope and love, what did Paul say was the greatest?

3.   Psalms 37:1-11
     a.   Why did the Psalmist say not to fret because of evil men?

     b.   What four things does the Psalmist encourage his listeners to do beside trusting in the Lord?

     c.   What will the Lord give one, if they delight themselves in him?

     d.   What will happen when one commits his way to the lord and trusts in him?

     e.   What does the Psalmist encourage the people to do before the Lord?

     f.   From what should the people refrain and from what should they turn away?

     g.   What will happen to the meek?

4.   Proverbs 21:23-24
     a.   How does one keep himself from calamity?

     b.   How does a proud and arrogant man behave?

STUDY QUESTIONS FOR AUGUST 21

1. Job 1:1-3:26
   a. How was Job described in the first verse of chapter one?

   b. How did he compare to the other people of the East?

   c. Who came with the angels when they came to present themselves to the Lord?

   d. What did the Lord ask Satan about the Lord's servant Job?

   e. What did Satan think would happen if Job lost everything?

   f. What did the Lord allow Satan to do? What restriction did he place on Satan?

   g. How many messengers came and gave Job the bad news?

   h. How did Job respond to the bad news?

   i. What question did the Lord ask again of Satan the next time he came before the Lord?

   j. What did the Lord allow Satan to do to job this time? What restriction did the Lord place on Satan?

   k. What did Job's wife suggest that Job do?

   l. What question did Job ask his wife? Did Job sin in what he said?

   m. What did Job's friends do? How long did they sit on the ground with him, saying nothing?

   n. What did Job do when he opened his mouth?

   o. Instead of celebrating his birthday what did he want to happen to that day on the calendar?

   p. What came to Job instead of food?

   q. What happened about Job's fears?

2. I Corinthians 14:1-17
   a. What way does Paul encourage the Corinthians to follow and what are they to eagerly desire?

b. Who does the one that speaks in tongues speak to?

c. Who does the one that prophesies speak to?

d. Who does the one that speaks in tongues edify?

e. Who does the one that prophesies edify?

f. Paul said he would like everyone to speak in tongues but he would rather have them do what?``

g. What illustration did Paul use of the flute, the harp, and the trumpet?

h. What should one pray for that speaks in tongues?

i. What question does Paul ask if you are praising God with your spirit?

3. Psalms 37:12-29
   a. What two things do the wicked do against the righteous?

   b. What does the Lord do to the wicked?

   c. What happens to the sword of the wicked and what happens their bows?

   d. What happens to the power of the wicked?

   e. What about the days of the blameless?

   f. When did the Psalmist see the righteous forsaken or their children begging bread?

4. Proverbs 21:25-26
   a. What will be the death of the sluggard? Why will that be the death of him?

   b. While the sluggard is craving more what do the righteous do?

1.   Job 4:1-7:21
        a.   Who was Eliphaz?

        b.   He encourages Job to look back on his life, how should Job be encouraged by that?

        c.   What is his question about mortal man and a righteous God?

        d.   What does he say about a man that is corrected by God?

        e.   What will Job do about destruction and famine and beasts of the earth?

        f.   What about his children?

        g.   How would he come to the grave?

        h.   What did Job say about his anguish?

        i.   Where did Job say the arrows of God were? What happened to the poison?

        j.   What did Job say about the white of an egg?

        k.   What did Job say about his friends?

        l.   What did Job say he would do if his friends taught him?

        m.   How do honest words feel?

        n.   Why did Job ask them to look at him?

        o.   How swift were his days?

        p.   How did Job say he will complain?

        q.   What did he say about the meaning of his life?

        r.   What did Job think that his bed would do for him?

        s.   Where was he going lie to down?

2.   I Corinthians 14:18-40
        a.   Did Paul speak in tongues?

b. How did he prefer to speak in the church?

c. How were the brothers thinking?

d. "Tongues, then, are a sign not for _____ but for _____"

e. How many are to speak in tongues when the church comes together?

f. What should the speaker do if there is not interpreter?

g. How many prophets should speak? What are the others to do?

h. "For God is not a God of _____ but of _____" I Corinthians chapter fourteen verse thirty-three a

i. What should the brothers be eager to do?

j. What should they not forbid?

k. How should everything be done?

3. Psalms 37:30-40
   a. What does the mouth of the righteous man do? What about his tongue?

   b. What do the wicked do to the righteous?

   c. What will happen to all sinners? What about the future of the wicked?

   d. From where does the salvation of the righteous come?

   e. Who helps them and delivers them?

   f. Where do they take refuge?

4. Proverbs 21:27
   a. What kind of sacrifice is detestable?

   b. What is even more detestable?

STUDY QUESTIONS FOR AUGUST 23

1.   Job 8:1-11:20
      a.   What three men are giving speeches in this reading in Job?

      b.   Who talks first in chapter eight?

      c.   What did he say Job's words were like? What did he ask if God does?

      d.   What did he say that God would do for Job if he looked to God and pleaded with the almighty?

      e.   What did he say was the destiny of all who forget God?

      f.   With what did he say that Job's mouth and tongue will be filled?

      g.   In chapter nine what was Job's comment on what Bildad had said? What was the first question that Job wondered about a mortal?

      h.   How many times did Job speculate that a man might be able to answer God if he wished to dispute with God?

      i.   Who did Job say made the Bear and Orion, the Pleiades and the constellations?

      j.   How fast did Job say his days were? (Four illustrations)

      k.   In chapter ten, verse eight, what did Job say about God's hands? What question did he ask God?

      l.   What question does he ask in chapter ten, verse eighteen? What did he wish for in chapter ten verses eighteen and nineteen?

      m.   What four questions does Zophar ask of Job in chapter ten verses two and three?

      n.   How high and deep and wide did Zophar say the mysteries of God were?

      o.   According to Zophar, could a witless man become wise?

      p.   According to Zophar, what would happen to the wicked?

2.   I Corinthians 15:1-28
      a.   What did Paul want to remind the brothers?

      b.   How were they saved?

    c.   Who are the ones listed here to whom Christ appeared? To whom did he appear last of all?

    d.   Why did Paul say he was not worthy to be called an apostle?

    e.   What question did Paul have for some that say there is no resurrection of the dead?

    f.   Who was the first fruit of those who have fallen asleep?

    g.   What is the last enemy to be destroyed?

3.   Psalms 38:1-22
    a.   What three things does the Psalmist say that the Lord did to him before he admits that it was because of his sin?

    b.   What did his guilt do? What was it like?

    c.   Why did his wounds fester and become loathsome?

    d.   Where did the longings of the Psalmist lie?

    e.   What did his friends and companions do? Why?

    f.   On whom did the Psalmist wait? What did the Psalmist affirm that the Lord would do?

    g.   What does the Psalmist say about his enemies in verse nineteen?

    h.   With what three requests does the Psalmist conclude this Psalm?

4.   Proverbs 21:28-29
    a.   What happens to a false witness? What happens to the one that listens to a false witness?

    b.   What does a wicked man do? What does an upright man do?

1. Job 12:1-15:35
   a. Who is speaking in chapters twelve through fourteen?

   b. What does he say in the second verse that sounds like a put down?

   c. What does he say in defense of himself?

   d. What had Job become to his friends?

   e. What did he tell his comforters to do about the animals? What does he say that the animals know?

   f. What does the ear test? Where is wisdom found?

   g. To whom does wisdom, power and counsel belong?

   h. Who makes nations great and destroys them?

   i. In chapter thirteen verse three, what did Job desire?

   j. What did Job say about the maxims of his friends?

   k. What did Job say he would do even if the Lord slew him?

   l. What did Job know now that he had prepared his case?

   m. What two things did Job ask God to grant him?

   n. In the first two verses of chapter fourteen, how does Job describe men's lives?

   o. Who determines man's days? According to Job, what happens to man as compared to a tree?

   p. Who speaks next in chapter fifteen? What is the first question he asks Job? What did he say condemned Job?

   q. According to Eliphaz, what happens to all the days of a wicked man?

   r. According to Eliphaz, what will happen to those who love bribes?

2. I Corinthians 15:29-58
   a. How often did Paul say that he died? What question did Paul ask them about fighting wild beasts in Ephesus?

b. What does bad company do? What did Paul tell them that they should come back to their senses and do?

c. What has to happen to the seed sown before it can spring to life?

d. Who gives the plant its body?

e. What are the four kinds of flesh mentioned here?

f. Talking about the resurrection, what four contrasts are made between the body that is sown and the body that is raised?

g. What was written about he first Adam and the second Adam?

h. Can flesh and blood inherit the kingdom of God?

i. Paul says we will not all sleep but what?

j. Why does Paul say that they should always give themselves fully to the work of the Lord?

3. Psalms 39:1-13
   a. How was the Psalmist going to keep from saying the wrong thing?

   b. What were his comments on the length of life?

   c. Who will get man's wealth that he has heaped up?

   d. In whom did the Psalmist hope?

   e. What does the Psalmist request in verse twelve?

4. Proverbs 21:30-31
   a. What wisdom, insight, or plan can succeed against the Lord?

   b. With whom does victory rest?

STUDY QUESTIONS FOR AUGUST 25

1.   Job 16:1-19:29
      a.   What does Job call his comforters?

      b.   What would Job do different if their roles were reversed?

      c.   What happens to his pain if he speaks or he doesn't speak?

      d.   Who does Job blame for assailing, tearing and gnashing his teeth at him?

      e.   In chapter sixteen verse twelve through verse sixteen, what discouraging things happened even though his hands had been free from violence and his prayer pure?

      f.   Where was Job's witness and advocate?

      g.   What will happen to a man that denounces his friends for reward?

      h.   Who replied to Job in chapter eighteen?

      i.   What four questions does this person ask of Job in the first part of chapter eighteen?

      j.   What did this person use the rest of chapter eighteen to describe? Do you think he was inferring that this description described Job?

      k.   What question does Job ask his comforters? How many times did he say that they had reproached him?

      l.   Whose concern did Job say that it was if it was true that he had gone astray?

      m.   What happened even though he cried that he had been wronged?

      n.   What happened to Job's brothers, his acquaintances, his kinsmen, his friends, guests and maidservants?

      o.   What did he say about his breath?

      p.   What would Job see after his skin was destroyed?

2.   I Corinthians 16:1-24
      a.   What had Paul asked the Galatian church to do about the offering.

      b.   What was Paul going to do when he arrived? Would he go with the men to Jerusalem?

c.   When was Paul going to come to them?

d.   How much longer was he going to stay at Ephesus?

e.   What did Paul ask them to do for Timothy?

f.   What had Paul urged Apollos to do? How did Appolos feel about this?

g.   Who were the first converts in Achaia?

h.   Why was Paul glad when Stephanas, Fortunatus, and Achaicus arrived?

i.   How were they to greet one another?

3.   Psalms 40:1-10
      a.   For whom did the Psalmist wait patiently?

      b.   In verse two and three, what four things did the lord do for the Psalmist?

      c.   What man is blessed?

      d.   What did the Lord not desire?

      e.   In verse seven and eight, what did the Psalmist say?

      f.   What did the Psalmist proclaim? Where did he proclaim it?

      g.   Of what two things did the Psalmist speak?

      h.   What did the Psalmist not conceal?

4.   Proverbs 22:1
      a.   What is more desirable than great riches?

      b.   What is better than silver or gold?

STUDY QUESTIONS FOR AUGUST 26

1.   Job 20:1-22:30
        a.   What is meant by the expression, "Job's comforters"?

        b.   Why did Zophar decide to answer what had been said?

        c.   What does Zophar say about mirth of the wicked and the joy of the godless?

        d.   What happens to the evil that is sweet in the mouth of the wicked man? What does God make his stomach do?

        e.   According to Zophar, why will the wicked man fail to enjoy profit from his trading?

        f.   What would expose the guilt of the wicked man?

        g.   Do you think Zophar was referring to Job when he was talking about the wicked man?

        h.   What did Job tell his friends to do in chapter twenty-one, verse one and two?

        i.   In chapter twenty-one, verses seven through twenty-one, what is Job questioning?

        j.   What question did Job ask about the knowledge of God?

        k.   What did Job say about his friends consoling?

        l.   What question did Eliphaz ask about man and God?

        m.   What did Eliphaz say about how Job treated his brothers, the weary, the hungry, the widows and the fatherless?

        n.   What advice does Eliphaz give Job in chapter twenty-two, verse twenty-one and twenty-two?

        o.   According to Eliphaz what must Job do to be restored?

        p.   What does Eliphaz say will become Job's gold when he assigns his nuggets to the dust and his gold of Ophir to the rocks in the ravines?

2.   II Corinthians 1:1-11
        a.   How did Paul become an apostle of Christ Jesus?

        b.   To what church did Paul address this letter? What other group of people did he include?

    c.   What did Paul extend to them from God the Father?

    d.   To who was praise to be given?

    e.   Who comforted Paul and company in all their troubles? Why were they comforted?

    f.   Why did Paul and company come under hardship and pressure while they were in the province of Asia?

    g.   How was the gracious favor granted to Paul and company?

3.   Psalms 40:11-17
    a.   For what two things does the Psalmist ask in verse eleven?

    b.   What does the Psalmist say about his troubles and his sins?

    c.   What request does the Psalmist make about the ones that seek to take his life?

    d.   What is his request for the one that says, "aha! Aha!"?

    e.   What is his request for the ones who seek the Lord?

    f.   What does he want the Lord to do even though he, himself is poor and needy?

    g.   Who was the Psalmist's help and deliverer?

4.   Proverbs 22:2-4
    a.   What do rich and poor have in common?

    b.   What does a prudent man do when he sees danger?

    c.   What brings wealth and honor and life?

STUDY QUESTIONS FOR AUGUST 27

1.   Job 23:1-27:23
       a.   What did Job say about his complaint today?

       b.   Who was Job looking for? Where did he look?

       c.   What did Job say would happen when he was tested by God?

       d.   What three things did Job say that he did to follow God?

       e.   Why was Job terrified before God?

       f.   How were men treating the orphan, the widow and the poor?

       g.   What does the murderer do when daylight is gone?

       h.   What does the eye of the adulterer watch for? Why?

       i.   What does God do to the mighty?

       j.   What does Bildad the Shuhite say about dominion and awe?

       k.   What question does Bildad ask about the righteousness of mankind?

       l.   Over what does God spread the northern skies? How does God wrap up the waters?

       m.   As long as Job had life within him, what does he promise that his lips will not speak?

       n.   In chapter twenty-seven verse eleven, what did Job promise to teach them?

       o.   What is the fate of the wicked man?

       p.   What happens to the silver and the clothes of the wicked man?

       q.   What happens when the wicked man lies down wealthy?

       r.   What does the east wind do to the wicked man?

2.   II Corinthians 1:12-2:11
       a.   What was the boast of Paul and Timothy?

       b.   Paul said they had not acted by worldly wisdom but according to what?

c.   Could the Corinthians understand what Paul wrote?

d.   When had Paul planned to visit Corinth?

e.   Did Paul make his plans in the worldly manner?

f.   What was the message of Jesus Christ? What about the promises God has made?

g.   Why did Paul write as he did to the Corinthians?

h.   Did Paul have confidence in the Corinthians?

i.   In chapter two verse seven to eight how does Paul say that the church should now treat the one that had sinned?

3.   Psalms 41:1-13

        a.   Who is blessed? What does the Lord do for this person?

        b.   What did the Psalmist say?

        c.   What did the enemies of the Psalmist say about him?

        d.   What does the enemy do with the slander he gathers?

        e.   What did his enemies imagine and what did they say?

        f.   What did his close friend do to him?

        g.   How does the Psalmist finish this Psalm?

4.   Proverbs 22:5-6

        a.   What is found in the paths of the wicked? What about the one that guards his soul?

        b.   What happens to the child that is trained in the way he should go?

1.   Job 28:1-30:31

    a.   Look back at chapter twenty- six of Job, who is giving this discourse?

    b.   What illustration does he use in the first part of chapter twenty-eight of finding something of value to purchase wisdom?

    c.   How did he say that sapphires were transformed?

    d.   Were birds of prey able to find precious stones?

    e.   Does man comprehend the worth of wisdom?

    f.   Can wisdom be purchased with gold or precious stones?

    g.   Who understands the way to wisdom?

    h.   What did God say to man in Job chapter twenty-eight verse twenty-eight?

    i.   In chapter twenty-nine, what did Job long for? How does Job describe his former life?

    j.   How did men listen to him?

    k.   How did things change in chapter thirty?

    l.   Who mocked Job? How did they mock Job verse nine?

    m.   What did they do to his face?

    n.   How is his dignity driven away?

    o.   What happened to his safety?

    p.   What happened when Job cried out to God?

    q.   What happened to Job before the wind and what happened to him in the storm?

    r.   What two questions did Job ask in chapter thirty verse twenty-five?

    s.   What happened when he hoped for good?

    t.   What happened when he looked for light?

u.   Did Job's skin turn black because of the sun?

v.   For what was his harp and flute used?

2.   II Corinthians 2:12-17
   a.   Where did Paul go?

   b.   Did he have peace of mind?

   c.   Where did he go next?

   d.   To whom did Paul give thanks? Why was he giving him thanks?

   e.   What were Paul and his workers to God? To what did he liken their smell and their fragrance?

   f.   Did they peddle the word of God for profit?

3.   Psalms 42:1-11
   a.   What does the deer do?

   b.   What does the Psalmist's soul do?

   c.   What had been the Psalmist's food day and night?

   d.   What did the men ask him?

   e.   As the Psalmist remembered, what did he do about the house of God?

   f.   What did the Psalmist ask his soul? What did he tell his soul to do?

   g.   What does the Lord do at night?

   h.   In verse eleven, the Psalmist repeats his conversation with his soul, what does he say?

4.   Proverbs 22:7
   a.   Who do the rich rule over?

   b.   Who is a servant to the lender?

1.	Job 31:1-33:33
	a.	What covenant did Job make with his eyes?

	b.	What did Job say God would find if God weighed Job in honest scales?

	c.	What five things did Job say should cause him to loose his arm?

	d.	What three things did Job say would be sins that should be judged?

	e.	What three things would cause briars to come up instead of wheat and weeds instead of barley?

	f.	Why was Elihu angry?

	g.	How did Elihu compare in age to the other men?

	h.	Did Elihu think that only the old were wise?

	i.	What compelled Elihu?

	j.	From where did his words come?

	k.	Who did Elihu say made him and what gave him life?

	l.	What did he say Job was wrong about?

	m.	How did he say that God speaks to men?

	n.	How did he say a man could be chastened?

	o.	What did he say about an angel being on a mans side?

	p.	Why did he say God does all these things to man?

	q.	"Pay attention Job, and listen to me; be_____ and I will_____." Job chapter thirty-three verse thirty-one

	r.	What did he tell Job to do if he had anything to say?

	s.	Why did he want Job to be silent?

2.	II Corinthians 3:1-18
	a.	What two questions did Paul ask the Corinthians at the beginning of this chapter?

b. What was the letter written on their hearts that was known and read by everybody?

c. The letter was not written with ink but with what? From where does their competence come?

d. What kills and what gives life?

e. Why could the children of Israel not look on the face of Moses?

f. How does Paul compare the ministry that condemns men, to the ministry that brings righteousness? Why was Paul bold?

g. How is the veil that was over the old covenant taken away? Where is freedom?

3. Psalms 43:1-5
    a. Who did the Psalmist ask to vindicate him?

    b. Who did he want to plead his case?

    c. Who was his stronghold?

    d. What were his two questions to God?

    e. What was God's light and truth going to do for him?

    f. Where was the Psalmist going to go?

    g. How was he going to praise God?

    h. What questions did he ask his soul?

    i. What did he tell his soul to do?

4. Proverbs 43:1-5
    a. What will be reaped when wickedness is sown?

    b. When will a generous man be blessed?

1.   Job 34:1-36:33
      a.   Who is the speaker in this section of Job?

      b.   What quote did he give from Job?

      c.   What did he say that Job was doing?

      d.   In chapter thirty-four verses ten through twelve, what does he say about God?

      e.   According to Elihu, what would happen to mankind if God withdrew his spirit and breath?

      f.   Whose eyes does he say that are on the ways of men? Can evildoers hide from God?

      g.   What did Elihu think was the root of Job's problem in chapter thirty-four verse thirty-three through thirty-seven?

      h.   What is Elihu's thinking on how Job's sin or righteousness affect God?

      i.   With what does Elihu accuse Job in the last verse of chapter thirty-five?

      j.   As Elihu continues in chapter thirty-six, what seems to be his goal expressed in verse two?

      k.   What does he say about God in verse five?

      l.   According to Elihu, what will happen to the man that obeys and serves God? What about the one that does not listen?

      m.   What warning does he give Job in verse eighteen? What about verse twenty-one?

      n.   In chapter thirty-six verse twenty-six, what two things docs he say about God?

      o.   What does God's thunder do? According to Elihu, what does the same thing?

2.   II Corinthians 4:1-12
      a.   How did Paul and his group have their ministry?

      b.   What did they do instead of losing heart?

      c.   If their gospel was veiled, from whom was it veiled? Who blinded their eyes?

d. What were they preaching?

e. What did God say about the light? Where did he make his light shine?

f. Where did they have this treasure stored? To what do you think Paul was referring?

g. Why were the ones that were alive always being given over to death for Jesus' sake?

3. Psalms 44:1-8
a. How did they hear?

b. How did God drive out the nations?

c. What did God do to the people? What did God do for their fathers?

d. Was it by their sword that they won the land? Was it their arm that brought them victory? What did bring them victory?

e. How did the Psalmist push back his enemies? How did he trample his foes?

f. In whom did they make their boast? How long would they praise God's name?

4. Proverbs 22:10-12
a. What happens if the mocker is driven out?

b. Who will the one that loves with a pure heart and whose speech is gracious, have as a friend?

c. Over what will the eyes of the Lord keep watch? What does the Lord do to the words of the unfaithful?

STUDY QUESTIONS FOR AUGUST 31

1.   Job 37:1-39:30
     a.   Who is speaking here in chapter thirty-seven? (Look back to the first of chapter thirty-six)

     b.   What is he describing in the first fourteen verses of this chapter?

     c.   What happens to men's labor and what did the animals do?

     d.   What did he tell Job that he should do?

     e.   What does he say about the sun?

     f.   Who talks to Job in chapter thirty-eight and chapter thirty-nine?

     g.   What was the first question that the Lord asks Job.

     h.   List the next seven questions.

     i.   Do you think that the Lord was kind of mocking Job in chapter thirty-eight, verse twenty-one?

     j.   What does the Lord ask Job about the snow and the hail?

     k.   What does the Lord ask about the raven?

     l.   What do the wings of the ostrich do? To what can they not compare?

     m.   How does a stork treat her eggs and her young?

     n.   What does a horse do about fear? What can a horse not do when he hears the trumpet sound?

     o.   What are the next two questions that the Lord asks Job?

     p.   Where does an eagle dwell and stay at night?

     q.   On what does an eagle's young feed?

     r.   What do you think Job felt like after all these questions?

2.   II Corinthians 4:19-5:10
     a.   What did Paul and friends do because they believed?

b.   What was all this for?

c.   Though outwardly they were wasting away, what was happening inwardly?

d.   What were their light and momentary troubles achieving for them?

e.   On what did they fix their eyes? What did Paul say about what was seen? What about unseen?

f.   What did they know if their earthly tent was destroyed?

g.   What did they do in the mean time?

h.   Who made them for this very purpose? What did God give them as a guaranty of what is to come?

i.   How were they to live?

j.   Where must all men appear?

3.   Psalms 44:9-26
    a.   What eleven things did the Psalmist say that God had done to them?

    b.   What was before the Psalmist all day long?

    c.   What four things did the Psalmist say that they had not done?

    d.   For whose sake did they face death all day long?

    e.   As what were they considered?

    f.   For what things does the Psalmist ask the Lord in verse twenty-three?

    g.   For what reason does the Psalmist ask God to help him?

4.   Proverbs 22:13
    a.   What does the sluggard say?

STUDY QUESTIONS FOR SEPTEMBER 1

1. Job 40:1-42:17
    a. What question does the Lord ask Job in verse two?

    b. How did Job respond?

    c. What did the Lord tell Job to do in chapter forty verse seven?

    d. What four questions does the Lord ask Job in verses eight and nine? What eight things did the Lord tell him to do if he answered in the affirmative?

    e. What would the Lord admit if Job did these things?

    f. Where does the behemoth lie? What surrounds him? What does it say about him when the river rages?

    g. What does the Lord describe in chapter forty-one? What twelve questions does the Lord ask about this being?

    h. When Job replied to the Lord in chapter forty-two verse two, what did Job say that he knows? How did he repent?

    i. Why was the Lord angry with Eliphaz and his two friends? (Chapter forty-two verse seven)

    j. What did the Lord instruct them to do? What did the Lord say that Job would do for them?

    k. Did Eliphaz and his two friends do what the Lord asked them to do?

    l. What happened to Job after he prayed for his friends?

    m. What did all Job's brothers and sisters and everyone who had known job before, do for job and what did they bring him?

    n. Who were the most beautiful women in the land?

    o. How long did Job live after this?

    p. How many generations of his family was Job able to see?

2. II Corinthians 5:11-21
    a. "Since then" what did Paul, et all come to know?

125

b.   What were they trying to persuade men?

c.   What were Paul and group not trying to do? What were they trying to do?

d.   What did they say would be the case if they were out of their mind? What would be the case if they were in their right mind?

e.   What compelled Paul and company? For whom did Christ die?

f.   What happens to anyone that is in Christ? Who did Paul say were Christ's ambassadors?

g.   What did Paul implore his hearers to do?

3.   Psalms 45:1-17
     a.   What stirred the Psalmist's heart? What was he doing when he was stirred?

     b.   To what did the Psalmist liken his tongue?

     c.   To whom is the Psalmist referring in chapter forty-five verse six? (See Hebrews chapter one verse eight and nine)

     d.   What does the Son of God love, and what does he hate?

     e.   How are his robes described?

     f.   Who was among his honored women?

     g.   What would the daughter of Tyre bring?

     h.   How is the princess described?

     i.   What were the nations going to do?

4.   Proverbs 22:14
     a.   To what was the mouth of an adulteress likened?

     b.   What will happen to one that is under the Lord's wrath?

STUDY QUESTIONS FOR SEPTEMBER 2

1. Ecclesiastes 1:1-3:22
   a. Who wrote the book of Ecclesiastes?

   b. What is his assessment of "everything"?

   c. Generations come and go but what happens to the earth?

   d. Where do the streams flow? What happens to the sea?

   e. Of what can the eye never get enough? What about the ear?

   f. What is new under the sun?

   g. What kingdom was the teacher, king of? To what did he devote himself?

   h. What did he learn when he applied himself to the understanding of wisdom and madness and folly?

   i. What did he find out about pleasure? What did he say about laughter?

   j. What eight great projects did Solomon undertake?

   k. What did he deny himself that his eyes desired?

   l. What happened when he surveyed all that his hands had done?

   m. What was better than folly?

   n. Why did he say that he hated life?

   o. To whom does God give wisdom, knowledge and happiness? What does God give to the sinner?

   p. In chapter three, Solomon says that there is a time for every activity, how many examples does he give?

   q. What conclusion does Solomon come to in chapter three, verse twenty-two?

2. II Corinthians 6:1-13
   a. What did Paul urge the Corinthians not to do about the grace of God?

   b. What did God say in verse two?

c.   When is the day of salvation?

d.   What did Paul say about putting a stumbling block in one's path?

e.   List the things for which Paul and his friends commend themselves?

f.   Paul and friends were not withholding their affections from the Corinthians, what were the Corinthians withholding from them? What did Paul ask them to do?

3.   Psalms 46:1-11
   a.   Who was their refuge and strength?

   b.   Why were they not going to fear? What could happen to the earth, mountains, and water and they would still not fear?

   c.   Who was with them and who was their fortress?

   d.   What does the Psalmist ask them to come and see?

   e.   Who makes the wars cease?

   f.   What does he do to the bow, spear, and the shield?

   g.   The Psalmist asks them to be still and what?

   h.   Who will be exalted among the nations?

   i.   Who will be exalted in the earth?

   j.   Who was with them and was their fortress?

4.   Proverbs 22:15
   a.   What is bound up in the heart of a child?

   b.   What will drive it far from him?

STUDY QUESTIONS FOR SEPTEMBER 3

1. Ecclesiastes 4:1-6:12
   a. Who wrote the book of Ecclesiastes?

   b. What conclusion did the author make about the living and the dead?

   c. From where did he say that all labor and all achievement spring?

   d. In chapter four verse four, what phrase is used that is repeated many, many times in the book of Ecclesiastes?

   e. What did he say about the man that was alone, that had neither son or brother, yet he was not content with his wealth?

   f. In chapter four verse nine through twelve, what four reasons are given that two are better than one??

   g. When is it better to be a youth than an old king?

   h. What should one do when he goes to the house of God?

   i. What should one do when he makes a vow to God? What is better to do, in regard to a vow?

   j. Who takes the increase of the land?

   k. What happens to the person that loves money and the one that loves wealth?

   l. What happens as goods increase?

   m. What is said about the sleep of the laborer and the rich man?

   n. How does a man come from his mother's womb and how does he leave this earth?

   o. What is said about the man that has a hundred children and lives many years?

   p. What is said about more words?

2. II Corinthians 6:14-7:7
   a. What do we usually think of when we hear about being yoked together in chapter six verse fourteen?

   b. Could that verse refer to other areas of life also? If so what?

c.   What five questions are asked about the relationship between good and evil?

d.   What did God say about the people and being their God?

e.   What two things does God tell his people to do?

f.   What was God going to be to the people and what were the people going to be to him?

g.   Why were the people to purify them selves from everything that contaminates the body?

h.   What did Paul ask the people to make room for in their hearts?

i.   How did God comfort Paul and his group?

3.   Psalms 47:1-9
        a.   What did the Psalmist tell the people of all the nations to do with their hands and with their voices?

        b.   Who did the Psalmist say was awesome?

        c.   Who is the great king over all the earth?

        d.   How did God ascend?

        e.   To whom should one sing praises?

        f.   Who reigns over the nations? To whom do the kings of the earth belong? Who is greatly exalted?

4.   Proverbs 22:16
        a.   What happens to the one that oppresses the poor to increase his own wealth?

        b.   What happens to the one that gives gifts to the rich?

STUDY QUESTIONS FOR SEPTEMBER 4

1. Ecclesiastes 7:1-9:18

   a. In the book of Ecclesiastes, what is king Solomon searching for?

   b. What is better than fine perfume?

   c. Where is the heart of the wise? Where is the heart of a fool?

   d. It is better to heed the rebuke of a wise man than what?

   e. What does extortion and bribes do?

   f. Why should one not be quickly provoked in their spirit?

   g. What does wisdom do for the life of its possessor?

   h. Solomon points out three things that one should not go overboard on, what are these three things?

   i. In chapter seven verse eighteen what will the man who fears God avoid?

   j. Why should one not pay attention to every word people say?

   k. What did Solomon find more bitter than death?

   l. How many upright men did he find in a thousand? How many upright women did he find in a thousand?

   m. What man has power over the wind to contain it?

   n. What happens when the sentence for a crime is not quickly carried out?

   o. What is a live dog better than?

   p. Why did he say that "What ever your hand finds to do, do it with your might"?

   q. "The quiet words of the wise are more to heeded" than what?

2. II Corinthians 7:8-16

   a. What did Paul not regret? Why was Paul happy?

   b. What does godly sorrow bring?

   c. What does worldly sorrow bring?

d.   What encouraged Paul?

e.   What happened to Titus that especially delighted Paul?

f.   Who did Paul boast about? Was he embarrassed?

g.   What made Titus' affection for the Corinthians even greater?

h.   Why was Paul glad?

3.   Psalms 48:1-14
   a.   Who is great and worthy of praise?

   b.   Where is God's holy mountain?

   c.   How does the Psalmist describe God's mountain?

   d.   What happened when the kings joined forces to advance on the mountain of God?

   e.   What was the pain like that they experienced?

   f.   What did God do to these forces?

   g.   What did the people do within God's temple?

   h.   How far do the praises of God reach?

   i.   Why did mount Zion rejoice?

   j.   How long would God be their God?

4.   Proverbs 22:17-19
   a.   What is the student of Proverbs supposed to do?

   b.   In whom is the student to trust?

STUDY QUESTIONS FOR SEPTEMBER 5

1.   Ecclesiastes 10:1-12:14
   a.   What do dead flies do to perfume?

   b.   What is one to do if the anger of a ruler is raised against him?

   c.   What may happen to the one that digs a pit?

   d.   What may happen to the one that quarries?

   e.   What about the one who splits logs?

   f.   How does he compare the words of a wise man to the words of a fool?

   g.   What happens to the house of a lazy man?

   h.   Why did he say do not revile the king even in your thoughts or curse the rich in you bedroom?

   i.   What did he say to do with your bread?

   j.   What two illustrations did he use to show that we can not understand the work of God?

   k.   What should you do in the morning? What about the evening?

   l.   What should be remembered in the days of your youth?

   m.   How is old age described in this section?

   n.   What happens at the end of old age?

   o.   What does the teacher say about everything?

   p.   What did the teacher do with knowledge?

   q.   How was the teacher's writing described?

   r.   When will the making of books end?

   s.   What is the conclusion of the whole matter?

2.   II Corinthians 8:1-15
   a.   What did Paul want the brothers to know in regard to the Macedonian churches?

b.   What came out of their most severe trial and their extreme poverty?

c.   What was Paul's testimony about the Macedonian churches?

d.   Paul said that the Corinthians excelled in everything-in faith, in speech, in knowledge, in complete earnestness and in your love for us. In what else did he want them to excel?

e.   How was Paul going to test the love of the Corinthians?

f.   What did the Corinthians know about the grace of the Lord Jesus Christ?

g.   What was Paul's desire for those involved?

h.   What was the plenty of the Corinthians for?

i.   What was written?

3.   Psalms 49:1-20
a.   Who did the Psalmist ask to listen to him?

b.   What was his mouth going to speak?

c.   Can a man redeem the life of another?

d.   What happens to a wise man? A foolish man? A senseless man?

e.   What happens to their forms (bodies) that lie in the grave?

f.   How does the Psalmist tell us to respond to the man that grows rich?

4.   Proverbs 22:20-21
a.   How many sayings did he write?

b.   What was the purpose of these sayings?

STUDY QUESTIONS FOR SEPTEMBER 6

1.   Songs of Songs 1:1-4:16
     a.   Several translations have inserted notations to identify the speaker in each portion of Song of Songs. What three people or groups of people are shown?

     b.   To what did the beloved compare the love of her lover?

     c.   What did she say his name was like?

     d.   What did she request from her lover?

     e.   What did the friends say?

     f.   Why was the beloved so dark? Why was her own vineyard neglected?

     g.   To what did the lover liken his beloved?

     h.   To what did the lover liken the eyes of his beloved?

     i.   What did the lover say that the beams of their house were?

     j.   In chapter two verse four, where had the lover taken his beloved? What was his banner over her?

     k.   What did the beloved charge the daughters of Jerusalem?

     l.   In chapter two verse fourteen, what did he say about his beloved's voice?

     m.   How was Solomon's carriage described?

     n.   What did Solomon's heart do on the day of his wedding?

     o.   In the first verse of chapter three, what did the beloved say about her lover?

     p.   The lover mentions seven body parts, how does he describe each of these? In verse seven, what does the lover say about the beauty of his beloved?

     q.   What request does the beloved make of the wind? Why does she make this request?

2.   II Corinthians 8:16-24
     a.   For what did Paul thank God? What did Paul say about Titus?

     b.   Who was Paul sending along with Titus? Who had chosen this person to accompany Paul's group as they carried the offering to Jerusalem?

    c.   What did Paul want to avoid?

    d.   What were they taking pains to do?

    e.   In verse twenty-three, what did Paul say about Titus? What did he say about the brothers that went with Titus?

    f.   What did Paul request that the Corinthians show to these men?

3.   Psalms 50:1-23
    a.   Who is the Psalmist speaking of in this Psalm?

    b.   What devours before God? What rages around him?

    c.   What does God summon to judge his people?

    d.   What proclaims the righteousness of God?

    e.   Why does God not need a bull from the stall of his people?

    f.   Why wouldn't God tell his people if he was hungry?

    g.   In verse fourteen and fifteen, what two things does God tell his people to do? What promise does God give when they honor him?

    h.   In verse twenty-two, what warning does God give those that forget God?

    i.   In the last verse of this chapter, why should the people sacrifice thank offerings to honor God?

4.   Proverbs 22:22-23
    a.   What does he say about exploiting the poor.

    b.   Why does he say that we should follow this advice?

STUDY QUESTIONS FOR SEPTEMBER 7

1. Song of Songs 5:1-8:14
    a. To where did the lover come? What had he eaten and drunk?

    b. What did the beloved say about sleeping?

    c. What did she arise to do for her lover? What happened when she opened the door for her lover?

    d. What did she do then? What did the watchmen do to her?

    e. What did her friends ask when she asked them to help her find her lover?

    f. How does the beloved describe her lover?

    g. What is the next question that the friends ask? How did she answer them?

    h. What does the lover say about the queens and the concubines? What did the maidens call the beloved?

    i. How does the lover describe the neck and the eyes of the beloved?

    j. To whom does the beloved say she belongs? Where does the beloved suggest that they go and spend the night?

    k. What would the beloved give her lover to drink?

    l. What question do the friends ask?

    m. Where did the beloved ask her lover to place her?

    n. How strong is love? How does it burn?

    o. To whom was the beloved going to give her own vineyard? Who were the thousand shekels for?

    p. What did the beloved invite her lover to do? What did she say he should be like?

2. II Corinthians 9:1-15
    a. What is Paul talking about when he says, "This service to the saints"?

    b. Why was Paul sending the brothers?

    c. What happens to the one that sows sparingly? What happens to the one that sows generously?

      d.   What should each man give and how should it be given?

      e.   What does God love?

      f.   Who supplies the sower with seed and bread for food? Who will enlarge the harvest of your righteousness?

      g.   What would be the result of their generosity?

      h.   To whom does the final thanks go?

3.   Psalms 51:1-19
      a.   What four things does the Psalmist ask for in the first two verses?

      b.   Against whom did the Psalmist sin? How long had the Psalmist been sinful?

      c.   How clean would the Psalmist be when God cleansed him?

      d.   What did the Psalmist want God to create in him? What did he want God to renew? What did he want restored to him?

      e.   What would the Psalmist teach?

      f.   Of what would the Psalmist's tongue sing? What would his mouth declare?

      g.   What are the sacrifices of God? What does he say that God will not do?

      h.   What does he ask God to do for Zion?

4.   Proverbs 22:24-25
      a.   With whom should one not make friends?

      b.   With whom should one not associate?

STUDY QUESTIONS FOR SEPTEMBER 8

1. Isaiah 1:1- 2:22
   a. What did this vision concern that Isaiah saw?

   b. What four kings of Judah did Isaiah serve under as a prophet?

   c. What had the children of the Lord done?

   d. What question does the Lord ask his people?

   e. What parts of their bodies had been affected because of their sinfulness?

   f. How had their country been affected because of their sinfulness?

   g. What kept them from becoming like Sodom and Gomorrah?

   h. What kind of sacrifices did the Lord tell them to stop bringing?

   i. What did the Lord tell them that he could not bear?

   j. What would happen to them when they spread out their hands in prayer?

   k. What did the Lord promise when he said, "Come now let us reason together."?

   l. How will Zion be redeemed?

   m. In the last days, what will happen to the mountain of the Lord's temple?

   n. From where will the law go out?

   o. What would they do with their swords?

   p. Of what was their land full?

   q. What would happen to the arrogance of man?

   r. In what does Isaiah tell them to stop trusting?

2. II Corinthians 10:1-18
   a. By what was Paul appealing to the Corinthians?

   b. What was Paul when he was face to face with them? What was Paul when he was away from them?

c.   What did Paul beg them that he would not have to be when he came?

d.   What were their weapons not? What were their weapons?

e.   What should one that is confident that he belongs to Christ consider?

f.   What should the ones that said that Paul's letters were weighty and forceful, but in person he is unimpressive, realize?

g.   What does Paul say about the ones that measure themselves by themselves?

h.   What was Paul's hope for the Corinthians? If one is going to boast, in whom should he boast?

3.   Psalms 52:19
      a.   What was the first question the Psalmist asks in this passage?

      b.   What did their tongues plot? To what was their tongue likened?

      c.   What did they love rather than good? What about speaking the truth?

      d.   Who was going to bring down the tongue?

      e.   What would the righteous see and do?

      f.   In what was the Psalmist going to trust for ever and ever? For what was the Psalmist going to praise God?

4.   Proverbs 22:26-27
      a.   What does Solomon tell his son about debt?

      b.   If he lacked means to pay what would happen to his bed?

1.   Isaiah 3:1-5:30

     a.   What was the Lord about to do? or as they say in Oklahoma, "What was the Lord fixing to do"?

     b.   What were people going to do to each other?

     c.   How were they going to choose their leader?

     d.   What was Jerusalem and Judah doing?

     e.   What were they doing like Sodom?

     f.   Who brought the disaster on Jerusalem and Judah?

     g.   Who enters to judge God's people?

     h.   What did the Lord say about the women of Zion?

     i.   In that day, how many women would be chasing after one man?

     j.   What is the vineyard of the Lord Almighty?

     k.   What was going to happen to the great houses and the mansions?

     l.   How much wine would a ten-acre vineyard produce?

     m.   Why were God's people going into exile?

     n.   What would happen to mankind and what would happen to the Lord Almighty?

     o.   What is said about the person that calls evil good and good evil, who put darkness for light and light for darkness, who put bitter for sweet and sweet for bitter?

     p.   There are three other things that causes Isaiah to pronounce woes on the people, what are these three things?

     q.   In chapter five verse thirty, what will one see if he looks at the land?

2.   II Corinthians 11:1-15

     a.   What was Paul hoping for?

     b.   Why was Paul jealous with a godly jealousy?

c. Who did Paul think he was not inferior to?

d. What did he say about not being a trained speaker?

e. How had Paul robbed other churches?

f. Was Paul a burden to the Corinthians when he needed something? Who supplied what he needed?

g. What did Paul keep himself from being to the Corinthians? Was he going to continue to do this?

h. What did Paul say about the men that wanted to be considered equal with him?

3. Psalms 53:1-6
   a. What does the fool say in his heart?

   b. According to the Psalmist, who does good?

   c. Why does God look down from heaven on the sons of men?

   d. What has everyone done? What did they become?

   e. What does the Psalmist repeat in verse three that he said in verse one?

   f. What did God do with the bones of the ones that attacked the Psalmist?

   g. From where would the salvation for Israel come?

   h. What would Jacob and Israel do when God restores the fortunes of his people?

4. Proverbs 22:28-29
   a. What is said about boundary stones?

   b. What will a man that is skilled in his work do?

STUDY QUESTIONS FOR SEPTEMBER 10

1. Isaiah 6:1-7:25
    a. When did Isaiah receive this vision?

    b. Who did Isaiah see seated on a throne?

    c. How does he describe the seraphs?

    d. What were the seraphs calling to each other?

    e. What did Isaiah realize when he was in the presence of God. What did one of the seraphs do for Isaiah?

    f. What question did the voice of the Lord ask?

    g. Who marched up to fight against Jerusalem? Did they conquer Jerusalem?

    h. What did the Lord tell Isaiah to do?

    i. What did the Lord promise to do for his people?

    j. What was going to happen to Ephraim within sixty five years?

    k. What was said about standing firm in your faith?

    l. Why did Ahaz refuse to ask for a sign?

    m. What was the sign that the Lord himself would give? To whom did this sign refer?

    n. What would happen to the land of the two kings that Israel dreaded?

    o. The Lord promised to bring a time on the people unlike any since what time?

    p. What was going to happen to God's people when the Lord hires a razor from beyond the river-the king of Assyria?

    q. What were all that remained in the land going to eat?

    r. What would happen to the hills they once cultivated?

2. II Corinthians 11:16-33
    a. What did Paul repeat?

b.   What was Paul going to do if they thought of him as a fool?

c.   If Paul did some boasting, would he be talking as the Lord? How would he be talking?

d.   In verses nineteen through twenty-one it sounds like he is making fun of the Corinthians, in your own words, what is he saying?

e.   What three things were others boasting about that he could also boast about?

f.   Name at least twenty things that Paul endured that showed that he was a servant of Christ.

g.   If Paul had to boast, what was he going boast of?

h.   What happened to Paul when King Aretas had the city guarded in order to arrest Paul?

3.   Psalms 54:1-7
   a.   How did the Psalmist want God to save him? How did he want to be vindicated?

   b.   Who was attacking the Psalmist? Who was seeking his life?

   c.   Who was the Psalmist's help? Who sustained him?

   d.   On whom did the Psalmist request that evil recoil? What did the Psalmist request that God do to them

   e.   What was he going to sacrifice to God? Who was he going to praise?

   f.   Why was he going to praise?

4.   Proverbs 54:1-7
   a.   When dining with a ruler, what did Solomon say one should do if he was given to gluttony?

   b.   What did he say about craving the delicacies of a ruler?

1.　　Isaiah 8:1-9:21
　　　a.　　What did the Lord tell Isaiah to do?

　　　b.　　How soon would the king of Assyria carry off the wealth of Damascus and the plunder of Samaria?

　　　c.　　What did Isaiah prophecy would happen to the nations when they prepared for battle against Judah? Why was this going to happen?

　　　d.　　Who were they to regard a holy? Who were they to fear? Who were they to dread?

　　　e.　　For who was Isaiah going to wait? In whom was he going to put his trust?

　　　f.　　What were Isaiah and the children that the Lord had given him?

　　　g.　　What will the people see when they look toward the earth?

　　　h.　　In chapter nine, what does Isaiah say about gloom?

　　　i.　　What did the people walking in darkness see?

　　　j.　　What had God done for the nation?

　　　k.　　Who is Isaiah referring to in chapter nine verses six and seven?

　　　l.　　 Who did God send the next message against?

　　　m.　　What was the boast of Ephraim and the inhabitants of Samaria?

　　　n.　　Who devoured Israel with open mouth from the east and the west?

　　　o.　　Why did God cut off from Israel both head and tail?

　　　p.　　After all this was God's anger turned away?

　　　q.　　How was the land going to be scorched?

2.　　II Corinthians 12:1-10
　　　a.　　Why do you think Paul felt like he must go on boasting even though there was nothing to be gained?

　　　b.　　What did Paul talk about next?

c.	How long before this discourse did the experience happen that Paul is relating?

d.	In verse two Paul starts out like he was talking about another person but in verses five through seven it becomes apparent that Paul was talking about himself. Was Paul conscious or unconscious?

e.	What would Paul boast about?

f.	What happened to Paul so that he would not become conceited?

g.	How many times did Paul plead with the Lord to take away this thing?

h.	What was God's answer?

i.	In what did Paul delight for Christ's sake?

3.	Psalms 55:1-23
a.	What two things made the Psalmist distraught?

b.	What did he say about his heart?

c.	What did the Psalmist ask the Lord to do to the wicked?

d.	What was at work in the city? What never leaves its streets?

e.	What did he want death to do to his enemies?

f.	On whom is one to cast his cares? What will happen if he we does that?

4.	Proverbs 23:4-5
a.	For what should man not wear himself out?

b.	What happens to riches?

STUDY QUESTIONS FOR SEPTEMBER 12

1.   Isaiah 10:1-11:16
       a.   What does God say to those that make unjust laws and who issue oppressive decrees that deprive the poor of their rights?

       b.   When the day of reckoning comes, from where will disaster come?

       c.   Was God's anger satisfied?

       d.   God had dealt with the nations around Jerusalem, now what question does God ask about Jerusalem?

       e.   Why was God going to punish the king of Assyria?

       f.   What did God do to the boundaries of nations and to their treasuries?

       g.   What kind of a disease was the Lord going to send upon his sturdy warriors?

       h.   What did Isaiah prophesy that Israel was going to do to Assyria?

       i.   In that day on whom will the remnant of Israel rely?

       j.   Israel is like the sand of the sea, but how many will return to God?

       k.   Who will carry out the destruction of the whole land?

       l.   God promised that his anger against Israel would end, then where will his wrath turn?

       m.   Isaiah uses the illustration of trees, what was going to happen to the trees of Lebanon? What about the root of Jesse?

       n.   How was the root of Jesse going to judge the needy and the poor?

       o.   To what period of time is chapter eleven verses six through nine referring?

2.   II Corinthians 12:11-21
       a.   What caused Paul to make a fool out of himself? Was Paul inferior to the other apostles?

       b.   Would he be a burden to them on his next visit? What did Paul want from them?

       c.   Why does he say in verse sixteen "Yet crafty fellow that I am, I caught you by trickery!"?

147

d. What was Paul's question about Titus?

e. The Corinthians thought they were defending themselves, but what did Paul say they were doing?

f. What was Paul afraid would happen?

g. What would make Paul grieve?

3. Psalms 56:1-13
   a. Why did the Psalmist want God to be merciful to him?

   b. What was he going to do when he was afraid?

   c. What did men do to the words of the Psalmist? What else did they do to him?

   d. What was his request to God about the men that were giving him a bad time?

   e. What did he want God to record?

   f. How would he know that God was with him?

   g. In who would he trust? Why would he not be afraid ?

   h. To whom was he under vows?

   i. Who delivered him from death and his feet from stumbling? Why was he delivered?

4. Proverbs 23:6-8
   a. Why should one not eat the food of a stingy man?

   b. What does the stingy man say? What about his heart?

1.   Isaiah 12:1-14:32
   a.   Looking back to chapter eleven we find that the root of Jesse will gather the scattered exiles of Israel and Judah. In chapter twelve, what will these people say?

   b.   Who would be their strength, song and salvation?

   c.   What would they do to the Lord? What would they make known to the nations?

   d.   To whom did the oracle, related in chapter thirteen, concern?

   e.   Why did the Lord summon his warriors?

   f.   What did the uproar among the kingdoms sound like? What was the Lord Almighty doing?

   g.   What day was coming? How was the day described?

   h.   What would happen to the captured ones? What about the ones that were caught?

   i.   What would happen to the glory and pride of Babylon?

   j.   What would fill the houses of Babylon?

   k.   In chapter fourteen, what would the Lord do for Israel?

   l.   Who has broken the rod of the wicked and the scepter of the rulers?

   m.   In chapter fourteen verses twelve through seventeen, who else is being referred to other than Babylon?

   n.   In verse twenty-three, what was the Lord going to turn Babylon into?

   o.   Why did the Lord tell the Philistines not to rejoice that the rod that struck them was broken?

   p.   In the last verse of this section, what answer would be given to the envoys of the Philistines?

2.   II Corinthians 13:1-14
   a.   How must every matter be established?

   b.   When had Paul given them a warning? What was he doing about the warning at this time?

      c.   What were the Corinthians demanding of Paul?

      d.   What were the Corinthians to look for when they examined themselves?

      e.   What did he ask them if they did not realize? What did he pray to God about the Corinthians?

      f.   What did Paul say that he and his group could not do?

      g.   Why did Paul write these things to the Corinthians while he was absent?

      h.   After he told them his good-by, what three things did he tell them to do? What promise does he make to them?

      i.   How were they to greet one another? Quote the benediction that Paul gives in verse fourteen.

3.   Psalms 57:1-11
      a.   Where does the Psalmist take refuge?

      b.   How long does he take refuge?

      c.   To whom does he cry out?

      d.   Who is to be exalted?

      e.   What was to be the extent of God's exaltation?

      f.   Where is he going to praise the Lord?

      g.   How does he describe God's love?

4.   Proverbs 23:9-11
      a.   Why should one not speak to a fool?

      b.   Why should one not move an ancient boundary stone or encroach on the field of the fatherless?

1.   Isaiah 15:1-18:7
       a.   What did the first oracle in chapter fifteen concern? What was to happen to Ar and Kir in Moab?

       b.   What would happen to every head and every beard?

       c.   What would they wear in the streets? What would they do on the roofs and the public squares?

       d.   What happened to the waters of Nimrim? What about the grass and the vegetation?

       e.   What would happen to the waters of Dimon?

       f.   To what did Isaiah liken the women of Moab at the fords of Arnon?

       g.   What will happen to the oppressor and the destruction? What will happen to the aggressor?

       h.   How would a throne be established? Who would sit on this throne?

       i.   What was taken away from the orchards?

       j.   What happens when Moab appears at her high places?

       k.   What did the Lord say would happen to Moab within three years? How would these years be counted?

       l.   What did the next oracle concern?

       m.   What would the city of Damascus become?

       n.   In that day where will men look and turn their eyes? Where will they not look?

       o.   What was going to happen to the harvest even though they planted well?

       p.   In chapter eighteen, where were the messengers to go?

       q.   At that time who would bring gifts to the Lord almighty?

2.   Galatians 1:1-24
       a.   Who sent Paul out as an apostle?

b.   To whom was Paul sending this letter?

c.   What was Paul sending to this people?

d.   Why was Paul astonished?

e.   What did Paul say that was "evidently" happening to these people?

f.   Whose approval was Paul seeking?

g.   What did Paul want them to know?

h.   Why did God set Paul apart from birth and call him by God's grace?

i.   What did the people do when they heard what God had done in Paul's life?

3.   Psalms 58:1-11
        a.   What question does the Psalmist ask in the first verse of this chapter? How does he answer his own question?

        b.   What do the wicked do even from birth?

        c.   What illustration does the Psalmist use of the lies they speak?

        d.   What five things does the Psalmist request that God do to the wicked?

        e.   How soon will the righteous be avenged?

        f.   How will the righteous react when they are avenged?

        g.   Then what two things will men say?

4.   Proverbs 23:12
        a.   To what should one apply his heart?

        b.   To what should one apply his ears?

STUDY QUESTIONS FOR SEPTEMBER 15

1. Isaiah 19:1-21:17
    a. What did the first oracle concern?

    b. What did the idols of Egypt do before the Lord?

    c. What would happen when the Lord stirred up Egyptian against Egyptian?

    d. What was going to happen to the river of Egypt?

    e. What would happen to the fishermen?

    f. What would happen to those that work with combed flax, and the workers in cloth?

    g. What is said about the officials of Zoan and the counselors of Pharaoh?

    h. What kind of a spirit did the Lord pour into the officials of Zoan and the leaders of Memphis? What did they make Egypt do?

    i. "In that day", what will Egyptians be like?

    j. "In that day", what kind of an altar will be in the heart of Egypt?

    k. What does the Lord say about each of the three nations mentioned in chapter nineteen verse twenty-five?

    l. What did the Lord instruct Isaiah to do in chapter twenty verse two? What was the king of Assyria going to do to Egypt?

    m. What did the next oracle concern? What did the Lord tell Isaiah to do in chapter twenty-one verse six?

    n. What did the man in the chariot say?

    o. What does the oracle concerning Dumah say?

    p. What does the Lord say at the end of the oracle concerning Arabia?

2. Galatians 2:1-16
    a. Where did Paul go? Who went with him?

    b. Who did Paul talk to? What did he set before them?

c. Why did the matter of circumcision arise? Did Paul give in to this group of people? Why?

d. By what does God not judge?

e. What did those men add to Paul's message?

f. To whom was Peter an apostle? To whom was Paul an apostle?

g. Who did Paul oppose at Antioch? Why did he oppose him?

h. What did Paul say to Peter in front of them all?

i. How is a man not justified? How is a man justified?

3. Psalms 59:1-17
   a. What three requests does the Psalmist make in the first two verses?

   b. In verses three and four, what does the Psalmist complain about his enemies and what request does he make?

   c. What request does he make about the nations? To what does he liken the traitor nations?

   d. What does the Lord do to those nations?

   e. Who was the Psalmist's strength and fortress? Who was going to go before him?

   f. What request is made by the Psalmist for God's people, Israel, so the world will know that God rules over Jacob?

   g. Quote Psalms chapter fifty-nine verse seventeen.

4. Proverbs 23:13-14
   a. What should not be withheld from a child?

   b. Why should a child be punished with a rod?

STUDY QUESTIONS FOR SEPTEMBER 16

1.   Isaiah 22:1-24:23
      a.   What did the first oracle of this reading concern?

      b.   In chapter twenty-two verses two and three, how does Isaiah describe what is going on in the city?

      c.   Of what were their choicest valleys full?

      d.   How did the people prepare for war with their water?

      e.   What did they do to strengthen their walls?

      f.   In chapter twenty-two verse twelve, what did the Lord call the people to do? What did the people say?

      g.   What was Shebna doing? How did God describe what he was going to do to Shebna?

      h.   Who would take Shebna's place?

      i.   What did the next oracle concern? What was going to happen to that city?

      j.   What did the Assyrians make of the land of Babylonia?

      k.   How long would Tyre be forgotten?

      l.   What will the merrymakers do when the earth dries up and withers and the new wine dries up and the vine withers?

      m.   What happens to the entrance to every house?

      n.   What will happen to all joy and what is said about gaiety?

      o.   What happens to everyone that flees at the sound of terror?

      p.   What happens to the moon and the sun?

      q.   Who will reign on Mount Zion and in Jerusalem and before its elders, gloriously?

2.   Galatians 2:17-3:9
      a.   What does Paul say that it will prove if he rebuilds what he destroyed?

      b.   Paul says, "For through the law I died to the law" so that he may what?

c.   What does Paul say about being crucified and living?

d.   What does he say about Christ's death if righteousness could be gained through the law?

e.   Why did he call the Galatians foolish?

f.   Why did God give his Spirit and work miracles among the Galatians?

g.   What was credited to Abraham as righteousness?

h.   What promise did God make to Abraham that included the Gentiles?

3.   Psalms 60:1-12
        a.   In chapter sixty verse one, what did God do to them? What request did the Psalmist make?

        b.   What did God do for those that feared him?

        c.   How does the Psalmist ask that God save and help them? Why does he ask for this help?

        d.   What are the six areas that God claims for his own?

        e.   Who would bring David to the fortified city?

        f.   What two requests does David make about his enemies?

        g.   How much is man's help worth?

        h.   How would they gain the victory over their enemies?

4.   Proverbs 23:15-16
        a.   What would happen if the son's heart is wise?

        b.   When would the writer's inmost being rejoice?

STUDY QUESTIONS FOR SEPTEMBER 17

1. Isaiah 25:1-28:13
   a. Who was Isaiah going to exalt and praise? Why was he going to praise and exalt him?

   b. Why were strong people going to honor God and cities of ruthless nations going to revere him?

   c. What was the Lord almighty going to prepare on the mountain?

   d. What was the Lord going to destroy on the mountain?

   e. In chapter twenty-five verse n nine, what will the people say?

   f. What was God going to do to the high fortified walls of Moab?

   g. Who was going to sing the song given in chapter twenty-six?

   h. Who was going to watch over, water, and guard day and night, the fruitful vineyard?

   i. In the days to come, what would happen to Jacob? What about Israel?

   j. What were those who were perishing in Assyria and the ones exiled in Egypt, going to do?

   k. What were some of the things that would happen to the wreath of Ephraim (the northen kingdom)?

   l. In chapter twenty eight, what is said about the Lord Almighty, in that day?

   m. How are the actions of the priest and prophets described in chapter twenty eight?

   n. Who is being taught?

   o. In chapter twenty-eight verses ten and thirteen, how are they being taught?

2. Galatians 3:10-22
   a. What does this scripture say about those that observe the law?

   b. Who is cursed?

   c. Can one be justified by the law?

d. How will the righteous live?

e. In verse fourteen, why did God redeem them through Jesus Christ?

f. Did the inheritance depend on the law?

g. To whom did God give his promise?

h. What was the purpose of the law?

i. Is the law opposed to the promises of God?

j. In verse twenty two, to whom was the promise given? How was this promise obtained?

3. Psalms 6:1-8
   a. Who did the Psalmist ask to hear his cry?

   b. From where was the Psalmist going to call to God?

   c. To whom did the Psalmist ask to be led?

   d. Who was the Psalmist's refuge?

   e. Where did he long to dwell? How long did he desire to dwell there?

   f. What did he pray for the king?

   g. To whose name was the Psalmist going to sing praises? When was he going to fulfill his vows?

4. Proverbs 23:17-18
   a. What is said about feelings toward sinners?

   b. What is said about future hope?

STUDY QUESTIONS FOR SEPTEMBER 18

1.   Isaiah 28:14-30:11
    a.   In verse fourteen, who did Isaiah tell to hear the word of the Lord?

    b.   What boast did these people make?

    c.   What did the lord say about a cornerstone? To whom was the prophet referring?

    d.   What was going to happen to the peoples covenant with death?

    e.   What would the understanding of the message bring?

    f.   What would happen to the people if they didn't stop their mocking?

    g.   What was going to happen to the city where David settled?

    h.   Will the hordes of all the nations that fight against Mount Zion be satisfied? What illustration does Isaiah use to show this?

    i.   What does God say about the heart of his people that come near him with their mouths?

    j.   Of what was their worship made up?

    k.   What did the Lord who redeemed Abraham, say to the house of Jacob?

    l.   How were the obstinate children described? Where were they looking for help?

    m.   What would Egypt's shade bring?

    n.   What did he say about Egypt's help?

    o.   What did the rebellious people say to the seers? What did they say to the prophets?

    p.   What did they want to hear?

2.   Galatians 3:23-4:31
    a.   How were they held prisoners?

    b.   What happened so that they were no longer prisoners?

    c.   How were they sons of God?

d. How did Gentiles become Abraham's seed? What about slave or free? What about male or female?

e. What happened when the time was fully come?

f. What did you become when you became a son?

g. What was Paul worried about when he saw the Galatians turning back to weak and miserable principles?

h. How had the Galatians welcomed Paul?

i. Which woman was the mother of Paul and the brethren?

3. Psalms 62:1-12
a. Where did the Psalmist's soul find rest?

b. Who is the fortress of the Psalmist? Would he be shaken?

c. What did the Psalmist remind his soul to do? (Something that he already said his soul does in verse one)

d. Who alone is his rock and salvation?

e. In verse eight, what did the Psalmist tell the people to do?

f. In verse ten what did he tell the people not to do?

g. What two things had the Psalmist heard?

h. How was the Lord going to reward each person?

4. Proverbs 23:19-21
a. What was the son to do with his heart?

b. What was Solomon's advice about drinking and eating?

c. What happens to drunkards and gluttons?

STUDY QUESTIONS FOR SEPTEMBER 19

1.   Isaiah 30:12-33:12
     a.   Who is talking in this passage?

     b.   What three things did they do to deserve the promised punishment?

     c.   The destruction of the wall was going to be so great that they would not be able to find big enough pieces to do what two chores?

     d.   Israel's enemies were going to pursue them, how many would flee at the threat of one? How many at the threat of five?

     e.   What did the Lord long to do?

     f.   What was going to happen when Israel cried out for help?

     g.   What were their ears going to hear?

     h.   Who was going to send the rain?

     i.   What was going to shatter Assyria?

     j.   What did he say about the ones that go down to Egypt for help and rely on horses?

     k.   Are the Egyptians god? What about their horses?

     l.   How will the Assyrians fall?

     m.   What will happen to the stammering tongue?

     n.   What does he say about the fool?

     o.   What will the fruit of righteousness be?

     p.   What is Isaiah's prayer in Isaiah chapter thirty-three verse two?

     q.   Who will be Israel's sure foundation?

     r.   Who is going to arise and be exalted?

2.   Galatians 5:1-12
     a.   Why has Christ set us free?

     b.   In Christ what value is there in circumcision or in uncircumcision?

c. What is the only thing that counts? How does it express itself?

d. Paul said they were running a good race, what question did he ask them?

e. Does that kind of persuasion come from God?

f. What does Paul say about yeast?

g. What will happen to the one throwing them into confusion?

3. Psalms 63:1-11
   a. Who was the Psalmist going to seek earnestly?

   b. For what does his soul thirst?

   c. For what does his body long?

   d. Who did he see in the sanctuary?

   e. Why do his lips glorify God?

   f. How long was he going to praise God?

   g. Where was he going to remember God through the night watches?

   h. What upholds the Psalmist?

   i. In whom will the king rejoice?

   j. What will happen to the mouths of liars?

4. Proverbs 23:22
   a. To whom was the young man to listen?

   b. Who was he not to despise?

STUDY QUESTIONS FOR SEPTEMBER 20

1.	Isaiah 33:13-36:22
	a.	What did the Lord tell the ones that were far away to do? What about the ones that were near? What happened to the sinners of Zion?

	b.	What would the eyes of the righteous see? What would they ponder in their thoughts?

	c.	Who would be their mighty one?

	d.	What was going to happen to the spoils? What does it say about even the lame?

	e.	In chapter thirty-four, with what nation was the Lord angry?

	f.	What was going to happen to the all the stars of heavens, the sky and the starry host?

	g.	What would happen to the streams of Edom? What would her land become?

	h.	In chapter thirty-five, what would happen to the desert and the wilderness?

	i.	What would the highway that is in the restored land be called? What would be on the highway and what would not be on the highway?

	j.	How would the people enter Zion?

	k.	What happened in the fourteenth year of King Hezekiah's reign?

	l.	What did Sennacherib, through his field commander, say about Egypt?

	m.	What was the field commander's response when asked to speak in Aramaic? What language did he use?

	n.	When he was trying to convince the people to surrender to the king of Assyria, what question did he ask the people? How did the people respond?

2.	Galatians 5:13-26
	a.	What were the brothers called to be? What was the warning not to use?

	b.	What were they to do instead?

	c.	How is the entire law summed up?

	d.	What would happen if they continued to bite and devoured each other?

e. How were they to live?

f. What does the sinful nature desire? What does the Spirit desire?

g. What acts of the sinful nature are listed here?

h. What is the fruit of the Spirit listed here?

i. Is there any law against the fruit of the Spirit?

j. Since they lived by the spirit what were they to do with the Spirit?

k. How does Paul conclude Galations?

3. Psalms 64:1-10
   a. For what three things does the Psalmist pray?

   b. The Psalmist says that the evildoers do four things what are the four things?

   c. What three things will God do to the evildoers?

   d. What will the observers do?

   e. What three things will all mankind do?

   f. What are the righteous to do?

4. Proverbs 23:23
   a. What should one do with the truth?

   b. What three things should one get?

STUDY QUESTIONS FOR SEPTEMBER 21

1.   Isaiah 37:1-38:22
     a.   What had Hezekiah heard? (Look back to yesterday's reading) what did Hezekiah do?

     b.   What did Isaiah say to the officials that Hezekiah sent to him?

     c.   What did the field commander do when he heard that the king of Assyria had left Lachish?

     d.   What message did Sennacherib send to King Hezekiah through his messengers?

     e.   What did Hezekiah do when he received the letter from the messengers? What request did Hezekiah make of the Lord?

     f.   In chapter thirty-seven, verse twenty-nine, what does God promise that he will do to Sennachrib?

     g.   What would the sign be to Hezekiah?

     h.   What will come out of Jerusalem. What will come out of Mount Zion? What would accomplish that?

     i.   What four things did the Lord say the king of Assyria would not do?

     j.   How many men did the angel of the Lord put to death? Where did the king of Assyria return and stay?

     k.   What happened to Hezekiah in the thirty-eighth chapter of Isaiah?

     l.   How did Hezekiah respond to the prophecy, given by Isaiah?

     m.   What did the Lord do for Hezekiah? What sign did the Lord give that the promise would be fulfilled?

     n.   What could the grave and death not do?

     o.   What did Isaiah tell Hezekiah to do to the boil? What would happen when he did this?

2.   Galatians 6:1-18
     a.   What should the brothers that are spiritual do if someone is caught in a sin? What word of cautions does Paul give with this advice?

165

b. What should they do with other's burdens?

c. Who does one deceive if he thinks he is something when he is nothing?

d. What does Paul tell them about not being deceived?

e. What happens when one sows to his sinful nature?

f. Why do you think that Paul used such large letters?

g. In what was the only thing that Paul wanted to boast?

3. Psalms 65:1-13
   a. What awaited God in Zion?

   b. What did God do when the Psalmist was overwhelmed by sin?

   c. Who is the hope of all the ends of the earth?

   d. What do those living far away do?

   e. What did God do for the land?

   f. What does God do to the furrows of the earth. What does God do with the ridges? How does he soften the earth?

   g. How does God crown the year?

   h. What does the grasslands of the desert do? What about the hills?

   i. With what are the meadows covered? How are the valleys mantled?

4. Proverbs 23:24-25
   a. What gives the father great joy?

   b. What does the one that has a wise son do?

STUDY QUESTIONS FOR SEPTEMBER 22

1.   Isaiah 39:1-41:16
        a.   Who sent Hezekiah letters and a gift?

        b.   What did Hezekiah do for the envoys that brought the letters and gift?

        c.   What two questions did Isaiah ask Hezekiah? What was Hezekiah's answer?

        d.   What was the word of the Lord that Isaiah gave to Hezekiah? What was Hezekiah's response?

        e.   In chapter forty, what did God tell Isaiah to do for God's people?

        f.   To whom was the prophecy of chapter forty verses three through four, referring?

        g.   What happens to the grass and flowers? What does he say about the word of God?

        h.   In chapter forty verses twelve through fourteen, Isaiah asks who did a list of things, what is the answer to his questions?

        i.   What are the nations like? How are they regarded? What does God do with the islands?

        j.   How did they go about making idols? What does the man too poor to present such an offering do?

        k.   Who is the everlasting God and creator of the ends of the earth?

        l.   In chapter forty verse thirty-one, what will those that hope in the Lord do?

        m.   What does the Lord tell the islands to do?

        n.   What would happen to all who rage against Israel?

        o.   What was the Lord going to make Israel into, in chapter forty-one verse fifteen?

2.   Ephesians 1:1-23
        a.   To whom was this letter written?

        b.   To whom did Paul give praise?

        c.   How were they adopted as sons of God?

d. In whom did they have redemption?

e. Under what were all things in heaven and earth going to be brought together?

f. How were the ones that believe marked?

g. What had Paul not stopped doing since he heard about the faith of the Ephesians?

h. What did he keep asking God to give them? What else did he pray for?

i. Who was Paul talking about when he said, "And God placed all things under his feet and appointed him to be head over everything for the church"?

3. Psalms 66:1-20
   a. Who was to shout with joy to God?

   b. What were the people to say to God?

   c. What were the people to come and see?

   d. How long does God rule?

   e. Who were the people to praise?

   f. When the people went through fire and water, who brought them to a place of abundance?

   g. What was the Psalmist going to bring to the temple? What would happen if the Psalmist cherished sin in his heart?

4. Proverbs 23:26-28
   a. What did Solomon ask his son to do with his heart?

   b. What does Solomon say that a wayward wife is?

STUDY QUESTIONS FOR SEPTEMBER 23

1. Isaiah 41:17-43:13
   a. Who searched for water? Did they find any?

   b. Who would answer them? Who would not forsake them?

   c. What was God going to do so that the people would see and know that the hand of the Lord has done this?

   d. Why did God tell them to bring in their idols?

   e. In chapter forty-one verse twenty-nine, what did God say about the idols?

   f. In chapter forty-two who is God talking about when he said, "Here is my servant."?

   g. In chapter forty-two verse ten, what kind of a song were they to sing to the Lord?

   h. In chapter forty-two verse sixteen, what was God going to do for the blind?

   i. What did he say about those that trust in idols?

   j. What did it please the Lord to do?

   k. Who handed Jacob over to become loot, and Israel to the plunderers?

   l. In chapter forty-three, what does God promise to do for Jacob?

   m. What was Jacob in the sight of God?

   n. God declared that the people of Jacob were God's witnesses and what?

   o. What "God" was formed before the true God?

   p. Who was the true God?

   q. Who can deliver out of God's hand?

2. Ephesians 2:1-22
   a. Who was dead in their transgressions and sins?

   b. Who also lived among them at one time gratifying the cravings of their sinful nature?

169

c.   Who made them alive with Christ even when they were dead in transgressions?

d.   By what were they saved?

e.   Where did God seat the believers? Why did God do this?

f.   How were they saved? How much of one's salvation is dependant on their works?

g.   How were the ones that were far away brought near?

h.   Who is the chief cornerstone?

3.   Psalms 67:1-7
     a.   What two things does the Psalmist ask for in verse one?

     b.   Why does he ask for this?

     c.   Why should the people praise God and the nations be glad and sing for joy?

     d.   What theme is repeated two more times in verse five of this Psalm ?

     e.   Then what will happen to the land?

     f.   Who will bless us?

     g.   What will the ends of the earth do?

4.   Proverbs 23:29-35
     a.   Who has woe, sorrow, strife, complaints, needless bruises, and bloodshot eyes?

     b.   When should one not gaze into the wine?

     c.   What does that kind of wine do to the partaker?

STUDY QUESTIONS FOR SEPTEMBER 24

1. Isaiah 43:14-45:10
   a. What was God going to do to the Babylonians?

   b. What did God tell his people to do about former things? What about the past? What were they to see?

   c. Why did the wild animals honor God?

   d. What did God remind the people that they had not brought to him?

   e. With what did they burden God? With what had they wearied God?

   f. When God asked the people to review the past, what did their first father do? What did their spokesmen do?

   g. What did God promise to Jacob and Jeshrun?

   h. God says there is no other God beside him, is that right?

   i. There are people that make idols that God said are nothing, how much are their treasures worth?

   j. What are some of the things that a carpenter makes with the same piece of wood that he makes an idol?

   k. What does an idol know, see, or understand?

   l. List the things that God does in chapter forty four, verses twenty four through verse twenty eight.

   m. What does God promise to do through Cyrus?

   n. For whose sake did God do these things? Did Cyrus acknowledge God?

   o. How wide spread would the knowledge of the true God extend?

   p. What did God say about the one that quarrels with his maker?

2. Ephesians 3:1-21
   a. In the first verse, what is Paul in regard to Christ Jesus?

   b. What was given to Paul for the Gentiles?

c. How was the mystery made known to Paul?

d. This mystery was not made known to other generations, how was it given to Paul's generation?

e. What was the mystery that Paul was talking about?

f. Why was Paul given God's grace?

g. Through whom did God accomplish his eternal purpose?

h. How were the Gentiles able to approach God with freedom and confidence?

i. What did Paul pray for the Ephesians?

j. Quote the benediction given in verse twenty.

3. Psalms 68:1-18
   a. What does the Psalmist say about God's enemies?

   b. What does he say about the righteous?

   c. What does the Psalmist invite the people to do?

   d. What does God become to the fatherless and the widows?

   e. What happens to the rebellious?

   f. How does the Psalmist describe when God went out before his people?

   g. What does he say about the mountains of Bashan?

   h. How many are the chariots of God?

4. Proverbs 24:1-2
   a. What did Solomon say about wicked men?

   b. Why did he give that advice?

1.   Isaiah 45:11-48:11
       a.   Who made the earth and created mankind on it?

       b.   Whose hand stretched out the heavens?

       c.   What will happen to all the makers of idols?

       d.   How will Israel be saved?

       e.   Did God create the earth to be empty?

       f.   What does he say about people that carry about idols of wood, who pray to gods that cannot save?

       g.   To whom will every knee bow?

       h.   How were the idols of Bel and Nebo borne?

       i.   What did God promise the house of Jacob and all that remained of the house of Israel?

       j.   God's promise to Isaiah chapter forty-six verse four: "Even to your _____ _____ and _____ _____ I am _____, I am _____ who will _____ you."

       k.   What do some do with their bags of gold and their silver?

       l.   What happens when someone cries out to these gods?

       m.   What did God tell the virgin daughter of Babylon to do?

       n.   Why did God desecrate his inheritance and give them into the hands of the daughter of Babylonians?

       o.   What was going to overtake the daughter of Babylon?

       p.   In what had she trusted?

       q.   Why did God tell Israel and Jacob things long before they happened?

       r.   How did God test Israel and Jacob?

2.   Ephesians 4:1-16
       a.   Whose prisoner was Paul?

b.   Of what did Paul urge the Ephesians to live their life worthy?

c.   What were the Ephesians to make every effort to keep?

d.   What are the seven ones that Paul lists here?

e.   Who gave some to be apostles, some to be prophets, etc?

f.   Why did he give these?

g.   What would the Ephesians avoid when they were no longer infants?

h.   What would they do instead?

i.   Who holds the whole body together by every supporting ligament?

3.   Psalms 68:19-35
       a.   Who daily bears our burdens?

       b.   "Our God is a God who _____."

       c.   What will God do to the heads of his enemies?

       d.   What is the order of God's procession?

       e.   Where were they to praise God?

       f.   What tribe was leading them?

       g.   Who would submit herself to God?

       h.   What did the Psalmist say about God in his sanctuary?

4.   Proverbs 24:3-4
       a.   How is a house built?

       b.   How is a house established?

       c.   How is a house filled with rare and beautiful treasures?

STUDY QUESTIONS FOR SEPTEMBER 26

1. Isaiah 48:12 - 50:11
    a. Who is the first and the last? In this prophesy, Who was going to carry out God's purpose against Babylon?

    b. What five things would have happened to God's people if they had paid attention to God's commands?

    c. How were they to make their announcement as they left Babylon?

    d. True or false - the wicked have peace.

    e. Isaiah chapter forty-nine verse eight "This is what the Lord says: 'In the time of my favor I will _____ you, and in the day of salvation I will _____ you; I will _____ you and make you to be a _____ for the people, to restore the land.'"

    f. What was God's promise to his people about hunger, thirst and the desert heat?

    g. What did God tell the heavens, the earth, and the mountains to do?

    h. How did Zion (God's people) think the Lord was treating them?

    i. God promises many good things to his people then in Isaiah chapter forty-nine verse twenty-three he says "Then you will_____ that I am the _____ those who _____ in me will not be _____."

    j. What will all mankind know about the Lord when he does all these things he promised?

    k. The Lord asks "Was my arm to short to ransom you?" Was it?

    l. What two examples did God give of his power?

    m. To whom is Isaiah fifty verses four through nine referring?

    n. Who does God encourage the ones that walk in darkness to trust in and rely on?

2. Ephesians 4:1 - 32
    a. Paul told the Ephesians, "Don't live like the _____ do."

    b. What was wrong with the Gentile's understanding?

    c. To what did they give themselves over?

d. How did the Ephesians come to know Christ?

e. What should they not do in their anger?

f. What should they not let happen on their anger?

g. What six things did Paul tell the Ephesians to get rid of?

h. What two things should replace the things they were to get rid of?

i. Who should be their example?

3. Psalms 69:1 - 18
   a. How does the Psalmist describe his situation?

   b. How many hated him without reason?

   c. What was he forced to do?

   d. What did God know about the Psalmist?

   e. Why did he endure scorn?

   f. What happened when he put on sackcloth?

   g. To whom did he pray?

   h. For what things did he pray?

   i. What was the basis of God's answer to the Psalmist's prayer?

4. Proverbs 24:5 - 6
   a. What does a wise man have?

   b. What do you need to wage war? What do you need for victory?

STUDY QUESTIONS FOR SEPTEMBER 27

1. Isaiah 51:1-53:12
   a. Who did Isaiah call to listen to him? Where did he tell them to look?

   b. What was the Lord going to do for Zion?

   c. What were the islands going to do?

   d. How long would God's salvation last? What did he say about his righteousness?

   e. What did the Lord say they should not fear and by what they should not be terrified?

   f. How would the ransomed of the Lord enter Zion?

   g. Who is the one who churns up the sea so that it waves roar?

   h. Who said to Zion, "You are my people"?

   i. What was the Lord going to do with the cup that he had taken out of the hand of Zion that made them stager?

   j. What six things was Zion told to do in the first two verses of chapter fifty-two?

   k. Who was going to be the rear guard of those that return to Zion?

   l. To whom does the prophecy in chapter fifty-three refer?

   m. What is said about the beauty of this person?

   n. What did men think of him?

   o. What did he do for our infirmities and sorrows?

   p. Why was he pierced? Why was he crushed?

   q. Where was he assigned a grave?

   r. What did he do for the sin of many?

2. Ephesians 5:1-33
   a. What did Paul encourage the Ephesians to be?

   b. What kind of a life were they to live? What example of this did they have?

c.   What five things should not be among them? What should there be instead?

d.   What kind of a man has no inheritance in the kingdom of Christ and of God?

e.   What did Paul say that the Ephesians were once and what had they become? Of what three things does the fruit of the light consist?

f.   Why should they be very careful how they lived? What should they do instead of being drunk?

g.   How should they speak to one another?

h.   Why should they submit to one another? To whom should wives submit? How should husbands love their wives?

i.   For what reason would a man leave his father and mother?

j.   In verse thirty-three, what must a man do and what must a woman do?

3.   Psalms 69:19-36
   a.   What had the enemies done?

   b.   How many comforters were found?

   c.   What was put in his food and his drink?

   d.   What pleases the Lord more than an ox?

   e.   What happens to the poor and needy?

4.   Proverbs 24:7
   a.   What is too high for a fool?

   b.   What does a fool have to say in the assembly at the gate?

STUDY QUESTIONS FOR SEPTEMBER 28

1. Isaiah 54:1-57:13
   a. Why would the barren woman sing? (Look in chapter fifty-three)

   b. What were they to do with their tent? Why were they to do that?

   c. Of what two things were they not to be afraid?

   d. What would they forget and what would they not remember?

   e. Starting in chapter fifty-four verse seven, what did the Lord her redeemer say?

   f. With what was the Lord going to build the afflicted city?

   g. Who would teach their sons?

   h. What was God's promise about weapons formed against them?

   i. What does Isaiah tell the thirsty to do? What about those who have no money?

   j. When were they to seek the Lord? How about calling?

   k. Are God's thoughts our thoughts?

   l. What would grow instead of the thornbush and briers?

   m. In chapter fifty-six, what were they to do about justice?

   n. What would the Lord's house be called?

   o. What does Isaiah call the watchmen of Israel? How does he describe them?

   p. What were they doing to their children in the ravines and under the overhanging crags?

   q. What did they do behind their doors and doorposts ?

   r. What happens to the man that makes God his refuge?

2. Ephesians 6:1-24
   a. What is the first commandment with promise? What is the promise?

   b. What should fathers not do to their children? What should they do instead?

c. What should slaves do? The scripture says they should serve wholehearted as if what?

d. How should masters treat their slaves?

e. How should the Ephesians be strong? What were they to put on?

f. What were the six articles of armor that are mentioned here? How many were for offense?

g. What prayer request did Paul make for himself?

h. What would Tychicus tell the Ephesian church?

3. Psalms 70:1-5
   a. In verse one what does the Psalmist want God to do?

   b. What did the Psalmist pray about the ones that sought his life?

   c. What did he pray about the ones that desired the Psalmist's ruin?

   d. What did he pray for the ones that said, Aha! Aha!

   e. What was the Psalmist's desire for the ones that seek the Lord?

   f. What should the ones that love the Lord's salvation always say?

   g. How did the Psalmist describe himself? What did he ask of the Lord?

4. Proverbs 24:8
   a. As what will a man that plots evil be known?

STUDY QUESTIONS FOR SEPTEMBER 29

1.   Isaiah 57:14-59:21
     a.   In the first part of chapter fifty-seven, from yesterday's reading, God was talking about how his people followed idols and foreign "gods". In today's reading, verse sixteen through seventeen, what does God say about his anger? What was God going to do for the people even though God had seen man's ways?

     b.   What are the wicked like? What does he say about peace for the wicked?

     c.   In chapter fifty-eight, what was Isaiah to declare to God's people?

     d.   What were the people doing on their fast days that made the fast ineffective?

     e.   In the kind of a fast that God choose, what four things should happen because of the fast?

     f.   What three things should the one who is fasting be doing during the fast? If they do these things, who will be their rear guard?

     g.   When the people do a proper fast, what can they expect their light to do and what would their night become like?

     h.   What is said about the arm and the ear of the Lord? What had separated the people from their God?

     i.   What did the feet of the people rush into? What were they swift to do?

     j.   What were the people doing along the wall? To what were they likened? What were they doing at midday?

     k.   In chapter fifty-nine verse fifteen and sixteen, why was the Lord displeased? In verse twenty, what is promised to those who repent of their sins?

     l.   When would the words of God's covenant, spoken by Isaiah, depart from their mouths and the mouths of their children or the mouths of their descendants?

2.   Philippians 1:1-26
     a.   To whom were Paul and Timothy sending this letter?

     b.   How often did Paul thank God for this church? Why did he thank God for them?

     c.   Who shared with Paul in God's grace?

     d.   What was Paul's prayer for these people?

e.   What did Paul want the brothers to know about the results of what happened to him?

f.   What had happened to most of the brothers because of Paul's chains?

g.   How did the two groups of people preach Christ? How did Paul look at this?

h.   Why would Paul continue to rejoice? Between what two things was Paul torn? Of what was he convinced?

3.   Psalms 71:1-24
    a.   List the things that the Psalmist asks God to do for him in verses one through four.

b.   Who was the Psalmist's hope and confidence since his youth?

c.   What did the enemies of the Psalmist say about him?

d.   What does the Psalmist say he would always have and what will he do?

e.   To whom was the Psalmist going to declare God's power?

f.   What would the Psalmist's tongue tell?

4.   Proverbs 24:9-10
    a.   What are the schemes of folly?

b.   What do men detest?

c.   What does it show if one falters in times of trouble?

STUDY QUESTIONS FOR SEPTEMBER 30

1. Isaiah 60:1-62:5
   a. Why were the people encouraged to rise, shine?

   b. Why will the nations be drawn to Israel?

   c. What was going to happen to the wealth of the seas and the riches of the nations?

   d. Who endowed Israel with splendor?

   e. Who was going to rebuild Israel's walls and what would their kings do?

   f. When would the gates of the city be closed?

   g. What would happen to the nation or kingdom that would not serve the Lord?

   h. What would the sons of the oppressors of Israel do?

   i. What was God going to make of Jerusalem?

   j. Then what would Jerusalem know?

   k. What would no longer be heard in the land of Israel?

   l. Instead of the sun and the moon, what would be their everlasting light?

   m. In chapter sixty-one, who is Isaiah talking about? Can you find the scripture where this scripture was read in the New Testament?

   n. Instead of shame, what would the people of God receive?

   o. What does the Lord love? What does the Lord hate?

   p. Where will the descendants of God's people be known?

   q. What will all who see them acknowledge?

   r. What will they no longer call Jerusalem and its land? What will they now call them?

2. Philippians 1:27-2:18
   a. How were the Philippians to conduct themselves? Why did Paul ask for this kind of conduct?

b. What else were the Philippians going to experience beside believing in Christ? Was Paul experiencing the same thing?

c. How could the Phillipians complete Paul's joy?

d. What did Paul say about selfish ambition and vain conceit?

e. What should they do beside looking to their own interest? What kind of an attitude should they have?

f. What was to happen at the name of Jesus?

g. How were the Phillipians to do everything?

h. Why should the Phillipians be glad and rejoice with Paul?

3. Psalms 72:1-20
a. According to the "Spirit Filled Life Study Bible", this Psalm is about the glory and universality of the Messiah's reign. How long will the Messiah endure?

b. In the days of the Messiah, who will flourish?

c. What will the kings of Tarshish do for the Messiah? How about the kings of Sheba and Seba? How about the other kings?

d. What will happen to all the nations through the name of the Messiah?

e. To whom is praise due?

4. Proverbs 24:11-12
a. What was the son to do about the ones being led away to death and those staggering toward slaughter?

b. What does the one that weighs the heart perceive?

c. How was each person to be repaid?

STUDY QUESTIONS FOR OCTOBER 1

1.   Isaiah 62:6-65:25
     a.   Where were the watchmen posted? When would they be silent?

     b.   What did the Lord swear by his right hand and his mighty arm?

     c.   What proclamation was to be made to the daughter of Zion?

     d.   Who was the one coming from Edom, from Bozrah?

     e.   What kindnesses was Isaiah going to tell about?

     f.   How did God's people react when God, in his love and mercy redeemed them?

     g.   What were some of the things that the people remembered when they recalled the days of old?

     h.   What did Israel's enemies do to God's sanctuary?

     i.   What did the people wish that God would do in first part of chapter sixty-four?

     j.   What were their righteous acts like?

     k.   Who is the clay? Who is the potter? Who was the work of God's hand?

     l.   What happened to God's sacred cities?

     m.   In chapter sixty-five verse one, to whom did God reveal himself? By whom was God found? What did God say about the nation that did not call on his name?

     n.   What did God promise Jacob and Judah?

     o.   In chapter sixty-five verse seventeen, what will God create?

     p.   What is said about the wolf, the lamb, the lion and the ox?

     q.   What is going to happen in God's holy mountain?

2.   Philippians 2:19-3:4a
     a.   What did Paul hope to do?

     b.   Why was Paul excited about his plan?

     c.   Who served with Paul and had proved himself?

d.   Paul was sending Timothy but what did Paul hope to do himself?

e.   Who sent Epaphroditus to Paul and for what purpose?

f.   Why was Paul sending him back?

g.   Why did Paul say he was spared sorrow?

h.   How was the church to welcome back Epaphroditus and why?

i.

j.   In chapter three verse one, what did Paul say about his writings.

k.   For whom is the church to watch out?

l.   Who was the circumcision? How do they worship? In whom do they glory?

3.   Psalms 73:1-28
      a.   Who is good to Israel?

      b.   What mistake had the Psalmist made about the wicked? How did he feel about them?

      c.   What happened to the Psalmist all day long?

      d.   Did entering the sanctuary of God change his attitude?

      e.   Who did the Psalmist make his refuge? What was he going to tell?

4.   Proverbs 24:13-14
      a.   In these verses, to what does he liken the sweet taste of honey?

      b.   What is promised about our hope?

STUDY QUESTIONS FOR OCTOBER 2

1. Isaiah 66:1-24

    a. To God, what is heaven and what is earth?

    b. What did God ask about his house?

    c. Who made all things?

    d. Who does God esteem?

    e. What had these people done about their own way and in what did they delight?

    f. What did God choose for this people? What will God bring upon them?

    g. Why did God do this to his people?

    h. Who did Isaiah tell to hear the word of the lord?

    i. Who did he want to be glorified?

    j. What was the uproar from the city and the noise that was heard from the temple?

    k. How long will Zion be in labor before she brings forth children?

    l. How was God going to extend his peace to Jerusalem?

    m. In verse twelve what does "dandled" mean?

    n. What was going to be made known to the Lord's servants? What was going to be shown to the Lord's foes?

    o. How will God come and execute judgement on all men?

    p. What will all the nations and tongues come and see?

    q. Who would select the priests and Levites?

    r. What was going to endure like the new heavens and new earth?

    s. Who come and bow down before the Lord?

2. Philippians 3:4b-21

    a. What does Paul list that shows he has more reasons to put confidence in the flesh than anyone else?

187

b.   What does he now consider these things for the sake of Christ?

c.   To what did he compare these works?

d.   From where does Paul's righteousness come?

e.   How is this righteousness obtained?

f.   What did Paul want to know?

g.   Had Paul already obtained or was he perfect in all this? How was he going to continue from there?

h.   Whose example does Paul ask them to follow?

i.   What is the god of the enemies of the cross of Christ?

3.   Psalms 74:1-23
     a.   In this Psalm, what is the first question asked of God?

     b.   What request does the Psalmist make?

     c.   What did the foes of God do to the temple of God?

     d.   What did the foes of God say in their hearts?

     e.   In verses ten and eleven, what three questions are asked of God?

     f.   In verses thirteen through seventeen, what eight thing did God do?

     g.   What does the Psalmist ask God to remember about foolish people?

4.   Proverbs 24:15-16
     a.   Solomon says "Do not lie in wait", like what?

     b.   What happens to a righteous man even though he falls seven times? What about the wicked?

STUDY QUESTIONS FOR OCTOBER 3

1. Jeremiah 1:1-2:30
   a. Jeremiah prophesied during the reign of how many kings?

   b. When was Jeremiah set apart by God?

   c. Why did God say that Jeremiah should not be afraid of the people?

   d. What six jobs did God give Jeremiah to do to the nations and the kingdoms?

   e. Why did God pronounce judgement on his people?

   f. What did the Lord remember about Israel?

   g. What had their fathers done about worthless idols?

   h. Where did God bring their fathers?

   i. What did they do with God's land and the inheritance that God gave them?

   j. What did their leaders and prophets do?

   k. What did God's people exchange for their glory?

   l. How should the heavens respond?

   m. What were the two sins that God's people committed?

   n. How did God's people bring these problems on themselves?

   o. Could God's people get rid of the stain of their guilt by using soda or abundance of soap?

   p. What did the people say about foreign gods?

   q. What did the people say to wood? What did they say to stone?

   r. They turned their backs on God but what did they say when they were in trouble?

2. Philippians 4:1-23
   a. How did Paul describe the brothers he was addressing?

   b. When should they rejoice in the Lord?

c.   How should they guard against being anxious?

d.   List the things they should think about.

e.   Who was going to be with them?

f.   What could Paul do through Christ?

g.   Philippians chapter four verse nineteen "And my God will meet all your needs according to his glorious riches in Christ Jesus." is an often quoted promise. What is the context of this promise?

h.   As Paul closes this letter to whom does he give the glory?

3.   Psalms 75:1-10
      a.   To whom do we give thanks? Why do we give thanks?

      b.   Who is the psalmist talking about when he says, "**you** say '**I** choose the appointed time; it is **I** who judge uprightly. When the earth and all its people quake, it is **I** who hold its pillars firm.'"?

      c.   Who judges? Who brings one down and exalts another?

      d.   What was in the hand of the Lord?

      e.   What happened when the Lord poured it out?

      f.   To whom was the Psalmist going to sing?

      g.   What was going to happen to the horns of the wicked?

      h.   What was going to happen to the horns of the righteous?

4.   Proverbs 24:17-20
      a.   Should one gloat when their enemy falls? Should they rejoice when he stumbles? Why?

      b.   Should one fret or be envious of the wicked? Why?

STUDY QUESTIONS FOR OCTOBER 4

1. Jeremiah 2:31-4:18
    a. What did Jeremiah ask that generation to do?

    b. What three questions does the Lord ask his people through Jeremiah in verses thirty-one and thirty-two? What had God's people done?

    c. In verse thirty-five why was God going to pass judgement on his people?

    d. In chapter three verse two, how had the people defiled the land? How were they being punished?

    e. In chapter two verse ten, how did Judah return to the Lord? How should she have returned?

    f. What message does Jeremiah give to faithless Israel? What promise does he make? What did they need to acknowledge?

    g. At that time what would they call Jerusalem?

    h. In chapter three verse twenty-two, what would God do if the faithless people returned?

    i. In the last part of chapter three, against whom did the people admit that they sinned?

    j. What would happen to the men of Judah and Jerusalem if they did not break up their unplowed ground and circumcise themselves and their hearts?

    k. From where was the Lord bringing disaster?

    l. In chapter four verse eight, what were the people to do?

    m. In that day what would happen to the officials, the priests and the prophets?

    n. How swift would the invading horses be?

    o. What is said about their punishment in the last verse of this passage?

2. Colossians 1:1-20
    a. What two people were mentioned that were sending this letter?

    b. To whom was this letter addressed?

c.   What did they send from God the Father?

d.   Why did they always thank the Lord?

e.   What was the gospel doing over all the world? How did the church that was at Colosse hear about the gospel?

f.   With what was Paul asking God to fill the believers? He prayed that so that they might do what five things? So that they might have what two things?

g.   By whom were all things created? Who was before all things? In whom are all things held together?

h.   How did God reconcile all things to himself?

3.   Psalms 76:1-12

a.   Who is known in Judah?

b.   Whose name is great in Israel?

c.   The Psalmist says that God is more majestic than what?

d.   Who alone is to be feared?

e.   Who can stand against God when he is angry?

f.   What does God's wrath against men bring?

g.   What happens to the survivors of God's wrath?

h.   Who breaks the spirit of rulers?

i.   Who is feared by the kings of the earth?

4.   Proverbs 24:21-22

a.   Who should the son fear?

b.   Who should he not join?

STUDY QUESTIONS FOR OCTOBER 5

1. Jeremiah 4:19-6:14
    a. Jeremiah has been called "the weeping prophet", how does Jeremiah describe his feelings in chapter four, verse nineteen?

    b. How are God's people described in verse twenty-two?

    c. Will God completely destroy the land?

    d. In verse thirty one, what kind of a cry did God hear?

    e. In chapter five verse one, what did God promise if they could find but one person who deals honestly and seeks the truth?

    f. What question does God ask the Israelites in chapter five verse seven? What did God remind them that their children did?

    g. What did the Lord declare about the house of Israel and the house of Judah? (Jeremiah chapter five verse eleven)

    h. What was the Lord going to bring against the house of Israel?

    i. What does the Lord say about the case of the fatherless and the rights of the poor?

    j. What did the Lord tell the people of Benjamin to do?

    k. What warning does the Lord give to Jerusalem?

    l. What did the Lord say about gleaning the remnant of Israel?

    m. What was going to happen to their houses, their fields and their wives?

    n. Who was greedy for gain?

    o. What did prophets and priests alike do?

    p. What do the priests and prophets say?

2. Colossians 1:21-2:7
    a. At one time what was the relationship of the Colossians to God?

    b. Now what was their relationship to God? How did that change?

    c. Where has this gospel been proclaimed? What did Paul become?

d.   In what did Paul rejoice?

e.   What had God chosen to make known among the Gentiles?

f.   Who did Paul proclaim? How did he do this? Why did he do this?

g.   What did Paul want them to know?

h.   What was Paul's purpose?

i.   In whom are all the treasures of wisdom and knowledge hidden?

j.   What were the Colossians to do just as they had received Christ?

3.   Psalms 77:1-20
     a.   Who did the Psalmist cry out to for help?

     b.   What did the Psalmist do when he was in distress?

     c.   What did the Psalmist remember? (Verses three, six, and eleven)

     d.   On what was the Psalmist going to meditate and consider?

     e.   How did God lead his people?

4.   Proverbs 24:23-25
     a.   What is said about showing partiality in judging?

     b.   What happens to the one that says to the guilty, "You are innocent"?

     c.   What happens to those that convict the guilty?

STUDY QUESTIONS FOR OCTOBER 6

1. Jeremiah 6:15-8:7

    a. How does the Lord describe the actions of his people in verse fifteen? What was he going to do to them?

    b. What would they receive if they walked in the good way?

    c. What was the Lord going to bring on this people? Why was he going to do that?

    d. What was the Lord going to put before his people? What would happen to the fathers and sons?

    e. From where would the army be coming? What would they sound like?

    f. Why were God's people called, "rejected silver"?

    g. In chapter seven, who were invited to hear the word of the Lord? What were they asked to do? What would the Lord do in return?

    h. While his people were doing bad things, what did the Lord do again and again? How did the people react?

    i. What did the Lord tell Jeremiah not to do in chapter seven verse sixteen?

    j. In chapter seven verse twenty, on what things will the Lord's anger be poured out?

    k. What did the people do instead of listening and paying attention to the Lord?

    l. To what was the Lord going to bring to an end in chapter seven verse thirty-four?

    m. In chapter eight, what was going to happen to the bones?

    n. What would the survivors prefer?

    o. What did the people do when the Lord listened attentively? What did the Lord say his people did not know?

2. Colossians 2:8-23

    a. How was Paul worried that the Colossians might be taken captive? On what did this philosophy depend?

    b. In whom did the fullness of the deity live in bodily form?

    c. What kind of circumcision is Paul talking about here?

d. What did God do for the Colosians when they were dead in their sins?

e. How did God forgive all their sins, having disarmed the powers and authorities?

f. What did Paul say about people judging them? Where is the reality found?

g. What does Paul say about the one who delights in false humility?

h. In verse twenty, what does Paul say about submitting to the rules of the world?

i. How do the rules appear? What do the rules lack?

3. Psalms 78:1-31
   a. What were the people to do? What was going to come out of his mouth?

   b. What were they going to tell the next generation?

   c. Where would the children put their trust?

   d. What were their forefathers like?

   e. What did the men of Ephraim do even though they were armed with bows?

   f. How did God guide them in the day time and how did he guide them at night?

   g. What happened when God's anger arose?

4. Proverbs 24:26
   a. What is an honest answer like?

1. Jeremiah 8:8-9:26
    a. In the first verse of today's reading, the people were looking to the law of the Lord, what was the problem with this?

    b. Why will the wise be put to shame?

    c. What was God going to do with the wives and the fields of these men?

    d. What were their prophets and priests doing?

    e. What were the prophets and priests saying about peace?

    f. Were the prophets and priests ashamed of their loathsome conduct?

    g. Because of their actions, what was God going to do with their harvest?

    h. How were the people provoking God to anger?

    i. Quote Jeremiah chapter eight verse twenty.

    j. Read chapter nine verse one, Jeremiah is known as the "_____ prophet"

    k. What did the people do with their tongues?

    l. How did the people speak with his mouth to his neighbor? What did they do with their heart?

    m. What was God going to make of Jerusalem? What did the Lord say was the reason that this was going to happen to Jerusalem?

    n. What did the Lord declare in chapter nine verse twenty-two?

    o. What does the Lord say about the wise man, the strong man, and the rich man?

    p. Who was the Lord going to punish?

2. Colossians 3:1-17
    a. On what was the Christian to set his heart? Why were they to do this?

    b. What will the Christian do when Christ appears in glory?

    c. What is the Christian to do with whatever belongs to his earthly nature?

d.   Name the five things that Paul uses as examples of things the Christian should get rid of.

e.   With what five things should the Christian clothe themselves?

f.   How were they to forgive?

g.   What were they to put on over all these virtues?

h.   What were the believers to do with the peace of Christ?

3.   Psalms 78:32-55
      a.   In verse thirty-two, what is the Psalmist referring to when he says "In spite of all this"? (Look back to yesterday's reading)

      b.   How did God end their days?

      c.   What did the people do when God slew them?

      d.   What did the people remember about God?

      e.   In verse thirty-eight, how did God respond to his unfaithful people?

      f.   What did the people fail to remember?

      g.   To what did the Psalmist liken God bringing out his people?

      h.   What did God do to the nations before Israel?

4.   Proverbs 24:27
      a.   What is the son told that he should do before he builds his house?

STUDY QUESTIONS FOR OCTOBER 8

1. Jeremiah 10:1-11:23
    a. What did God say to the house of Israel? Why did he tell them not to do this?

    b. Who is like the Lord?

    c. How were the people of the nations taught?

    d. Where did they get silver and gold to make their idols?

    e. How did the craftsmen clothe the idols?

    f. Who is the true God? How is he described?

    g. What will happen to the god's who did not make the heavens or the earth?

    h. Who made the earth?

    i. In chapter ten verses fourteen through fifteen, how does Jeremiah describe the idols that were being made?

    j. The Lord Almighty is the maker of all things and those that are of his inheritance, what were their instructions and warnings?

    k. Give a brief description of what was happening in the towns of the north.

    l. In chapter ten, verses twenty-three to twenty-five, what was the essence of Jeremiah's prayer?

    m. In chapter eleven, give highlights of what the Lord answered Jeremiah.

    n. Who was Jeremiah to tell?

    o. Who broke the covenant that the Lord made with their forefathers?

    p. What happened to the people that broke God's covenant?

    q. In chapter eleven verse seventeen, what provoked the Lord to anger?

2. Colossians 3:18-4:18
    a. What should wives do? What should husbands do? What should children do? What should fathers do? What should slaves do? What should masters do?

    b. Paul reminds the Colossians to pray, who does he ask them to pray for?

c.   What did Paul say their conversation (actions) should be like?

d.   What was Tychicus going to do? How does Paul describe him?

e.   Among Paul and his workers, how many were Jews?

f.   Who was always wrestling in prayer for the Colosians?

g.   What were the Colosians to do with this letter after it had been read to them?

h.   Who wrote this greeting in his own hand?

3.   Psalms 78:56-72
   a.   What did the Israelites do to God? What did they do about God's statutes?

   b.   How were these people like their forefathers?

   c.   To what did God give his people over? What happened to their young men?
         What happened to their maidens?

   d.   What did God do to his enemies?

   e.   What tribe did God choose?

   f.   What mount did God choose?

   g.   What servant did God choose? How did this servant shepherd God's people?

4.   Proverbs 24:28-29
   a.   What is said about testifying against your neighbor?

   b.   What was not to be said?

STUDY QUESTIONS FOR OCTOBER 9

1. Jeremiah 12:1-14:10
   a. Who is always righteous?

   b. Who knew Jeremiah and tested his thoughts about God?

   c. What were the people saying about God?

   d. Whose sword would devour from one end of the land to the other? Would anyone be safe?

   e. When they sowed wheat, what would they reap? What would they gain when they wear themselves out?

   f. What did God promise to do to any nation that does not listen?

   g. What did God tell Jeremiah to do about a linen belt?

   h. What prophecy did this story illustrate?

   i. In chapter thirteen verse twelve, what did the Lord instruct Jeremiah to tell the people?

   j. To whom were they to give glory?

   k. What was the answer to the question people might ask themselves, "Why has this happened to me.?"?

   l. What was God going to do to the people? Why was God going to do this?

   m. In chapter fourteen, what does the word of the Lord concern?

   n. What did the nobles ask their servants to do? What did the servants find when they tried to do what the nobles asked?

   o. What request did the people make of their God?

   p. What did the Lord say about this people?

   q. Would the Lord accept the people? What would the Lord do?

2. I Thessalonians 1:1-2:9
   a. Who is sending this letter?

b.   To whom was this letter being sent?

c.   What is said in the salutation?

d.   How did their gospel come to the brothers?

e.   What did the Thessalonians become to all the believers in Macedonia and Achaia?

f.   Was their visit a failure?

g.   Who were the senders of this letter trying to please?

h.   Were Paul, Silas and Timothy a burden to the Thessalonians?

3.   Psalms 79:1-13
   a.   Who had invaded God's inheritance and defiled his holy temple?

   b.   What did they do with God's servants and saints?

   c.   What three question did the Psalmist ask the Lord?

   d.   What did the Psalmist ask the Lord to do to the nations that did not acknowledge God?

   e.   The Psalmist requested that God do several things and not do several things for his people, list these requests.

   f.   How many times did the Psalmist want God to pay back into the laps of their neighbors?

   g.   Then what did the Psalmist promise God that the people would do? How long would they do it?

4.   Proverbs 24:30-34
   a.   What did he see when he went past the field of the sluggard?

   b.   What was the result of a little sleep, a little slumber, and a little folding of the hands?

STUDY QUESTIONS FOR OCTOBER 10

1. Jeremiah 14:11-16:15
    a. What messages were the prophets preaching?

    b. Why was God upset with the prophets?

    c. What did God say was going to happen to the prophets?

    d. Why is Jeremiah called the weeping prophet?

    e. What questions did Jeremiah ask of God?

    f. Who sends the rain? In whom was their hope?

    g. God said his heart would not go out to the people even if what two Bible characters stood before him?

    h. What two things did Jerusalem do to reap God's wrath?

    i. How did Jeremiah describe the number of widows that would be in Jerusalem?

    j. God promised to deliver them for a good purpose, what was he going to make their enemies do?

    k. What was God going to do with their wealth and treasures? Why was he going to do that?

    l. What did Jeremiah do with God's word and what did they become? Why did Jeremiah sit alone?

    m. From whose hand was God going to rescue Jeremiah?

    n. What did God say was going to happen to the fathers and the mothers born in this land?

    o. Why did God say they were not to mourn or show sympathy for the people?

    p. When the people ask "Why has the Lord decreed such a great disaster against us?" what was Jeremiah to answer?

    q. What was God's final promise to his people in chapter sixteen verse fifteen?

2. I Thessalonians 2:10-3:13
    a. Who were the witnesses that Paul and his group were holy, righteous, and

blameless?

b.   How did Paul deal with the Thessalonians?

c.   Why did Paul thank God continually?

d.   What was Paul's glory and joy?

e.   Who did Paul send to encourage to strengthen them in their faith?

f.   What had Paul told them about persecution?

g.   What was Paul's fear for the Thessalonians?

h.   What good news did Timothy bring?

i.   What was Paul's prayer night and day?

j.   I Thessalonians chapter three verse thirteen "May _____ _____ your _____ so that you will be _____ and _____ in the _____ of our God and father when our Lord Jesus comes with all his holy ones."

3.   Psalms 80:1-19
    a.   To whom is this prayer addressed?

    b.   What four things does the Psalmist request in the first three verses?

    c.   What do their enemies do?

    d.   What did God bring out of Egypt?

    e.   What two requests does the Psalmist make in verse nineteen?

4.   Proverbs 25:1-5
    a.   What is the glory of God? What is the glory of kings?

    b.   What does he say about the heart of a king? What happens when one removes the wicked from the presence of the king?

STUDY QUESTIONS FOR OCTOBER 11

1. Jeremiah 16:16-18:23
   a. The fishermen and hunters refers to the conquers of the land, where were they going to find God's people that escaped? How was God going to repay them for their wickedness and sin? Why were they going to be punished?

   b. When the nations come to the Lord, what are they going to say?

   c. What will the nations know when the Lord teaches them?

   d. Whose fault was it that Judah lost her inheritance? To whom was Judah going to be enslaved? Where would they be enslaved?

   e. What man will be blessed? What will he be like?

   f. What is said about the heart?

   g. What will happen to all that forsake the Lord?

   h. In chapter seventeen verse eighteen, what three request are made about the persecutors?

   i. What was promised if the people kept the Sabbath? What was promised if they did not keep the Sabbath?

   j. In chapter eighteen, where did the Lord tell Jeremiah to go?

   k. What happened to the pot the potter was working on? How did that apply to the house of Israel?

   l. In chapter eighteen verses eleven through twelve, what was the Lord preparing for Jerusalem and what did he ask them to do? Did they do it?

   m. Did God's people remember God? To whom did God's people burn incense?

   n. In verse eighteen, what were the people doing to Jeremiah?

   o. In the last verse, what does Jeremiah request of the Lord?

2. I Thessalonians 4:1-5:3
   a. What did Paul encourage the brothers to do with the instruction that he had already given them?

   b. What should they avoid? What should they learn to control?

c. Who does the one that rejects their instructions reject?

d. By whom were the brothers taught in brotherly love?

e. What does Paul encourage them to have as their ambition?

f. Of what does Paul not want the believers to be ignorant?

g. How is the Lord himself going to come down from heaven?

h. In what order will believers be taken into heaven?

i. How is the day of the Lord going to come? What will happen as people are saying, "peace and safety,"?

3. Psalms 81:1-16
   a. What six things were the people asked to do when they came together in celebration at the new moon, when the moon is full, on the day of their feast?

   b. Who removed the burden from the people's shoulders and set their hands free from the basket?

   c. What did the people do in their distress? What did God do and how did he do it?

   d. Of what does God warn in verses eight and nine?

   e. Of what does the Lord remind the people in verse ten?

   f. Did the people listen? What happened to the people?

4. Proverbs 25:6-7
   a. What two things does Solomon tell his son not to do in these two verses?

   b. What is better for the king to say?

1. Jeremiah 19:1-21:14
    a. What did the Lord tell Jeremiah to do?

    b. What did the Lord say he was going to do to "this place"? Why was he going to do that?

    c. In verses eight and nine, what was God going to do to the city?

    d. What was Jeremiah to do with the jar? What was he to say to the people?

    e. Then what did Jeremiah do?

    f. What did Pashhur, the priest do when he heard Jeremiah prophesying these things?

    g. What was the Lord going to do to Pashhur?

    h. What did the word of the Lord bring Jeremiah all day long?

    i. What did Jeremiah say would happen to his persecutors?

    j. What was Jeremiah lamenting in chapter twenty, verses fourteen through eighteen?

    k. Who did King Zedekiah send to inquire of Jeremiah?

    l. What did they say to Jeremiah? What did they say that perhaps the Lord might do?

    m. How did Jeremiah answer them?

    n. What was the Lord going to do to Zedekiah and to his officials?

    o. What kind of mercy, compassion and pity would Nebuchadnezzar have on the king and his officials?

    p. What did Jeremiah tell the people to do to live?

    q. What were the people saying that the Lord didn't like?

2. I Thessalonians 5:4-28
    a. Were the Thessalonian brothers in darkness about this day?

b.　Who does Paul say they should not be like?

c.　Since they belonged to the day, what should they do?

d.　What were they to do for each other as they were doing?

e.　What were they to do for the ones that worked hard among them?

f.　What were they to do with the idle, the timid, the weak and everyone? What were they to avoid?

g.　What were they to do continually?

h.　 How does Paul close this book?

3.　Psalms 82:1-8
　　a.　Who presides in the great assembly?

　　b.　Who gives judgement?

　　c.　In verse two, what question does the Psalmist ask the judges?

　　d.　What two things does he tell the judges that they should do?

　　e.　How does he describe the judges in verse five?

　　f.　What were the judges called in verse six?

　　g.　How would the judges die?

　　h.　What request is made of God because of the corruption of the judges?

4.　Proverbs 25:8-10
　　a.　What does Solomon say about going into court?

　　b.　What does he say about betraying another man's confidence?

1.   Jeremiah 22:1-23:20
    a.   In chapter twenty-two, what did the Lord say to Jeremiah?

    b.   How did the Lord say that the king should treat the alien, the fatherless or the widow?

    c.   What did the Lord promise would happen if the king did not obey these commands?

    d.   What would the people from many nations ask? What was the answer to their question?

    e.   In chapter twenty-two verse seventeen, on what was Jehoiakim eyes and heart set?

    f.   What kind of a burial would Jehoiakim have?

    g.   What was the Lord going to do with Jehoichin and his mother?

    h.   How many of Jehoiachin's offspring would sit on the throne of David?

    i.   In chapter twenty-three verse four, what was the Lord going to do for his people?

    j.   What will the king that the Lord raises up be called? To whom is this prophecy referring?

    k.   In the coming days, what would the people say instead of "As surely as the Lord lives, who brought the Israelites up out of Egypt."? Where would they live?

    l.   Why was Jeremiah's heart broken within him? What was the land full of?

    m.   What two things did the prophets of Samaria do?

    n.   What spread ungodliness across the land?

    o.   In the last verse of chapter twenty-three, what would happen in the days to come?

2.   II Thessalonians 1:1-12
    a.   Who were sending the letter to the Thessalonians?

    b.   What two things did they send to the Thessalonians from God?

    c.   Why should they thank God for the brothers?

d.   What were Paul and group doing among God's churches?

e.   Who would God punish? How would they be punished?

f.   What were they praying for the Thessalonians? Why were they praying this?

3.   Psalms 83:1-18
      a.   In verse one, what does the Psalmist request in three different ways?

      b.   What does the Psalmist point out that the enemies of God were doing to his people? What were these enemies saying about the nation of God's people?

      c.   What were these enemies doing together?

      d.   In verse nine and ten, what did the Psalmist ask God to do to these enemies?

      e.   What did the Psalmist want their nobles and princes to be like?

      f.   Why did the Psalmist want the faces of the enemies to be covered with shame?

      g.   How did the Psalmist want them to perish?

      h.   In verse eighteen, what did the Psalmist want the enemies to know about God?

4.   Proverbs 25:11-14
      a.   What is like apples of gold in settings of silver?

      b.   What is a wise man's rebuke to a listening ear like?

      c.   What is like clouds and wind without rain?

STUDY QUESTIONS FOR OCTOBER 14

1. Jeremiah 23:21-25:38

    a. What does the Lord say about the prophets in chapter twenty-three verses twenty-one and twenty-two?

    b. What did the Lord hear the prophets say?

    c. What two things did the Lord say his word was like?

    d. What kind of prophets was the Lord against?

    e. What was God going to do to the prophets because they said, "This is the oracle of the Lord." Even though it wasn't an oracle of God?

    f. In chapter twenty-four, what did the Lord show Jeremiah?

    g. To what were the good figs likened?

    h. To what were the bad figs likened?

    i. How was the Lord going to deal with Zedekiah, his officials and the survivors from Jerusalem?

    j. Jeremiah spoke to the people again and again but did the people listen?

    k. How long could the people stay in the land if they turned from their evil ways and their evil practices?

    l. How did he people provoke the Lord?

    m. How long would the nations serve the king of Babylon?

    n. What would God do to the king of Babylon and his nation after that period of time?

    o. What did Jeremiah do with the cup filled with the wine of God's wrath that the Lord gave him?

    p. What did the Lord almighty say in chapter twenty-five verse thirty two?

    q. Who was likened to a lion leaving his lair?

2. II Thessalonians 2:1-17

    a. What did Paul ask of the Thessalonians believers?

b.   What did Paul say must happen before the day of the Lord will come?

c.   What was the man of lawlessness going to proclaim?

d.   When will the lawlessness one be revealed? Who is holding him back?

e.   How will the Lord Jesus overthrow the lawless one?

f.   How will the coming of the lawless one be displayed?

g.   Why should Paul thank God for the Thessalonians?

h.   In verse sixteen, what was Paul asking God to do for the believers?

3.   Psalms 84:1-12
   a.   For what did the Psalmist's soul yearn and even faint?

   b.   What found a place near God's altar?

   c.   In this Psalm there are three types of people that are blessed, name them.

   d.   What request does the Psalmist make regarding prayer?

   e.   What does the Psalmist pray for in verse nine?

   f.   What is better than one-thousand days on a tropical island?

   g.   What would the Psalmist rather do than to dwell in the tents of the wicked?

   h.   What good thing does God withhold from the people whose walk is blameless?

4.   Proverbs 25:15
   a.   What can persuade a ruler?

   b.   What can a gentle tongue do?

STUDY QUESTIONS FOR OCTOBER 15

1.   Jeremiah 26:1-27:22
        a.   When did this word come from the Lord?

        b.   What did the Lord instruct Jeremiah to do? What would be the consequences if
                the people did not listen?

        c.   What did the priests, the prophets and all the people do to Jeremiah when he
                finished telling them all that the Lord had commanded him to say?

        d.   How did Jeremiah respond to the accusations of the people?

        e.   What was the advice of the elders of the land that stepped forward?

        f.   What happened to Uriah?

        g.   In chapter twenty-seven, what did God instruct Jeremiah to do? What message
                about Nebuchadnezzar did God give to Jeremiah?

        h.   Which prophets, diviners, interpreters of dreams, mediums, and sorcerers, did
                Jeremiah warn the people not to listen to?

        i.   What would happen to the nation that bowed to Babylon?

        j.   What were some of the prophets prophesying about Babylon? What did Jeremiah
                say about those prophets?

        k.   What did Jeremiah tell them to do for the king of Babylon? Can you see why
                some of the people thought that Jeremiah was a traitor?

        l.   What did the Lord Almighty say about the pillars, the sea, the movable stands and
                other furnishings left in the city?

        m.   How long would the furnishings be left in Babylon?

2.   II Thessalonians 3:1-18
        a.   What prayer request does Paul make?

        b.   What does Paul say about the Lord?

        c.   What did Paul command the brothers to do?

        d.   Whose example should the brothers follow?

e.   When did Paul and his crew labor? Why did they labor like that?

f.   What rule was given to the brothers when Paul was with them?

g.   What was said about the ones that were not busy? What was commanded and urged of these people?

h.   How were they to treat the ones that did not obey the instructions of II Thessalonians?

i.   In verse sixteen, what is Paul's wish for the brothers?

j.   How does he close this book in verse eighteen?

3.   Psalms 85:1-13
   a.   Who showed favor on the land? Whose fortunes did he restore?

   b.   What request does the Psalmist make of God?

   c.   What three questions does the Psalmist ask?

   d.   What kind of love did the Psalmist want God to show?

   e.   To what was the Psalmist going to listen?

   f.   What did he say about salvation?

   g.   What will the Lord give?

   h.   What goes before God?

4.   Proverbs 25:16
   a.   In this verse, against what does Solomon warn?

STUDY QUESTIONS FOR OCTOBER 16

1. Jeremiah 28:1-29:32
    a. In what month and year was this prophecy given?

    b. At this time who was king of Judah?

    c. What did Hananiah say that the God of Israel was going to do to the king of Babylon?

    d. What did Hananiah say that God was going to do for the exiles of Judah?

    e. Did Jeremiah agree with this prophecy?

    f. What did Jeremiah say had to take place for a prophet that prophesies peace to be recognized?

    g. What did the word of the Lord tell Jeremiah to say to Hananiah the prophet?

    h. Who were the nations going to serve? What was said about the wild animals?

    i. What did Jeremiah then go on to say about Hananiah the prophet?

    j. What happened to Hananiah in the seventh month of the same year?

    k. In the letter that Jeremiah sent to the exiles, were they to increase or decrease in population?

    l. What were they to seek?

    m. What would happen when seventy years were completed?

    n. What did Jeremiah say about his people that did not go into exile?

    o. What did he say about his people that did go into exile?

    p. What punishment was Shemaiah going to receive? Why was he to receive this punishment?

2. I Timothy 1:1-20
    a. How did Paul describe himself and by whose command did he write this epistle?

    b. To whom was this letter addressed?

    c. What blessing did Paul ask for the addressee?

d.   Where was the addressee asked to stay? Why was he asked to stay there?

e.   What do myths and endless genealogies promote? Rather than what?

f.   What comes from a pure heart and a good conscience and a sincere faith?

g.   What did Paul say about the ones that wanted to be teachers of the law?

h.   I Timothy chapter one verse eight "We know that the law is good..." if what?

i.   In verse twelve, for what did Paul thank Christ Jesus?

j.   Why did Christ Jesus come into the world?

k.   Why was Paul giving these instructions to Timothy?

3.   Psalms 86:1-17
      a.   How long did the Psalmist call out to the Lord?

      b.   Who was forgiving and good?

      c.   What god was like the Lord?

      d.   What did the Psalmist say he would do if God would teach him his ways?

      e.   Why did the Psalmist want God to give him a sign of his goodness?

4.   Proverbs 25:17
      a.   How often should you set foot in the house of your neighbor?

      b.   What happens if you go to often?

STUDY QUESTIONS FOR OCTOBER 17

1. Jeremiah 30:1-31:26
    a. What people were the object of this prophecy?

    b. What did he ask about men bearing children?

    c. What did Jeremiah see happening to every strong man?

    d. What did God say about the yoke and their bonds?

    e. What was God's promise to his people when he destroys completely all the nations?

    f. What happened to Israel and Jacob's allies?

    g. What was going to happen to the ones that devoured Israel and Jacob?

    h. What was God's promise to Israel and Jacob?

    i. How long until God's fierce anger will be turned back?

    j. With what kind of love did God love his people?

    k. Who scattered Israel and who will gather them?

    l. Who was going to ransom Jacob?

    m. What was God going to turn their mourning into?

    n. How was God going to satisfy the priests? What was God going to do for his people?

    o. Why were the people to restrain their voices from weeping and their eyes from tears?

    p. What did God declare about the future of this people?

    q. What did Ephraim say in what God called Ephaim's moaning?

    r. What was God going to do for the weary and the faint?

2. I Timothy 2:1-15
    a. What did Paul urge Timothy to do first of all?

b.   What about kings and those in authority? Why should they be included?

c.   What pleases God our savior?

d.   What is God's desire?

e.   How many gods are there?

f.   How many mediators between God and man? Who is the mediator?

g.   What was Paul's purpose? Was he telling the truth?

h.   What did Paul want the men to do?

i.   What did Paul want the women to do?

j.   How should women learn?

k.   Who was formed first?

l.   What will happen for women if they continue in faith, love and holiness?

3.   Psalms 87:1-7
      a.   Who set his foundation on the holy mountain?

      b.   What does the Lord love more than the dwellings of Jacob?

      c.   Who will establish Zion?

      d.   Who will write in the register of the peoples: "This one was born in Zion."?

      e.   Where did the people find their fountains of joy?

4.   Proverbs 25:18-19
      a.   How is a man who gives false testimony described?

      b.   To what is reliance on the unfaithful in times of trouble likened?

1.   Jeremiah 31:27-32:44

    a.   What was the Lord going to do for the house of Israel and the house of Judah just as he had done when they were uprooted, torn down, overthrown, and destroyed?

    b.   What was said about when the fathers ate sour grapes? How would that saying change?

    c.   What would have to happen before Israel would cease to be a nation before God? What would have to take place before the Lord rejects all the descendants of Israel because of all they have done?

    d.   How does the Lord describe the days that are coming?

    e.   When the word of the Lord came to Jeremiah in the tenth year of Zedekiah, what was the army of the king of Babylon doing? Where was Jeremiah?

    f.   In chapter thirty-two verse eight, what was Zedekiah's cousin going to do? What did Zedekiah do? What did these actions foretell?

    g.   In verse eighteen, what did Zedekiah say about the Lord's love and punishment of the fathers?

    h.   How long did the Lord's miraculous signs and wonders that started in Egypt continue?

    i.   In chapter thirty-two verses twenty-nine through thirty-five, list at least nine things that God's people did that provoked God's anger.

    j.   The rest of the chapter gives God's promise to his people. From where would the Lord gather his people? Where would he let them live in safety?

    k.   What kind of a covenant was he going to make with them? How long was he going to do good for them?

    l.   As he brought this great calamity on them, what was he going to give them? What was he going to restore to them?

2.   I Timothy 3:1-16

    a.   What is said about desiring to be an overseer (bishop)?

    b.   What seven things should an overseer be? What four things should he not be? What two things should he do?

c.   What are the first two things that Paul says that deacons should be like? What must they do?

d.   What must first happen to one that is being considered as a deacon? What must be the result of this?

e.   What is required of the wife of a deacon?

f.   What else is said about a deacon's wife, his children and his household?

g.   What did Paul hope to do soon?

h.   Why did Paul write this letter?

i.   What did Paul say was beyond all question?

j.   What six things did Paul say about the work of Christ?

3.   Psalms 88:1-18
     a.   What declaration does the Psalmist make in verse one?

     b.   What two requests does he make in verse two?

     c.   What five things does the Psalmist mention that describe his life?

     d.   What four things does he say the Lord did to him?

     e.   What two things did the Psalmist do?

     f.   What six things does he ask the Lord?

     g.   What does the Psalmist say is his closest friend?

4.   Proverbs 25:20-22
     a.   To what is one likened who sings songs to a heavy heart?

     b.   What two things should one do for his enemies?

1. Jeremiah 33:1-34:22

    a. What happened to Jeremiah while he was still confined in the courtyard of the guard?

    b. Even though this prophecy starts out with punishment, how does the prophecy change starting with chapter thirty-three, verse six?

    c. What was going to happen to the streets of Jerusalem?

    d. What was the Lord going to restore?

    e. What "days" are coming?

    f. What was God going to make sprout out of David's line?

    g. What did God promise to Judah and Jerusalem in those days.

    h. What did God promise to David's descendants and descendants of the Levites?

    i. What word came to Jeremiah while Nebuchadnezzar king of Babylon and all his army and all his kingdom and his people were fighting against Jerusalem?

    j. Who was Zedekiah king of Judah going to see and with whom was he going to speak face to face?

    k. How was Zedekiah going to die and what would his funeral be like?

    l. What were the only fortified cities left in Judah?

    m. What covenant did king Zedekiah make with all the people in Jerusalem? What happened afterward?

    n. In chapter thirty-four, verse seventeen, what did God say about them not proclaiming freedom for their fellow countrymen?

    o. In the last verse of this section, what was God going to do to the towns of Judah?

2. I Timothy 4:1-16

    a. What does the Spirit say will happen in later times?

    b. From where does such teaching come? What did these teachers forbid the people to do?

c.	What did Paul say about God's creation?

d.	With what was Timothy told that he should have nothing to do? What was he to do instead?

e.	Where did they put their hope?

f.	What did Paul tell Timothy that he should command and teach?

g.	To what should Timothy devote himself until Paul came? What was Timothy to watch closely?

3.	Psalms 89:1-13
a.	What was the Psalmist going to sing about?

b.	What two things was he going to declare?

c.	What did God swear to David?

d.	What do the heavens do?

e.	Where is God greatly feared? Why was he greatly feared?

f.	Who rules over the surging sea? What does he do when the waves mount up?

g.	With what did God scatter his enemies?

h.	What did the Psalmist say about God's arm, his hand and his right hand?

4.	Proverbs 25:23-24
a.	What does a north wind bring? What does a sly tongue bring?

b.	What is better than sharing a house with a quarrelsome wife?

1. Jeremiah 35:1-36:32
    a. When did this word of the Lord come to Jeremiah?

    b. Where did Jeremiah invite the Recabite family to come? What did he set before them?

    c. What did he say to them? What was their answer?

    d. Where did the Recabite's go when Nebuchadnezzar invaded the land?

    e. What did the Lord almighty, the God of Israel say to the men of Judah and the people of Jerusalem about the Recabite's? Did the people of Jerusalem obey God when he spoke to them again and again?

    f. What was the Lord God Almighty going to bring on Judah and everyone living in Jerusalem because they had not obeyed God?

    g. What was the Lord God Almighty going to do for Jonadab the son of Recab because he had obeyed the command of his forefather?

    h. What did the Lord say might happen when Jeremiah writes the words God spoke to him on a scroll?

    i. Who did Jeremiah call to be the scribe to take his dictation? What did Jeremiah ask the scribe to do?

    j. What did Micaiah do when he heard all the words of the Lord from the scroll?

    k. What did this group of officials ask Baruch to do?

    l. What did the officials tell Baruch and Jeremiah to do?

    m. What did the king do as the words on the scroll were being read to him? What did the king command?

    n. What did the word of the Lord tell Jeremiah to do?

    o. What punishment did the Lord pronounce on Jehoikim?

2. I Timothy 5:1-25
    a. How should Timothy treat older men? Younger men? Older women? Younger women? What did he stipulate about the younger women?

223

b.   What was he supposed to do for the widows who were really in need?

c.   What was pleasing to God?

d.   What is said about the one that does not provide for his relatives?

e.   What was required of a widow before she could be placed on the list of widows?

f.   How did Paul counsel young widows?

g.   What should Timothy not be hasty to do?

3.   Psalms 89:14-37
   a.   What is the foundation of God's throne?

   b.   Who are blessed?

   c.   To whom did the shield of the Psalmist belong?

   d.   What is said about the Lord finding David? With what did the Lord anoint David?

   e.   What was the hand of the Lord going to do for David? What about the Lord's arm?

   f.   What was God going to do to David's foes and his adversaries?

   g.   How long will David's line continue?

4.   Proverbs 25:25-37
   a.   What is news from a distant land like?

   b.   What is a righteous man that gives way to the wicked like?

   c.   What two things are said not to be good?

STUDY QUESTIONS FOR OCTOBER 21

1.   Jeremiah 37:1-38:28
       a.   Who made Zedekiah king of Judah? What king did he replace?

       b.   What request did Zedekiah make of Jeremiah?

       c.   What was the word of the Lord that came to Jeremiah?

       d.   What accusation did Hananiah make against Jeremiah? How did Jeremiah
              answer? What did they do to Jeremiah?

       e.   What did Zedekiah ask Jeremiah when he brought him to the palace?

       f.   What did Jeremiah ask the king?

       g.   What petition did Jeremiah bring before the king? Did the king grant his petition?

       h.   What did the officials hear Jeremiah saying to all the people?

       i.   What did they do to Jeremiah?

       j.   What Cushite went to the king to plead for Jeremiah? What did the king allow
              him to do?

       k.   How did Jeremiah respond to the king's questions when the king brought him to
              the third entrance to the temple?

       l.   What oath did Zedekiah swear secretly to Jeremiah?

       m.   What did the Lord say through Jeremiah to Zedekiah if he surrendered to the
              officers of the king of Babylon?

       n.   What was king Zedekiah afraid of?

       o.   How did Jeremiah answer the king?

       p.   What did Zedekiah tell Jeremiah to tell the officials if they asked about his
              conversation with the king?

       q.   How long did Jeremiah remain in the guard's courtyard?

2.   I Timothy 6:1-21
       a.   How were the slaves to treat their masters?

b. Are the believing slaves that have believing master supposed to treat their masters with less respect because they are brothers? Could the same principle hold true today for believing employee's with their believing boss?

c. What does Paul say about the man that has an unhealthy interest in controversies and quarrels?

d. What is godliness with contentment?

e. What did they bring into the world and what are they taking out of the world?

f. What is said about the person that wants to get rich?

g. What did Paul tell Timothy to do?

h. What was Timothy to command those who are rich in this present world?

i. What was Timothy to guard?

3. Psalms 89:38-52
a. To whom is the Psalmist referring in verse thirty-eight when he says "You" have rejected, "you" have spurned?

b. Who had the edge of his sword turned back?

c. The "Spirit Filled Life Study Bible" calls Psalm eighty-nine a messianic psalm, what does that mean?

d. What two questions does the Psalmist ask in verse forty-six?

e. What does the Psalmist ask God to remember in verse forty-seven?

f. How does this Psalm conclude?

4. Proverbs 25:28
a. What is like a city whose walls are broken down?

STUDY QUESTIONS FOR OCTOBER 22

1.   Jeremiah 39:1-41:18
      a.   What happened in the ninth year of king Zedekiah, in the tenth month?

      b.   How long did it take King Nebuchadnezzar to break through the walls of Jerusalem?

      c.   Who took seats at the middle gate? What did king Zedekiah do?

      d.   What sentence did king of Babylon pronounce on Zedekiah?

      e.   What orders did the king of Babylon give in regard to Jeremiah?

      f.   What word did Jeremiah receive while he was confined in the courtyard of the guard for Ebed Melech?

      g.   Where did the commander of the imperial guard find Jeremiah? What choices did he give Jeremiah?

      h.   Who did the king of Babylon appoint as governor of the land?

      i.   What did the Jews in the surrounding lands do when they heard that the king of Babylon had left a remnant in Judah?

      j.   Who sent Ismael? What mistake did Gedaliah make about Ishmael?

      k.   What did Ishmael do to Gedaliah? Who helped him?

      l.   What did Ismael do to the eighty men that went to the house of the Lord to worship?

      m.   What did Johanan do when he heard about all the crimes Ishmael had committed?

      n.   What happened to Ismael? How many men were with him?   Where did they go?

2.   II Timothy 1:1-18
      a.   Who wrote a letter to Timothy?

      b.   What was Paul's position? By who's will did he have this position?

      c.   What were Timothy's mother and grandmother's names?

      d.   What did Paul remind Timothy about in verses six and seven?

e.   Of what should they not be ashamed? What should they not be ashamed to do?

f.   What is the reason that they should not be ashamed?

g.   Why was Paul not ashamed?

h.   Who in the province of Asia deserted Paul?

i.   Why did Paul ask God to show mercy to the household of Onesiphorus?

3.   Psalms 90:1-91:16
      a.   How long is God, God?

      b.   What is a thousand years like in the sight of God?

      c.   What is the life span of men like?

      d.   Where did God set men's iniquities and secret sins?

      e.   What is the length of man's days?

      f.   What did the Psalmist request God to teach them to do? Why did he request that?

      g.   What does the Psalmist say about the one that dwells in the shelter of the Most High?

      h.   In the last verse of chapter ninety one, how was God going to satisfy the one that follows him?

4.   Proverbs 26:1-2
      a.   What does Solomon say about honor for a fool?

      b.   What does he say about an undeserved curse?

1. Jeremiah 42:1-44:23

   a. What did the people ask Jeremiah to do?

   b. What was Jeremiah's response? What did he promise to do?

   c. What did the people promise to do?

   d. When did the word of the Lord come to Jeremiah?

   e. What did God tell the people?

   f. Did they obey God's direction?

   g. Into what country did the remnant go?

   h. What did the Lord instruct Jeremiah to do with the large stones? What did this represent?

   i. What was Nebuchadnezzar king of Babylon going to do to the gods of Egypt?

   j. In chapter forty-four the word of the Lord came to Jeremiah concerning what group of people?

   k. What did the Lord almighty, the God of Israel say to his people?

   l. What did the Israelites do wrong, why was God angry?

   m. In chapter forty-four verse eleven what was God determined to do to Judah?

   n. What was going to happen to the remnant of Judah who had gone to live in Egypt?

   o. What did the men that knew that their wives were burning incense to other gods answer Jeremiah?

   p. What did Jeremiah tell all the people both men and women, who were answering him?

   q. Why did Jeremiah say that disaster had come on the people?

2. II Timothy 2:1-21

   a. Who was Paul calling his son and what was he telling him to do?

b. Does one serving as a soldier get involved in civilian affairs?

c. How does an athlete compete?

d. Who did Paul tell Timothy to remember?

e. What was the trustworthy saying that Paul passed on to Timothy?

f. Against what was Timothy to warn the people?

g. What was Timothy to avoid? Why should he avoid this?

h. If a man cleanses himself from the ignoble what kind of an instrument will he become?

3. Psalms 92:1-93:5
   a. What four things did the Psalmist say it was good to do?

   b. Who made the Psalmist glad and what made him glad?

   c. Whose works are great and thoughts profound?

   d. What will happen to the wicked that spring up like grass and the evil doers that flourish?

   e. Who will be exalted forever?

   f. What would surely happen to the enemies of the Lord and all evildoers?

   g. What will happen to the righteous?

   h. What does this Psalm say about God's statutes?

4. Proverbs 26:3-5
   a. A whip for a horse and a halter for a donkey, what was for the backs of fools?

   b. What happens if you answer a fool according to his folly?

STUDY QUESTIONS FOR OCTOBER 24

1.   Jeremiah 44:24-47:7
       a.   What did Jeremiah say to all the people including the women?

       b.   How were the jews living in Egypt going to perish?

       c.   Would there be a large number of Jews that would escape the sword and return to Judah?

       d.   What was God going to do with Pharaoh Hophra king of Egypt?

       e.   What was the message to Egypt?

       f.   How long will the sword devour?

       g.   Who will offer sacrifice in the land of the north by the river Euphrates?

       h.   What will happen to the warriors of Egypt?

       i.   What king did Jeremiah talk about next that was going to attack Egypt?

       j.   Who was going to push the warriors down?

       k.   When will Egypt hiss like a fleeing serpent?

       l.   How were Egypt's enemies going to come against her?

       m.   Why should Jacob not fear?

       n.   Was Jacob going to go without punishment?

       o.   What group of people does he prophesy about next?

       p.   What will overflow the land and everything in it?

       q.   The people that dwell in the land will wail at what sound?

       r.   Will fathers help their children?

       s.   What is the Lord about to destroy?

2.   II Timothy 2:22-3:17
       a.   What was Timothy supposed to do about the evil desires of youth?

b.   What four things was he to pursue instead?

c.   Why was he to avoid foolish and stupid arguments?

d.   What will people be like in the last days? (Nine verses)

e.   What did Timothy know about Paul's teaching and way of life? What did the Lord do for Paul?

f.   What is special about scripture and in what way is it useful?

3.   Psalms 94:1-23
      a.   What does the Psalmist ask God about the wicked?

      b.   What do the wicked do to God's people?

      c.   What do they do to the widows, aliens, and the fatherless?

      d.   What do they say about the Lord?

      e.   What four questions does the Psalmist ask the senseless ones among the people?

      f.   What does he say about the man that is disciplined of the Lord?

      g.   Who became the Psalmist's fortress and the rock in whom he took refuge?

      h.   Who will repay the wicked for their sins?

4.   Proverbs 26:6-8
      a.   What is it like to send a message by the hand of a fool?

      b.   What is a proverb like in the mouth of a fool?

      c.   To what is tying a stone in a sling likened?

STUDY QUESTIONS FOR OCTOBER 25

1. Jeremiah 48:1-49:22
   a. What does the prophecy of Jeremiah in chapter forty-eight concern?

   b. Why did Jeremiah say woe to Nebo? What did he say would happen to Kiriathaim?

   c. What did Jeremiah say about Moab being praised? What would Heshbon do?

   d. What would happen to them because they trusted in their deeds and riches.

   e. A curse was called on two kinds of action of men, what were they?

   f. Of whom will Moab be ashamed?

   g. The Lord said her horn was cut off, what about her arm?

   h. Why was it said that they should make her (Moab) drunk? What was said about her vomit and about ridicule?

   i. What did the Lord declare about her insolence and her boasting?

   j. What was gone from the orchards and fields of Moab?

   k. "In that day" what will the hearts of Moab's warriors be like?

   l. What was the Lord going to do for the fortunes of Moab in the days to come?

   m. In chapter forty-nine verse two, what would happen to Rabbah of the Ammonites? What would Israel do?

   n. In verse six, what was the Lord going to do for the fortunes of the Ammonites?

   o. What was the Lord going to do to Esau?

   p. What will the hearts of Edom's warriors be like?

2. II Timothy 4:1-22
   a. Who will judge the living and the dead?

   b. What four things did Paul charge Timothy to do? With what two things was he supposed to do this?

   c. When the time comes, with what will men not put up? What will they do instead?

233

d.   In verse five, what four things does Paul tell Timothy to do?

e.   What three things did Paul say he had done? Now what was in store for Paul?

f.   What did Paul want Timothy to do his best to do? Why did Demas desert Paul?

g.   Where did Crescens go? Where did Titus go?

h.   Who was the only one left with Paul?

i.   What did Alexnder the metalworker do to Paul? Who came to Paul's defense at his first hearing? Who stood beside him and gave him strength?

3.   Psalms 95:1-96:13
     a.   What four things are the hearers asked to do in verse one and two of chapter ninety-five?

     b.   What did the fathers of this people do at Massah in the desert? How long was God angry with that generation?

     c.   What five things of God's creation will praise him in verse eleven and twelve?

     d.   In the last verse of chapter ninety-six, how will God judge the world? How will he judge the peoples?

4.   Proverbs 26:9-12
     a.   What is like a thornbush in a drunkard's hand? Who is like an archer who wounds at random? To what is a fool that repeats his folly likened?

     b.   What is said about a man wise in his own eyes?

STUDY QUESTIONS FOR OCTOBER 26

1. Jeremiah 49:23-50:46
    a. What was God going to do to the walls of Damascus?   Whose fortress would the fire consume?

    b. What did God tell the people to do to Kedar and the people of the East?

    c. Against whom had Nebuchadnezzar plotted? (See verse thirty)

    d. What would Hazor become?

    e. What eight things is the Lord Almighty going to do to Elam?

    f. What did the Lord, through Jeremiah, say was going to happen to Babylon? What would happen to Bel? What would happen to Marduk?

    g. From where would the nation come that would attack Babylon and lay waste to her land?

    h. In chapter fifty, verse nine, what was God going to bring against Babylon?

    i. What will the people that pass Babylon feel and do?

    j. Who was the first to devour Israel? Who was the last to crush Israel's bones?

    k. In chapter fifty, verse nineteen and twenty, what promises does God make to Israel and Judah?

    l. What seven things does the Lord tell the punishing nations to do to Babylon (verses twenty-six through twenty-nine)?

    m. In chapter fifty verse thirty-four, what was God going to bring to the land of Israel and Judah? What was he going to bring to the land of Babylon?

    n. The Lord was going to bring a sword against seven things in Babylon, what were they?

    o. What will the earth do at the sound of Babylon's capture?

2. Titus 1:1-16
    a. Who is writing this letter and to whom is he writing it?

    b. From whom does he send grace and peace?

c.   Why was the recipient of this letter left in Crete?

d.   What ten things must an elder be? What five things must an elder not be?

e.   Why must the rebellious people, mere talkers and deceivers be silenced?

f.   Paul talks about some people that claim to know God, but what do their actions show?

3.   Psalms 97:1-98:9
   a.   What should the earth do because the Lord reigns? What about the distant shores?

   b.   What is the foundation of God's throne?

   c.   What do the heavens proclaim?

   d.   Who is the most high over all the earth?

   e.   Who should rejoice in the Lord?

   f.   What were the people to sing to the Lord? Why?

   g.   What was to shout for joy to the Lord?

   h.   How will the Lord judge the world? How will he judge the people?

4.   Proverbs 26:13-16
   a.   What does the sluggard say?

   b.   How does the sluggard turn on his bed?

   c.   Why does the sluggard bury his hand in the dish?

1. Jeremiah 51:1-53
    a. Who was the spirit of a destroyer going to come against?

    b. Who was the Lord going to send to winnow and devastate her?

    c. What were they going to do to her army?

    d. In verse five, why was God going to do this for his people?

    e. What were the ones that lived in Babylon encouraged to do?

    f. How high did the judgement of Babylon reach?

    g. Why did the Lord stir up the kings of the Medes?

    h. What does the Lord send with the rain? From where does he bring the wind?

    i. How are the images that the goldsmith made, described? How is the God of Jacob different?

    j. What nine groups of things was the Lord going to shatter with Jacob?

    k. For what was the Lord going to repay Babylon and all who live in Babylonia?

    l. What kingdoms were summoned against Babylon?

    m. In verse thirty what had the Babylonian soldiers done? Where did they remain? What happened to their strength?

    n. What did one courier after another and one messenger after another, announce to the king?

    o. Why would heaven and earth shout for joy over Babylon? In verse forty-nine, for what reason must Babylon fall?

    p. What was the Lord going to do to Babylon even if she reached the sky?

2. Titus 2:1-15
    a. What was Titus to teach?

    b. What was he to teach the older men?

    c. What was he to teach the older women? After the older women received this teaching what were they to do for the younger women?

    d.   What was Titus to encourage the young men to do?

    e.   What three things were to show from his teaching? What would be the result of this kind of teaching?

    f.   What was he to teach the slaves?

    g.   To what does the grace of God that brings salvation teach men to say, "no"?

    h.   For what were the people waiting?

    i.   What would the people that God purified for himself be eager to do?

    j.   How was Titus to encourage and rebuke? What was he not to let anyone do?

3.   Psalms 99:1-9

    a.   Who reigns? What do the nations do?

    b.   Where does he sit enthroned?

    c.   Who is exalted over all the nations? What should these nations do?

    d.   How is the king described? What does he love?

    e.   What did the Lord do when Moses, Aaron, Samuel and others called on his name? What did these men do?

    f.   In the last verse, what were the people to do?

4.   Proverbs 26:17

    a.   To what is a passer-by who meddles in a quarrel not his own likened?

1.   Jeremiah 51:54-52:34
     a.   From where did the sound of a cry come?

     b.   What was the Lord going to do to Babylon?

     c.   Who was going to come against Babylon?

     d.   What did the Lord say in chapter fifty-one, verse fifty-eight?

     e.   To whom did Jeremiah give his message when he went to Babylon with Zedekiah king of Judah?

     f.   What had Jeremiah written on a scroll concerning Babylon?

     g.   What did Jeremiah instruct Seraiah to do when he got to Babylon? What was he to do with the scroll when he finished reading it?

     h.   How old was Zedekiah when he became king of Judah? How long did Zedekiah reign in Jerusalem?

     i.   What happened in the ninth year, the tenth day of the tenth month of Zedekiah's reign?

     j.   What did the Babylonian army do to Zedekiah?

     k.   What did Nebuzaradan commander of the imperial guard do to Jerusalem?

     l.   Where was the bronze from Judah taken?

     m.   How many people did Nebuchadnezzar carry into exile?

     n.   What happened in the thirty-seventh year of exile of Jehoiachin king of Judah?

     o.   How did the new king of Babylon treat Jehoichin?

     p.   What was Jehoiachin able to do with his prison clothes? Where did he eat for the rest of his life?

2.   Titus 3:1-15
     a.   Of what was Titus to remind the people?

     b.   What did Paul say they were like before they were saved?

c. What happened when the kindness and love of God appeared?

d. Were they saved by the righteous things they had done?

e. What things did Paul want Titus to stress? Why did he want Titus to stress these things?

f. What was Titus to avoid? Why was he to avoid these things?

g. How many times was he to warn a divisive person? What was he to do after that?

h. What did Paul tell Titus to do in regard to Zenas and Apollos?

3. Psalms 100:1-5
   a. Who was to shout for joy?

   b. Who were they to worship? How were they to worship? How were they to come before the Lord?

   c. Who made us?

   d. Fill in the blanks, "We are his people, ____ _____ __ ___ _____."

   e. How are we to enter his gates?

   f. How are we to enter his courts?

   g. Why should we do this?

   h. How long does God's faithfulness continue?

4. Proverbs 26:18-19
   a. To what is a man likened that deceives his neighbor and says, "I was only joking."?

STUDY QUESTIONS FOR OCTOBER 29

1.   Lamentations 1:1-2:19
    a.   Who wrote the book of Lamentations?

    b.   To what city is the author referring in this chapter?

    c.   What is said about the gateways of Zion? What were her priests doing? What about her maidens?

    d.   Why did God bring grief to Zion (Jerusalem)?

    e.   What did Jerusalem remember in the days of her affliction and wandering?

    f.   What did Jerusalem's enemies do?

    g.   In chapter one verse sixteen, why did the author weep?

    h.   What happened when Jerusalem called on her allies? What happened to her priests and elders?

    i.   Why did Jerusalem want God to bring the day he had announced?

    j.   What did God do with the splendor of Israel?

    k.   What did the Lord do with the dwellings of Jacob?

    l.   What did the Lord make Zion do about her feasts and Sabbaths?

    m.   What happened to the gates and bars of Zion? What about her king, her princes, her prophets, her elders, and her young women?

    n.   What did the children and infants ask their mothers?

    o.   What comments were made about the prophets of Zion?

    p.   In chapter two verse sixteen, what did the enemies of Jerusalem do?

    q.   In chapter two verses eighteen and nineteen, what things were they told to do?

2.   Philemon 1:1-25
    a.   Who sent this letter?

    b.   What was Philemon to them?

c.   Beside Philemon, who else was addressed in this letter?

d.   Why did Paul thank God as he remembered them in prayer?

e.   What was Paul's prayer for them?

f.   Did Paul order Phlemon to accept Onesimus?

g.   Who was Onesimus? What did he have to do with Philemon?

h.   In verses seventeen and eighteen, what did Paul ask Philemon to do for Onesimus?

i.   How much did Philemon owe Paul?

j.   In verse twenty two, what last request did Paul make of Philemon?

3.   Psalms 101:1-8
    a.   What was the Psalmist going to sing about? To whom was he going to sing?

    b.   What was the Psalmist going to be careful to do?

    c.   What was he going to set before his eyes?

    d.   Where would the men of perverse hearts be?

    e.   How did he feel about evil?

    f.   What was he going to do with the one that slanders his neighbor?

    g.   Who would the Psalmist allow to dwell with him?

    h.   Who would he not allow to dwell in his house?

4.   Proverbs 26:20
    a.   How would you interpret this scripture?

1. Lamentations 2:20-3:66
    a. In chapter two verses twenty and twenty-one what does Jeremiah lament?

    b. Who escaped from the Lord's anger? What happened to those that Jeremiah cared for and the ones that he reared?

    c. To whom was Jeremiah referring when he said "I am the man who has seen affliction by the rod of his wrath"?

    d. What happened even when Jeremiah cried out for help?

    e. What did God do with Jeremiah's paths?

    f. What did Jeremiah become to all his people? What did they do to him in song all day long?

    g. Why did he say "We are not consumed"? When does God's compassion fail?

    h. To whom is the Lord good?

    i. What two things does Jeremiah say that it is good to do?

    j. What will God show even though he brings grief? What is the cause of this?

    k. From whose mouth does calamities and good things come?

    l. What should happen when we examine our ways and test them?

    m. What had God's people become among the nations?

    n. How will Jeremiah's eyes flow?

    o. What did his enemies do?

    p. What did he do when his enemies gave him a bad time?

    q. What four things did Jeremiah request that the Lord do to his enemies?

2. Hebrews 1:1-14
    a. Who spoke to the forefathers? How did he speak? Through whom did he speak? What about the last days?

    b. Who were the angels to worship?

c. What does God make the angels? What does he make his servants?

d. How long will the throne of God the son last?

e. In regard to the son, what is said about righteousness and wickedness?

f. What did God use to anoint Jesus?

g. What will happen to Jesus when his creation wears out like a garment?

h. Where was Christ to sit?

3. Psalms 102:1-28
a. What was the Psalmist's first three request in this Psalm?

b. What happened to the Psalmist's days?

c. What do the enemies of the Psalmist do all day long?

d. How long is the Lord enthroned?

e. What will the nations do? Who would revere God's glory?

f. Who would rebuild Zion?

g. What will God do to the prayer of the destitute?

h. In the beginning, who laid the foundation of the earth?

i. How long will God remain?

4. Proverbs 26:21-22
a. How is a quarrelsome man described?

b. Where do choice morsels of gossip go?

STUDY QUESTIONS FOR OCTOBER 31

1. Lamentations 4:1-5:22
    a. What happened to the gold?

    b. How did the value of the sons of Zion change?

    c. What happened to the infant's tongue? What did the children have to do for bread?

    d. How did the experience of the rich change?

    e. Why were the ones killed by the sword better off?

    f. What does the story tell about compassionate women?

    g. For the sins of what two groups of people did this punishment take place?

    h. How fast were their pursuers? Where were they chased?

    i. What was the Lord asked to remember? What did they want God to see?

    j. What happened to their inheritance?

    k. "We have become _____ and _____, our mothers like _____." Lamentations chapter five verse three

    l. What did they have to do to get water to drink and wood to burn?

    m. Why did they submit to Egypt and Assyria?

    n. What happened to their princes and their elders?

    o. What happened to their joy and their dancing?

    p. How long does the Lord reign? How long does his throne endure? (Chapter five verse nineteen)

    q. What was asked of the Lord in regard to the relationship between God and man?

    r. What was he asked to renew?

2. Hebrews 2:1-18
    a. Why do we need to pay more careful attention to what we have heard?

b.   Can anyone escape if they neglect God's salvation?

c.   Who did God crown with glory and honor?

d.   Who was made a little lower than the angels?

e.   How did God perfect men's salvation?

f.   Who did Christ's death destroy?

g.   What did Christ's death do for those who were held in slavery by their fear of death?

h.   Was it angels that Jesus helped?

i.   Why was Jesus made like his brothers in every way?

j.   Why was Jesus tempted?

3.   Psalms 103:1-22
        a.   What did the Psalmist say that all his inmost being should do?

        b.   What did he want his soul not to forget?

        c.   What six things does the Psalmist mention that God does?

        d.   To whom did God make his ways known?

        e.   Will God keep his anger forever?

        f.   How great is God's love for those that fear him?

        g.   How long does God's love last for those that fear him?

        h.   Where has the Lord established his throne?

        i.   What part of the Psalmist was to praise the Lord?

4.   Proverbs 26:23
        a.   What are fervent lips with an evil heart like?

STUDY QUESTIONS FOR NOVEMBER 1

1. Ezekiel 1:1-3:15
    a. In verse one, what did Ezekiel see while he was among the exiles by the river Kebar?

    b. In chapter one verse four, how did he describe the windstorm? What was in the center of the storm? What was in the fire?

    c. How does Ezekiel describe the faces of the creatures?

    d. In chapter one verse fifteen, what did Ezekiel see beside each creature? How does he describe these?

    e. What was spread out above the heads of the living creatures? What did he say about the wings?

    f. How does he describe the figure like that of a man? What did he do when he saw it?

    g. In chapter two verse one, what did the Lord tell him to do?

    h. Where was the Lord sending Ezekiel? What did the Lord say about these people?

    i. What was written on the scroll that he saw?

    j. In chapter three what did the Lord tell Ezekiel to do with the scroll? How did it taste in his mouth?

    k. What did the Lord tell him to do after he ate the scroll?

    l. Why was the house of Israel not willing to listen to Ezekiel?

    m. What was the Lord going to make of Ezekiel?

    n. Where was Ezekiel to go? What was he to say to them?

    o. Who lifted Ezekiel up and took him away? How does Ezekiel describe his going?

    p. What did Ezekiel do for seven days?

2. Hebrews 3:1-19
    a. On whom were the holy brothers to fix their thoughts?

    b. What two people are mentioned here that were faithful to God? What is said about each one's faithfulness?

    c.   Why was God angry with the generation that was in the desert?

    d.   What were the brothers to do daily, as long as it is called today? Why were many Israelites unable to enter the promised land?

3.   Psalms 104:1-23
    a.   What is the Psalmist telling to praise the Lord?

    b.   What is said about God in verse one?

    c.   What four things does God do in regard to stretching out the heavens like a tent?

    d.   What did God do with the earth? How stable is the earth?

    e.   How did God cover the earth?

    f.   What happened to the waters at the rebuke of God? What about at the sound of God's thunder?

    g.   Where did the water go after it flowed over the mountains?

    h.   Who sets the boundary for the waters? What will they never do again? From where does God water the mountains?

    i.   Why do the lions roar? Where do they go when the sun rises?

4.   Proverbs 26:24-26
    a.   How does a malicious man disguise himself? What does he harbor in his heart?

    b.   How may his malice be concealed? What will happen to his wickedness?

STUDY QUESTIONS FOR NOVEMBER 2

1.   Ezekiel 3:16-6:14
     a.   What did the word of the Lord that came to Ezekiel say that the Lord had made Ezekiel?

     b.   What would the Lord do to Ezekiel if he did not warn the wicked man? What would happen if Ezekiel warned him but the wicked man did not turn from his wicked ways?

     c.   What if Ezekiel fails to warn a righteous man that turns from righteousness and does evil?

     d.   Where did the Spirit tell Ezekiel to go after the Spirit came into Ezekiel?

     e.   What was Ezekiel to do with the clay tablet?

     f.   What was he to do with the sin of the house Israel when he lay on his left side? How many days was he to lay on his left side? What did this number of days represent?

     g.   How many days was he to lay on his right side. What did this number of days represent?

     h.   How much food was the prophet to weigh out to eat each day? How much water was he to drink?

     i.   In chapter five, what was Ezekiel to do with the a sharp sword?

     j.   What does the Sovereign Lord say about Jerusalem in chapter five verse five and six?

     k.   This prophecy divides the people into thirds, what will happen to each third?

     l.   What will the people know when the Lord has spent his wrath on Jerusalem?

     m.   What was going to happen to the mountains of Israel?

     n.   When the Lord stretched out his hand against Israel, what was he going to do to the land?

2.   Hebrews 4:1-16
     a.   What are the Hebrew believers encouraged to do about God's rest?

     b.   Why was the gospel message of no value to some people?

c. What did the ones that believed enter?

d. What did God do on the seventh day?

e. What should they make every effort to do? Why should they do that?

f. What five things describe the word of God?

g. What in God's creation is hidden from God? To whom must they give an account?

h. Who was their high priest? What should they do with their faith?

i. How should they approach the throne of grace?

3. Psalms 104:24-35
a. What is the earth full of?

b. How many creatures live in the sea both large and small?

c. What do the ships do?

d. To whom do these creatures look to for their food?

e. What happens when God sends his Spirit?

f. How long does the Psalmist request that the glory of God endure?

g. What happens when God touches the mountains?

h. How does this Psalm end?

4. Proverbs 26:27
a. What will happen if a man digs a pit?

b. What will happen if a man rolls a stone?

STUDY QUESTIONS FOR NOVEMBER 3

1. Ezekiel 7:1-9:11
   a. In chapter seven, verses one through four, what did the word of the Lord say to Ezekiel?

   b. What kind of disaster was coming? In verse eight what did the Lord say he was about to do?

   c. What would they know when these things came about?

   d. Why would no one go into battle even though they blew the trumpet and got everything ready?

   e. How would those in the country die? How would those in the city die?

   f. What would happen to all who survive and escape?

   g. What would they do with their silver? What would happen to their gold? Would their silver and gold be able to save them in the day of the Lord's wrath?

   h. What did they do with their beautiful jewelry? What was God going to do with their jewelry?

   i. When the Spirit lifted Ezekiel up between heaven and earth, where did he take Ezekiel? What did he see when he looked to the north?

   j. What did the Spirit tell Ezekiel to do when he saw a hole in the wall? What did he find?

   k. What did Ezekiel see when the Spirit brought him to the entrance to the north gate of the house of the lord?

   l. What did he see in the inner court of the house of the Lord?

   m. What did God tell the man clothed in linen to do?

   n. What did God tell the others to do? Where were they to start? What did Ezekiel do when he was left alone?

   o. What word did the man clothed in linen bring back?

2. Hebrews 5:1-14
   a. From where were the high priests selected? What were they appointed to do?

b. Why was the high priest able to deal gently with those who are ignorant and going astray?

c. By whom are the high priests called?

d. What two things are listed here that God said about Christ?

e. Why were Jesus' prayers and petitions with cries and tears heard?

f. Why were these things hard to explain to the Hebrews?

g. Who lives on the milk of God's word? Who lives on the solid food of God's word?

3. Psalms 105:1-15
   a. In the first two verse of this Psalm, what five things does the Psalmist tell the people to do?

   b. What three things should the hearts of those that seek the Lord do?

   c. In verse six, to whom is the Psalmist addressing the following remarks?

   d. Where are the judgements of their God?

   e. How long does their God remember his covenant? How about the word he commanded?

   f. What promise did God make to Israel in verse eleven?

   g. As they wandered from nation to nation, what did God do?

   h. What instruction did God give to those around Israel?

4. Proverbs 26:28
   a. Who does a lying tongue hate?

   b. What does a flattering tongue do?

STUDY QUESTIONS FOR NOVEMBER 4

1.   Ezekiel 10:1-11:25
        a.   What did Ezekiel see above the expanse that was over the heads of the cherubim?

        b.   What did the Lord say to the man clothed in linen?

        c.   Where were the cherubim standing when the man went into the temple?

        d.   What filled the temple and what was the court full of?

        e.   What did the sound of the wings of the cherubim sound like?

        f.   What could be seen under the wings of the cherubim?

        g.   What four faces did each cherubim have? Compare this with Ezekiel chapter one, verse ten.

        h.   What were the twenty-five men at the entrance to the gate of the house of the Lord doing?

        i.   In chapter eleven verse twelve, what would cause the people to know that God is Lord?

        j.   What was God going to do for his people in verse seventeen?

        k.   What would the people do when they returned to their land?

        l.   What would God do with their hearts of stone?

        m.   What was God going to do to the ones whose hearts were devoted to their vile images and detestable idols?

        n.   When the cherubim spread their wings, what was above them?

        o.   What did Ezekiel tell the exiles?

2.   Hebrews 6:1-20
        a.   What does the writer of Hebrews say that the people should do about the elementary teachings about Christ?

        b.   What happens to the land that drinks in the rain and produces a crop useful to those for whom it is farmed?

        c.   What happens to the land that produces thorns and thistles?

d. What was the writer confident of even though he spoke like this?

e. The writer says, "We do not want you to become lazy, but," what?

f. By whom did God swear?

g. Who entered the inner sanctuary behind the curtain on our behalf?

3. Psalms 105:16-36
a. Who called down famine on the land?

b. Who did God send before his people?

c. What did the king do for this man?

d. When Israel entered Egypt, how did Jacob live?

e. Who made God's people fruitful?

f. How did this make problems for God's people?

g. Who did God chose to perform miracles in Egypt?

h. How many plagues are mentioned in this Psalm?

i. What was the final plague?

4. Proverbs 27:1-2
a. Why should one not boast about tomorrow?

b. Should one praise himself?

STUDY QUESTIONS FOR NOVEMBER 5

1.   Ezekiel 12:1 - 14:11
     a.   What kind of people was Ezekiel living among? What does God say about these people?

     b.   What did God instruct Ezekiel to do in the sight of all the people?

     c.   Did Ezekiel do what God asked him to do?

     d.   What was Ezekiel to answer the rebellious house of Israel when they asked "what are you doing?"?

     e.   When would the people know that God was Lord?

     f.   How would the people of the land eat their food and drink their water? Why was their land going to be stripped of every thing in it?

     g.   What was the proverb that the people of the land had been quoting? How was God going to change that proverb?

     h.   What was Ezekiel to say to the prophets that prophesied out of their own imaginations?

     i.   What was going to happen to the people when the whitewashed wall falls?

     j.   Who were the ones that whitewashed the wall (chapter thirteen verse sixteen)?

     k.   What was Ezekiel to prophesy against the daughters of your people that prophesy out of their own imaginations?

     l.   What did God reveal to Ezekiel about the elders that came and sat down in front of him?

     m.   What was Ezekiel to say to these elders?

     n.   What was he to say to the house of Israel?

     o.   What would the people know when God cut the men off from the people? In chapter fourteen verse eleven what would be the result of all this?
2.   Hebrews 7:1-17
     a.   What does verse one say about Melchizedek?

     b.   Where had Abraham been?

c.   What did Abraham give Melchizedek?

d.   What does the name Melchizedek mean?

e.   Who was Melchizedek's father and mother? When did his life begin and when did he die?

f.   Why does the author say that Melchizedek was great?

g.   Was Melchizedek a descendant of Levi?

h.   How does the author show that it could be said that Levi paid a tenth through Abraham?

i.   Could perfection be attained through the Levitical priesthood?

j.   Who is being referred to in verse seventeen, "You are a priest forever in the order of Melchizedek"?

3.   Psalms 105:37-45
   a.   Who brought out Israel, laden with silver and gold, and from their tribes no one faltered?

   b.   Why was Egypt glad when the Israelites left?

   c.   How did God provide a covering for daytime and a light for night?

   d.   How did God feed the Israelites?

   e.   How did God supply water?

   f.   How did God bring his people out?

   g.   Why did God give them the lands of the nations and make them heirs to what others had toiled?

4.   Proverbs 27:3
   a.   To what does the author liken provocation by a fool?

1.   Ezekiel 14:12-16:42
    a.   What was God going to do to the nation that was unfaithful to him? If Noah, Daniel, and Job were still around, could they save the nation?

    b.   What four dreadful judgements would the Sovereign Lord send on Jerusalem?

    c.   What would be the conclusion of the observers when they see the conduct and actions of Jerusalem?

    d.   What comparison does God make with the vine and Jerusalem? What would the fire do to them?

    e.   Did anyone care for Jerusalem when she was born?

    f.   Who took pity on Jerusalem?

    g.   Who made Jerusalem grow like a plant of the field?

    h.   With whom did Jerusalem enter into a contract?

    i.   What did God do to clean up Jerusalem?

    j.   What made Jerusalem's beauty perfect?

    k.   What did Jerusalem trust in? What did she become?

    l.   What did she do with the jewelry that God gave her? What about the oil and incense?

    m.   What did she do with her sons and daughters?

    n.   What had Jerusalem forgotten?

    o.   To what kind of a person did God liken the actions of Jerusalem?

    p.   What four nations were mentioned that used Jerusalem for a prostitute?

    q.   When would God's wrath subside and his jealous anger turn away from Jerusalem?

2.   Hebrews 7:18-28
    a.   Why was the former regulation set aside?

b.   What is introduced?

c.   Others became priest without any oath, but whom became a priest with an oath?

d.   What did this person become because of the oath?

e.   Before this, there were many priests, why was this priest different?

f.   How does this high priest meet our needs?

g.   How many times did this high priest have to offer a sacrifice?

h.   What sacrifice did he make?

3.   Psalms 106:1-12
     a.   To whom were they to give praise? Why were they to give praise?

     b.   Who are blessed?

     c.   What two things did the Psalmist ask the Lord to do?

     d.   What three reasons did he give for asking these favors?

     e.   What did the Psalmist confess that their fathers and they had done?

     f.   Why did he say that God saved them even though they had sinned?

     g.   What happened to their adversaries?

     h.   Then what did God's people do?

4.   Proverbs 27:4-6
     a.   What is said about anger, fury, and jealousy?

     b.   What is better than open rebuke?

     c.   What is said about wounds from a friend?

STUDY QUESTIONS FOR NOVEMBER 7

1.   Ezekiel 16:43-17:24
    a.   Look back to beginning of chapter sixteen and find out who the prophet Ezekiel is talking about.

    b.   Why did God say he was surely going to bring down on her head what she had done?

    c.   What proverb were people going to quote about her?

    d.   What did God do with Sodom?

    e.   How did Samaria's sin compare to hers?

    f.   How did she make her sisters seem?

    g.   God said he would restore the fortunes of Sodom and Samaria what was he going to do with Jerusalem and her daughters?

    h.   What was God going to remember?

    i.   How long was his covenant going to last with Jerusalem?

    j.   What allegory did Ezekiel receive from the Lord?

    k.   What was Ezekiel to say to the rebellious house of Jerusalem?

    l.   Will the king of Jerusalem succeed by calling on Egypt?

    m.   Why was God going to execute judgement on the king of Jerusalem?

    n.   What was going to happen to all his fleeing troops and the survivors?

    o.   What would the people know when this prophecy is fulfilled?

    p.   What was the Sovereign Lord going to do with the shoot from the top of the cedar tree?

    q.   How did this shoot compare with the preceding allegory?

2.   Hebrews 8:1-13
    a.   Who is the high priest that is referred to in verse one?

    b.   Who set up the true tabernacle?

c.	Why was Moses warned "See to it that you make everything according to the pattern shown you on the mountain"?

d.	What was the Lord going to do about a covenant in the coming time?

e.	Why did God turn away from his people?

f.	In the new covenant what was God going to do with his laws?

g.	What was the Lord going to be to the people and what were the people going to be to him?

h.	What was going to happen to the old covenant?

3.	Psalms 106:13-31
a.	How long did it take the people to forget what God had done for them?

b.	Verse fifteen says that God gave them what they asked for, what else did he send them?

c.	Where did they make a calf and worship the idol?

d.	Who did the people forget?

e.	What kept the wrath of God from destroying them?

f.	How did the people provoke God to anger?

g.	Who stood up and intervened and stopped the plague?

4.	Proverbs 27:7-9
a.	How does a man's appetites change when he is hungry compared to when he is full?

b.	What springs from the earnest council of a friend?

STUDY QUESTIONS FOR NOVEMBER 8

1.   Ezekiel 18:1-19:14
       a.   What proverb were the people quoting?

       b.   In chapter eighteen verse three, what did the Sovereign Lord declare? What will happen to the soul that sins?

       c.   What happens to the man who is righteous and does what is right?

       d.   What happens to the son of an unrighteous man and this son does all kinds of unrighteous things?

       e.   What about the son of the son of a righteous man and this son is righteous before God?

       f.   Will the son share in the guilt of the father? Will the father share in the guilt of a son?

       g.   What happens to a wicked man that turns away from all the sins he has committed and keeps God's decrees and does what is just and right? What about the righteous man that turns to evil?

       h.   What was the house of Israel saying about the way of the Lord? What did God ask them in response to their saying?

       i.   In chapter eighteen verses thirty through thirty-two, what does Ezekiel plead with the house of Israel to do?

       j.   What does the lament in chapter nineteen concern?

       k.   In this lament, to what was their mother likened? What did she do?

       l.   What did she do for one of her cubs? What did this lion become? What happened to the lion?

       m.   What did she do when she saw her hope unfulfilled? What happened to this lion?

       n.   To what is the mother likened in verses ten through fourteen?

2.   Hebrews 9:1-10
       a.   What two things are mentioned that the first covenant had?

       b.   What three things were in the first room of the sanctuary? What was this room called?

c. What was the room behind the second curtain called? What two things were in this room?

d. What three things did the ark contain?

e. What was above the ark?

f. Who entered the outer room regularly? Why did they enter?

g. Who was the only one that entered the inner room? How many times a year did he enter this room?

h. What was the Holy Spirit showing by this?

i. Of what was this an illustration?

3. Psalms 106:32-48
   a. In verse thirty-two, where did the Israelites anger the Lord?

   b. What did the Israelites do about destroying the people in the land?

   c. What did the Israelites do with their sons and daughters?

   d. How did the Israelites defile themselves? What did the Lord do to the Israelites?

   e. What did the Lord do when he heard the cry of the Israelites?

   f. What were the people to do in verse forty-eight?

4. Proverbs 27:10
   a. Whom does Solomon tell his son not to forget?

   b. What is better than a brother far away?

STUDY QUESTIONS FOR NOVEMBER 9

1. Ezekiel 20:1-49

    a. Who came to inquire of the Lord and sat down in front of Ezekiel?

    b. What did the Lord say about their inquiry?

    c. What did the Lord swear to the descendants of the house of Jacob?

    d. What did the Lord tell each of them to do?

    e. Did they do what the Lord told them to do?

    f. Why did the Lord give them his Sabbaths?

    g. What did the lord swear to them in the desert?   Why was he going to do that?

    h. To what was the Lord gong to give them over?

    i. How did the people become defiled? Why did the Lord let them become defiled?

    j. What did their fathers do when they entered the promised land and they saw a high hill or any leafy tree? How did the Lord react to these actions?

    k. Why would the Lord not allow the people to inquire of him?

    l. How would the Lord rule over the people?

    m. Who was the Lord going to purge from his people? Will these be gathered from where they are living? Will they enter the land of Israel?

    n. Where was the Lord going to show himself holy?

    o. How many times in this section of Ezekiel, does it say, "(you or they) will know that I am the lord." or similar wording?

    p. What were the people saying of Ezekiel?

2. Hebrews 9:11-28

    a. When Christ came as high priest, what kind of a tabernacle did he come through?

    b. Did Christ enter by the blood of goats and calves? If not, how?

    c. What does man need to cleanse their consciences from acts that lead to death?

263

d.   Who is the mediator of the new covenant?

e.   When is a will in force?

f.   What did Moses have to do to put the first covenant into effect?

g.   What does verse twenty-two say about the blood?

h.   Where did Christ enter? What was he doing there?

i.   How many times was Christ sacrificed?

3.   Psalms 107:1-43
        a.   Why should one give thanks to the Lord?

        b.   What happened to the people when they cried out to the Lord?

        c.   What does the Lord do for the thirsty and the hungry?

        d.   What did the Lord do for the people after they were disciplined with bitter labor and then they cried out to the Lord?

        e.   Four times in this chapter the Psalmist says, "Let them give thanks to the Lord", why were they to give thanks?

        f.   According to verse forty-three, what two things should the wise do?

4.   Proverbs 27:11
        a.   What did Solomon ask his son to do?

        b.   What would happen if he obeyed?

STUDY QUESTIONS FOR NOVEMBER 10

1.   Ezekiel 21:1-22:31
      a.   What four things did the word of the Lord tell Ezekiel to do in the first three verses of chapter twenty-one?

      b.   What would the people know when this prophecy was fulfilled?

      c.   What was the prophet to answer when the people asked why he was groaning?

      d.   Why was the prophet asked to cry out and wail?

      e.   In chapter twenty-one verse fourteen, how many times would the sword strike? What kind of a sword was it called?

      f.   Where had God stationed the sword?

      g.   In verse eighteen and following, what two roads was the prophet to mark out?

      h.   What was the king of Babylon going to do at the junction of the two roads?

      i.   What was going to happen to the people of Israel because of the open rebellion of the people?

      j.   What was going to happen to the lowly? What was going to happen to the exalted?

      k.   What is prophesied about the blood of the Ammonites in the last part of chapter twenty-one?

      l.   How did the "city of blood" (Jerusalem) bring on herself doom and how did she defile herself?

      m.   What eighteen things listed here, did the princes of Israel do that displeased the Lord?

      n.   To what was the house of Israel likened?

      o.   In the last two verses of chapter twenty-two, for what was the Lord looking? Did he find it?

2.   Hebrews 10:1-17
      a.   In verse one, what word picture does the writer of Hebrews use to describe the law?

265

b. Can the law make the ones that draw near to worship, perfect?

c. Of what did the annual sacrifices become a reminder? Why was this a reminder?

d. Why did Christ come into the world?

e. How were the Hebrews made holy?

f. What happened when this priest made the sacrifice?

g. Where was the Lord going to put the law in the new covenant?

3. Psalms 108:1-13
   a. In this Psalm of victory, what does the Psalmist assert about his heart?

   b. How was he going to make music? When would he start making music?

   c. Where would he praise the Lord? Where would he sing?

   d. How great is God's love? How big is God's faithfulness?

   e. How should God be exalted?

   f. What request is made of the Lord in verse six?

   g. From where did God speak?

   h. Who was God's helmet? Who was God's scepter?

   i. How good is the help of man? How would the Psalmist gain the victory?

4. Proverbs 27:12
   a. What do the prudent do when they see danger?

   b. What do the simple do and what happens to them?

1.   Ezekiel 23:1-49

    a.   How were the two women in this story from God, related?

    b.   What did they become in Egypt?

    c.   What was the name of each of these women? Who was older? What city did each woman represent?

    d.   Who did Oholah lust after?

    e.   What is said about the idols of everyone she lusted after?

    f.   What did God do with Oholah?

    g.   What did the Assyrians do with Oholah?

    h.   Did Oholibah learn anything from what happened to her sister?

    i.   In addition to the Assyrians, who did Oholibah lust after?

    j.   What did God do when Oholibah carried on her prostitution openly and exposed her nakedness ?

    k.   What did the sovereign Lord say that he would do through Oholibah's lovers?

    l.   What brought all this punishment on Oholibah?

    m.   What did the Lord tell Ezekiel to do to Oholah and Oholibah?

    n.   What did they do on the very same day?

    o.   How did they use the incense and oil that belonged to God?

    p.   What did God say about the one worn out by prostitution?

    q.   What was the mob going to do with Oholah and Oholibah?

    r.   Remember that this whole chapter is a picture of how Samaria and Jerusalem were acting toward God. What would they know when all this takes place?

2.   Hebrews 10:18-39

    a.   To what is verse eighteen referring when it says, "And where these have been forgiven, there is no longer any sacrifice for sin"? (See chapter ten verse ten.)

b.	By what means could the brothers enter the Most Holy Place?

c.	Since they had a great priest over the house of God what should they do?

d.	In verse twenty-four, what should they consider?

e.	What should they do about meeting together?

f.	What is a dreadful thing?

g.	Why could the brothers joyfully accept the confiscation of their property?

h.	What would happen if they did not throw away their confidence?

i.	Were they ones that shrank back and were destroyed?

3.	Psalms 109:1-31
	a.	In verses one through five, who is the Psalmist describing?

	b.	Who is the Psalmist praying for (or should it be "against") in verses six through twenty?

	c.	What did the Psalmist mean when he said, "May his children be fatherless and his wife a widow?"

	d.	Who is the Psalmist praying for in the next eight verses?

	e.	Why did the Psalmist's knees give way?

	f.	 How is the Psalmist going to extol the Lord?

	g.	Where does the Lord stand?

4.	Proverbs 27:13
	a.	What should one do if a garment is put up for security for a stranger?

1. Ezekiel 24:1-26:21

   a. In chapter twenty-four, when did the word of the Lord come to Ezekiel?

   b. To what people was Ezekiel to give this message from God?

   c. What did the Sovereign Lord tell them to do with the cooking pot?

   d. Why did the Lord put the blood of **Babylon** on a bare rock?

   e. After they cooked the meat and bones, what were they to do with the empty pot?

   f. In chapter twenty-four, verse fourteen, how were the **Babylonians** going to be judged?

   g. When the Lord took Ezekiel's delight of his eyes (his wife), what instructions did God give about weeping? How did this apply to what Israel would loose?

   h. Why was God going to punish the Ammonites?

   i. In these three chapters, how many times is it said, "Then they will know that I am the Lord?

   j. Who did Ezekiel prophesy against in the eleventh year on the first day of the month? What did they say about Jerusalem?

   k. Who was God going to bring against this city?

   l. What would be done with the stone, the timber, and the rubble?

   m. What would happen to their noisy songs and the music of their harps?

   n. What lament is given about this city?

   o. How is the end of this city described?

2. Hebrews 11:1-16

   a. What is faith?

   b. How can we understand how the universe was formed?

   c. How did Able offer a better sacrifice than Cain? How was he commended as a righteous man? How does he still speak, even though he is dead?

d.   What happened to Enoch and what enabled him to experience this?

e.   What one thing missing in their life would make it impossible to please God?

f.   What did Noah do by faith? What did his faith do to the world?

g.   What enabled Abraham to receive God's promise to have descendants as numerous as the stars in the sky and as countless as the sand of the seashore?

h.   Did these people receive their promises before they died?

i.   Because of this faith, what is said about God in the last verse?

3.   Psalms 110:1-7
      a.   To whom is this Psalm referring?

      b.   What is meant by "The Lord will extend your mighty scepter from Zion"? What about "You will rule in the midst of your enemies"?

      c.   Will God change his mind?

      d.   He was going to be a priest in the order of what person?

      e.   What would happen to the kings of that day?

      f.   Who is going to judge the nations?

4.   Proverbs 27:14
      a.   What will happen if a man blesses his neighbor loudly early in the morning?

STUDY QUESTIONS FOR NOVEMBER 13

1. Ezekiel 27:1-28:26
   a. Who is "me" referring to when the word says, "The word of the Lord came to me."?

   b. What city was Ezekiel to lament?

   c. What was this city's assessment of itself?

   d. Where was their domain?

   e. With what were their decks inlaid?

   f. Who came alongside to trade with them?

   g. From where did men come to serve in their army?

   h. Who served to protect their walls?

   i. Why did Tarshish do business with them?

   j. What did Aram exchange with Tyre for their many products?

   k. What did Judah and Israel trade with Tyre?

   l. What did the east wind do to Tyre's oarsmen and cargo?

   m. What was going to happen on the shorelands when the seamen cry out?

   n. At the end of chapter twenty seven, what will happen to Tyre in the end?

   o. What did Tyre say in the pride of her heart? Was what she said true?

   p. In chapter twenty-eight verse twelve, what lament did the Sovereign Lord tell Ezekiel to take up next?

   q. How did the king start out? How did the king end up?

   r. What will be Israel's reaction when God's people dwell in safety and God punishes their neighbors?

2. Hebrews 11:17-31
   a. What is the main theme of Hebrews chapter eleven?

b.   What did Abraham do by faith?

c.   How did Abraham think that God would fulfill his promise, "That through Isaac all of Abraham's offspring will be reckoned," if he sacrificed his son Isaac?

d.   What did Isaac do by faith?

e.   What did Jacob do by faith?

f.   What did Joseph speak about when his end was near? What instructions did he give?

g.   What did Moses refuse when he had grown up?

h.   How did the people pass through the Red Sea?

i.   What happened to the walls of Jericho because of faith?

j.   What happened to Rahab because of her faith?

3.   Psalms 111:1-10
      a.   Who is to be praised?

      b.   Who was the Psalmist going to extol with his heart?

      c.   Who ponders the works of the Lord?

      d.   How long does God's righteousness endure?

      e.   For whom does God provide food?

      f.   How long does God remember his covenant?

      g.   Who gave God's people the lands of other nations?

      h.   Who provided redemption for God's people?

4.   Proverbs 27:15-16
      a.   To what is a quarrelsome wife likened?

      b.   What is it like to restrain her?

STUDY QUESTIONS FOR NOVEMBER 14

1.   Ezekiel 29:1-30:26

    a.   When did God give this prophecy to Ezekiel? Who was the prophecy against?

    b.   When will all who live in Egypt know that God is the Lord?

    c.   How does the statement in Ezekiel chapter twenty-nine, verses, six and seven compare to what the Assyrian king's representative said to Israel in II Kings chapter eighteen verses nineteen and twenty

    d.   What did the Lord promise to do to Egypt?

    e.   What did Egypt say about the Nile River?

    f.   How long would the punishment of Egypt last?

    g.   How many years elapsed before the next prophecy that Ezekiel received?

    h.   What was the Lord going to give to Nebuchadnezzar king of Babylon?

    i.   Why was God going to reward Nebuchadnezzar?

    j.   Who else was going to fall with Egypt?

    k.   How does he describe Nebuchadnezzar and his army?

    l.   What was God going to do with the streams of the Nile? (Remember they were trusting in the Nile and said that they had made the Nile)

    m.   What would Egypt know when God inflicted punishment?

    n.   To what year did the next prophecy jump back?

    o.   What was God going to do to Pharaoh's arms?

    p.   Where was God going to disperse the Egyptians?

    q.   What was God going to do for the arms of the king of Babylon?

2.   Hebrews 11:32-12:13

    a.   What is the writer of Hebrews talking about in the eleventh chapter of Hebrews?

    b.   What did Gideon, Barak, Sampson, Jepthah, David, Samuel, and the prophets have in common with heroes that had already been mentioned?

c.   What ten things mentioned here were accomplished by faith?

d.   Why did some refuse to be released?

e.   What persecutions are mentioned here?

f.   In chapter twelve verse one what is the "therefore" referring?

g.   What needs to be thrown off?

h.   Where were they to fix their eyes?

i.   How were they to endure hardship?

j.   Does discipline seem pleasant at the time?

3.   Psalms 112:1-10
        a.   What man is blessed?

        b.   What will the blessed man's children be like?

        c.   What will be in his house?

        d.   What happens even in darkness to the upright?

        e.   What happens the one who is generous and lends freely?

        f.   How long will a righteous man be remembered?

        g.   What does the man that fears the Lord do with his gifts?

        h.   What happens to the wicked man?

4.   Proverbs 27:17
        a.   What does iron sharpen? What sharpens another man?

STUDY QUESTIONS FOR NOVEMBER 15

1.   Ezekiel 31:1-32:32
        a.   What title did the Lord use for Ezekiel?

        b.   What nation was Pharaoh, king of Egypt, asked to consider?

        c.   To what was Assyria likened? How did it compare to the other nations?

        d.   What did the birds of the air and the beasts of the field do? What about all the great nations?

        e.   What is said about the cedars and the pine trees in the garden of God?

        f.   Who made Assyria a beautiful tree?

        g.   What did the Lord do to this tree because of its pride?

        h.   What did the most ruthless of foreign nations do to the tree?

        i.   Would there ever be a tree that would reach the height of this tree? What is their destination?

        j.   In chapter thirty-one verse eighteen, what is said about Egypt?

        k.   In the first part of chapter thirty-two, what did the lament concern? To what were they likened?

        l.   The sword of what nation would come against them?

        m.   From within their graves, what will the mighty leaders say of Egypt and her allies?

        n.   Three nations or peoples are mentioned that received punishment before Egypt, what was their punishment? Why did they receive this punishment?

        o.   What was going to happen to Pharaoh and all his hordes even though the Lord had him spread terror in the land of the living?

2.   Hebrews 12:14-29
        a.   What four things were the believers instructed to do in verses fourteen through sixteen?

        b.   For what was Esau used as an example? What could he not change even though he sought it with tears?

c.   What did the author of Hebrews say that his hearers had not experienced? What did Moses say about the terrifying experience?

d.   What had they experienced? What speaks a better word than the blood of Able?

e.   What were the hearers "to see to it", that they did not do?

f.   What two things should they do in response to receiving a kingdom that cannot be shaken?

3.   Psalms 113:1-114:8
      a.   What were the servants of the Lord to do?

      b.   How long should the name of the Lord be praised? Where should it be praised?

      c.   What does the Lord do for the poor and needy? What does the Lord do for the barren woman?

      d.   What became God's sanctuary and his dominion?

      e.   What did the mountains do? What did the hills do?

      f.   What should the earth do at the presence of the Lord?

      g.   What is the last question in this Psalm? What is the answer to this question?

4.   Proverbs 27:18-20
      a.   Solomon talks about two things that will be rewarded, what are they?

      b.   What does a man's heart reflect?

      c.   What three things are never satisfied?

STUDY QUESTIONS FOR NOVEMBER 16

1.   Ezekiel 33:1-34:31
      a.   What came to Ezekiel?

      b.   What will the people of the land choose? What will happen if the man sees the
            sword coming and warns the people but the people do not head the warning?

      c.   What would God do to the watchman if he did not warn the people?

      d.   What did God say that he had made Ezekiel? What two things did God tell
            Ezekiel to do?

      e.   What was the house of Israel saying about their offences and sins?

      f.   Does the Lord take pleasure in the death of the wicked? What would the Lord
            rather that they do?

      g.   What does the Lord tell Ezekiel to say to his countrymen about the righteousness
            of the righteous man and the wickedness of the wicked man?

      h.   Whose way is not just? Whose way did Ezekiel's countrymen say was not just?

      i.   What three things does the Lord point out that the people were doing when he
            asks the question, "Should you then possess the land?"

      j.   What were the people doing with their mouths? What were their hearts doing?

      k.   What will the people know when all this comes true?

      l.   What six things does Ezekiel accuse the shepherds of not doing?

      m.   What was the Lord going to do to the shepherds?

      n.   Who would become their shepherd? How would he shepherd the flock?

      o.   Quote Ezekiel chapter thirty-four verse thirty-one.

2.   Hebrews 13:1-25
      a.   What should the Hebrews keep on doing to each other as brothers?

      b.   Why should one not forget to entertain strangers?

      c.   What should be done about marriage?

      d.   What can one say with confidence?

277

e.   What does the scripture say about Jesus Christ in Hebrews chapter thirteen verse eight?

f.   By what should one not be carried away?

g.   Why did Jesus suffer outside the city gate?

h.   What should we offer continually to God through Jesus?

i.   Why should we obey our leaders?

j.   What did the author say about Timothy?

3.   Psalms 115:1-18
      a.   To whose name is the glory?

      b.   What do the nations ask? How does the Psalmist answer?

      c.   How are the nation's idols made?

      d.   What seven body parts does an idol have that it cannot use?

      e.   What does the Psalmist say about the ones who make idols and the ones who worship them?

      f.   In whom were the house of Israel and the house of Aaron to trust?

      g.   Who is it that does not praise the Lord? Who is it that praises the Lord?

4.   Proverbs 27:21-22
      a.   How is a man tested?

      b.   Can folly be removed from a fool?

STUDY QUESTIONS FOR NOVEMBER 17

1.   Ezekiel 35:1-36:38
        a.   What did the Lord tell Ezekiel to set his face against?

        b.   What would the people know when the Lord turned their towns into ruins and made the people desolate?

        c.   Why was the Lord bringing this judgement on them?

        d.   In accordance with what was the Lord going to treat these people?

        e.   To what is Ezekiel to prophesy in chapter thirty-six?

        f.   What did the enemies of Israel say of them?

        g.   What had these enemies done to Israel?

        h.   How does the Lord describe the mountains, hills, ravines, valleys and towns?

        i.   What did the Lord do in his burning zeal? Why did he do that?

        j.   What were the nations around Israel going to suffer just as Israel had?

        k.   What were the mountains of Israel going to produce for Israel?

        l.   What would happen to the men and animals as the Lord increased their number?

        m.   In chapter thirty-six verse fifteen what would Israel hear no longer and suffer no longer?

        n.   What had Israel done with the Lord's holy name wherever they went among the nations?

        o.   In chapter thirty-six verse twenty-six through thirty, what ten promises did the Lord make to Israel?

        p.   Was the Lord doing this for the sake of Israel?

2.   James 1:1-18
        a.   Whose servant was James? To whom did he write the letter of James?

        b.   What were they to do when they faced many kinds of trials? Why?

        c.   What were they to do if they lacked wisdom? What must they do along with that action?

      d.   In what should the brother in humble circumstances, take pride? What about the rich man? What will happen to the rich man?

      e.   What should no one say when he is tempted? How is man tempted? How does the temptation progress?

      f.   From where does every perfect gift come? Who does not change?

3.   Psalms 116:1-19
      a.   In verse one and two the Psalmist states in three different ways one of the reasons he loves the Lord, what was it? How long would he call on the Lord?

      b.   What happened to the Psalmist before he called on the name of the Lord to save him?

      c.   In verse five, what three things does he say about the Lord? What does the Lord do for the simplehearted?

      d.   In verse eight, what three things had the Lord done for the Psalmist?

      e.   After saying, "How can I repay the Lord?" what three things was the Psalmist going to do for the Lord? In verse seventeen, what two things did the Psalmist add to the things he was going to do?

4.   Proverbs 27:23-27
      a.   What did Solomon want his son to know about his flocks?

      b.   What did he say about riches and a crown?

      c.   Of what would he have plenty?

1. Ezekiel 37:1-38:23

    a. What was in the valley where the Lord set Ezekiel?

    b. What question did the Lord ask Ezekiel? How did Ezekiel answer?

    c. What happened when Ezekiel prophesied over the bones?

    d. What did these bones represent?

    e. The next time the word of the Lord came to Ezekiel, what was he to write on the two sticks? What was he to do with the sticks?

    f. What was he to answer when people asked what that meant? Who would be king over them?

    g. In the next word from the Lord, who was the Sovereign Lord against?

    h. How was the Lord going to turn Gog around?

    i. What evil thoughts and evil schemes would Gog devise?

    j. In chapter thirty-eight, verse fourteen, what was Ezekiel to prophesy and say to Gog?

    k. What further did the Lord say in chapter thirty-eight verse seventeen?

    l. How will God react when Gog attacks the land of Israel?

    m. At that time what will happen to the earth in the land of Israel?

    n. What will the birds of the air, the beasts of the field, every creature that moves along the ground and all the people on the face of the earth do?

    o. What was God going to do against Gog?

    p. What did God say that the people would know when he made himself known in the sight of many nations?

2. James 1:19-2:17

    a. What should everyone be quick to do and what should they be slow to do?

    b. What were they to do beside listen to the word?

c. Who will be blessed in what he does?

d. Who does a man deceive if he considers himself righteous yet does not keep a tight reign on his tongue?

e. What should the believers do about favoritism?

f. Who chose the poor in the eyes of the world to be rich in faith?

g. Who were dragging them into court?

h. Who were the ones that were slandering the noble name of Jesus?

i. How were they to love their neighbors?

j. What is said about the one that keeps the whole law but stumbles at just one point?

k. How many laws must one break to be a lawbreaker?

l. What will happen to the one that has not been merciful?

m. What is faith that is not accompanied by action?

3. Psalms 117:1-2
   a. Who should praise the Lord?

   b. Why should they praise the Lord?

   c. How long does the faithfulness of the Lord endure?

   d. How does the Psalmist finish this Psalm?

4. Proverbs 28:1
   a. What happens to the wicked man?

   b. What happens to the righteous man?

STUDY QUESTIONS FOR NOVEMBER 19

1.   Ezekiel 39:1-40:27
        a.   In chapter thirty-nine, who was Ezekiel asked to prophesy against?

        b.   Who was the sovereign Lord against?

        c.   What was going to happen to Gog and all its troops?

        d.   In chapter thirty-nine, verse six, what would they know when this came about?

        e.   What was Israel going to do with the weapons for seven years?

        f.   Who would Israel plunder?

        g.   What were they going to call the valley where they buried Gog and all his hordes?

        h.   How long would it take Israel to bury all the men and cleanse the land?

        i.   What did Ezekiel tell the birds and the animals?

        j.   How was God going to display his glory?

        k.   In chapter thirty-nine, verse twenty-five what was God going to do for Judah and Israel? What will Israel know when God does this?

        l.   What was God going to do with his spirit for the house of Israel?

        m.   In the twenty fifth year of Israel's exile, where did the Lord take Ezekiel?

        n.   How were the faces of the projecting walls decorated?

        o.   What did Ezekiel see in the outer court?

        p.   How long was the courtyard?

        q.   How many steps led up to the courtyard?

2.   James 2:18-3:18
        a.   What is James discussing in this first chapter?

        b.   What does James want the people to show him? How does he ask them to show him? How would James show them his faith?

        c.   What does James point out about their faith in one God?

d.   What example did James give about Abraham?

e.   What was credited to Abraham as righteousness?

f.   What was said about Rahab?

g.   Why did James say that not many should presume to be teachers?

h.   What two pictures are given to illustrate the importance of the tongue even though it is such a small part of the body?

i.   What does he say about praise and cursing coming out of the same mouth?

j.   What is said about wisdom that comes from heaven?

3.   Psalms 118:1-18
        a.   Why should thanks be given to God?

        b.   What three groups of people should say, "His love endures forever"?

        c.   Why did the Psalmist say, "I will not be afraid"?

        d.   It is better to take refuse in the Lord than what two things?

        e.   What happened when the Psalmist was pushed back and about to fall?

4.   Proverbs 28:2
        a.   What is said about the rulers of a rebellious country?

        b.   What does a man of understanding do?

STUDY QUESTIONS FOR NOVEMBER 20

1. Ezekiel 40:28-41:26
    a. Where is Ezekiel now taken by the man in his vision?

    b. What decorated the jambs and the eight steps that led up to the gateway?

    c. Where was Ezekiel taken next?

    d. Did all of the gateways have the same measurements?

    e. For what were the eight tables near the north gate used?

    f. For what did they use the four tables of dressed stone? What was the measurements of these tables?

    g. Who used the room in the north that was facing south? Who used the room in the south that was facing north?

    h. Where was the altar?

    i. What was the size of the outer sanctuary? What was the size of the inner sanctuary?

    j. What did they use to cover the floor, the wall up to the windows and the windows?

    k. What was carved above the entrance to the inner sanctuary?

    l. How many faces did each cherub have?

    m. What was each like?

    n. How far did these carvings extend?

    o. What was the size of the wooden altar?

    p. How were the doors to the outer sanctuary and the most Holy Place described?

    q. What was carved on each side of the narrow windows?

2. James 4:1-17
    a. From where do fights and quarrels come?

    b. What are two things that cause believers to fail to receive what they want?

c. What does friendship with the word equal with God?

d. What does one that chooses to be a friend of the world, become to God?

e. What does God do to the proud? What does he do to the humble?

f. What happens when one submits themself to God and resists the devil?

g. What should be said instead of "Today or tomorrow we will go to this or that city, spend a year there, carry on business and make money."?

3. Psalms 118:19-29
   a. What did the Psalmist say he would do if the Lord opened the gates of righteousness to him?

   b. Why did the Psalmist say he would give thanks?

   c. Who was the stone the builders rejected? What did he become?

   d. Who made this day? What should one do about it?

   e. Who is blessed?

   f. Who made his light shine upon us?

   g. What two things was the Psalmist going to do because God was his God? How long does God's love endure?

4. Proverbs 28:3-5
   a. To what is an oppressive ruler likened?

   b. Who praise the wicked?

   c. Who understands justice? Who does not understand justice?

1.   Ezekiel 42:1-43:27
      a.   Look back at chapter forty verse two, where did the Lord take Ezekiel in this vision?

      b.   When did Ezekiel receive the vision in chapter forty starting at verse one?

      c.   In chapter forty-two, where did the man lead Ezekiel?

      d.   What was the size of this building?

      e.   Which floor did not have pillars?

      f.   For what were the north and south rooms facing the temple courtyard to be used?

      g.   What were the priests to do about their garments that they were wearing in the Holy Place?

      h.   What was the size of the area around the building?

      i.   How was the temple area set off from the common area?

      j.   From which direction did Ezekiel see the glory of God coming?

      k.   What was God's voice like?

      l.   Where did God say he would live among the Israelites forever?

      m.   What did the Israelites have to do to receive the promise that God would live among them forever?

      n.   Why was Ezekiel to describe the temple to the people of Israel?

      o.   What were they to give to the priests as a sin offering?

      p.   What were they to offer the second day?

      q.   When did God say he would accept them.

2.   James 5:1-20
      a.   What did James tell the rich people to do? What happened to their wealth, clothes, and gold and silver?

      b.   What was the corrosion going to do against them and what was it going to do to their flesh?

    c.   What were the rich people doing wrong?

    d.   What example did James use for being patient?

    e.   Why should they not grumble against each other?

    f.   What were they to do if they were in trouble?

    g.   What were they to do if they were sick?

    h.   What does James say about the prayer of a righteous man?

3.   Psalms 119:1-16

    a.   Psalms one hundred nineteen is an acrostic. In Hebrew each of these sections (eight verse each) starts with a letter of the Hebrew alphabet. What is the letter for verse one and what is the letter for verse nine?

    b.   Name four things that describe the blessed person.

    c.   What was the Psalmist's desire in regard to God's decrees?

    d.   What two things did the Psalmist promise to do?

    e.   "How can a young man keep his way pure?"

    f.   What did the Psalmist do with God's word? Why? What does he do with his lips?

    g.   In what does he rejoice? What does he do with God's precepts? What does he promise to do about God's word?

4.   Proverbs 28:6-7

    a.   What is better than being a rich man with perverse ways?

    b.   What does a companion of gluttons do to his father?

1.   Ezekiel 44:1-45:12
   a.   To what location did the man bring Ezekiel back?

   b.   What did the Lord say to him?

   c.   Where did the man take Ezekiel next? What did he see?

   d.   What three things did the Lord instruct Ezekiiel to do?

   e.   What was he to say to the rebellious house of Israel? What did he say about the foreigners in chapter forty-four verses seven and nine?

   f.   Who was to bear the consequences of the sins of the Levites?

   g.   Because of their sins, what were the Levites not allowed to do?

   h.   What did the Lord say about the priests that were Levites who faithfully carried out the duties of the sanctuary when Israel went astray?

   i.   What were they to wear when they entered the gates of the inner court? What were they to do with these clothes when they went out to the outer court where the people were? Why did they need to change?

   j.   Who was to serve as judges?

   k.   What was to be the only inheritance of the priests?

   l.   What size was the land that was to be a sacred district?

   m.   What size was the sanctuary to be? What size was the area of open land around the sanctuary to be?

   n.   Where were the houses of the priests to be?

   o.   Who was to have the land bordering each side of the area formed by the sacred district?

   p.   Of what is the shekel and the mina to consist?

2.   I Peter 1:1-12
   a.   Who was writing this letter and to whom was he writing?

   b.   What did God, in his great mercy, give us?

c.   Why did they have to suffer grief in all kinds of trials?

d.   What did these believers do even though they had not seen Jesus?

e.   What were they receiving?

f.   What did the prophets do concerning this salvation?

g.   What was revealed to these prophets?/

h.   What do even angels long to do?

3.   Psalms 119:17-32
      a.   What does the Psalmist ask the Lord to do for him? What does the Psalmist promise to do?

      b.   With what is the Psalmist's soul consumed?

      c.   What does he ask to be removed from him?

      d.   What was the Psalmist going to do even though rulers sit together and slander him?

      e.   What does the Psalmist say about God's statutes?

      f.   What did the Lord do for the Psalmist when he recounted his ways? What does he ask the Lord to teach him?

      g.   Where did the Psalmist run? Why did he run there?

4.   Proverbs 28:8-10
      a.   What will happen to the wealth of one who increases his wealth by exorbitant interest?

      b.   What happens to the one that turns a deaf ear to the law?

      c.   What happens to the one who leads the upright along an evil path?

STUDY QUESTIONS FOR NOVEMBER 23

1.   Ezekiel 45:13-46:24
     a.   What was the special gift that Ezekiel was to offer? Who else was to participate in this special gift?

     b.   Who was to provide the burnt offerings and fellowship offerings to make atonement for the house of Israel?

     c.   What did the Lord say they were to do on the first month on the first day? What were they to do on the seventh day of the month?

     d.   When were they to celebrate the Passover? How long was this feast to last?

     e.   When was the gate of the inner court facing east, to be closed and when was it to be opened? Who was to enter the gate through the portico of the gateway?

     f.   What time of the day was the gate to be closed?

     g.   Where were the people to worship in the presence of the Lord?

     h.   What offering was the prince to bring on the day of the new moon?

     i.   Were the people to go out the same gate they came in?

     j.   If the prince makes a gift to one of his sons from his inheritance, to who else will it belong?

     k.   What happens to the gift a prince makes to a servant from his inheritance in the seventh year?

     l.   What did Ezekiel see in the four corners of the outer court?

     m.   What was the size of each?

     n.   What was around the inside of each?

     o.   What were the ministers going to do in these areas?

2.   I Peter 1:13-2:10
     a.   What were they to do to their minds?

     b.   On what were they to set their hope?

     c.   How were they to live their lives?

d.   With what were they redeemed?

e.   What is like grass that withers? What stands forever?

f.   Who laid the stone in Zion?

g.   Why did the people stumble?

h.   In verse nine and ten how were the people described?

3.   Psalms 119:33-48
       a.   What does the Psalmist ask for, in verse thirty-three? Then what will the Psalmist do?

       b.   What would he do if the Lord gave him understanding?

       c.   Why did he want God to direct him in the path of God's commands?

       d.   What did the Psalmist want God to fulfill? Why did he want the promise fulfilled?

       e.   What did the Psalmist want God to take away?

       f.   What did the Psalmist long for?

       g.   How long would the Psalmist obey God's law?

       h.   How was the Psalmist going to walk about? Why would he be able to walk about like that?

       i.   Why did the Psalmist delight in God's commands?

       j.   What was he going to do with his hands? On what was he going to meditate?

4.   Proverbs 28:11
       a.   What can a poor man that has discernment do?

STUDY QUESTIONS FOR NOVEMBER 24

1. Ezekiel 47:1-48:35
   a. What did Ezekiel see coming out from under the threshold of the temple toward the east?

   b. From what side of the temple was it coming?

   c. What happened when the man measured off one thousand cubits? What about one thousand cubits more? How about the third one thousand cubits? And the fourth one thousand cubits?

   d. What did Ezekiel see on both sides of the river?

   e. What happened where the river flowed into the sea? Where will the swarms of living creatures live?

   f. What is said about the leaves and the fruit of the trees on both sides of the river? How often will they bear?

   g. When the people return to Jerusalem, how were they to distribute the land?

   h. How were they to treat the aliens that settled among them?

   i. In chapter forty-eight, verses eight through twelve, Ezekiel asks them to present a special gift. For what was that special gift to be used?

   j. What was to be in the center of this special gift?

   k. Where will the Levites have their allotment? What was the requirement in regards to them about selling or exchanging this land?

   l. How many gates are to be on each side of the city? For whom were the gates to be named?

   m. What was the length of each side of the city? What was the total distance around the city?

   n. What was the name of the city going to be from that time on?

2. I Peter 2:11-3:7
   a. What did Peter urge the friends to do?

   b. In what way were they asked to live? To whom were they to submit?

c. In chapter two verse fifteen, what is God's will? How were they to live?

d. What were the slaves to do?

e. List the things mentioned here that show how Christ was an example to the hearers.

f. Why is it important that the wives be in submission to their husbands? What were the husbands to do?

3. Psalms 119:49-64
    a. What does the Psalmist request?

    b. Where was the Psalmist's comfort?

    c. What did the arrogant do to him? What did he do about God's law?

    d. Why did indignation grip him?

    e. What did he say about god's decrees?

    f. What did the Psalmist do in the night?

    g. What was the Psalmist's practice?

    h. What did the Psalmist do when he considered his ways?

    i. What will the Psalmist do even though the wicked bound him with ropes?

4. Proverbs 28:12-13
    a. What happens when the righteous triumph?

    b. What happens when the wicked rise to power?

    c. What are the consequences if a person conceals his sins? What if he confesses his sin?

STUDY QUESTIONS FOR NOVEMBER 25

1. Daniel 1:1-2:23
   a. Where did king Nebuchadnezzar take the things he took from Jerusalem?

   b. What four men are talked about that were taken from Judah? What new name did the chief official give them?

   c. What did Daniel ask the chief official? What did the official tell Daniel?

   d. What did Daniel suggest?

   e. After ten days, what was the result of the test?

   f. What did the king find when the young Hebrew men were brought before him?

   g. How long did Daniel remain there?

   h. What did King Nebuchadnezzar do when his mind was troubled and he could not sleep?

   i. How did the astrologers respond to the king's request?

   j. What did the king do when the astrologers would not tell him his dream and the interpretation?

   k. How did Daniel get involved in the king's order?

   l. What did Daniel ask Arioch, the commander of the king's guard?

   m. What did Daniel do when he found out what was happening?

   n. What happened during the night?

   o. What did Daniel do after that night?

   p. What does God do about times and seasons and kings?

   q. Daniel praised the God of his fathers for several things, what were they?

2. I Peter 3:8-4:6
   a. What does Peter ask the people to do?

   b. What group of people is the Lord's face against?

c.   What is said about the person that suffers for what is right?

d.   What should they always be prepared to do?

e.   What thing is better to suffer for?

f.   How many people were saved in the ark? What did the water of the flood symbolize?

g.   What had the people spent enough time doing in the past?

h.   What are the pagans going to be required to do when they appear before God the judge?

3.   Psalms 119:65-80
      a.   What did the Psalmist ask to be taught?

      b.   When did the Psalmist go astray?

      c.   What did the arrogant do to the Psalmist?

      d.   How does the Psalmist feel about God's law?

      e.   Who made the Psalmist?

      f.   In what did the Psalmist put his hope?

      g.   What did he ask to be his comfort?

      h.   In what did he delight?

      i.   On what would he meditate?

4.   Proverbs 28:14
      a.   Who is blessed?

      b.   What happens to the one who hardens his heart?

1. Daniel 2:24-3:30
    a. To whom did Daniel go? What did Daniel tell this man?

    b. What did Daniel answer when the king asked, "Are you able to tell me what I saw in my dream and interpret it?"

    c. What did the king see in his dream?

    d. What did the dream mean?

    e. Who had given the king dominion and power and might and glory?

    f. Who will be the last to set up a kingdom that will never be destroyed.

    g. What was the reaction of king Nebuchadnezzar?

    h. What did the king do for Daniel?

    i. At Daniel's request, what did the king do for Shadrach, Meshach, and Abednego?

    j. Describe the image that King Nebuchadnezzar made.

    k. What did the king require the people to do? Did all the people follow the instruction?

    l. How did the king react to the actions of Shadrach, Meshach, and Abednego?

    m. What punishment did the king give out? What did the king instruct his men to do with the furnace?

    n. What happened to the soldiers that carried out the king's command?

    o. What did the king see when he looked into the fire? What did he instruct the three Hebrew men to do?

    p. Were the men hurt? What did Nebuchadnezzar say? What did he decree? What did he do to Shadrach, Meshach, and Abednego?

2. I Peter 4:7-5:14
    a. There are at lest four things that Peter tells his listeners that they should do because the end is near, what are they?

    b. How should one speak?

c. How should one serve? Why should one serve like that?

d. What did he say about painful trials? Why should one rejoice?

e.   What happens if you are insulted because of the name of Christ?

f. In chapter four, verse seventeen, what is it time for?

g. What should the ones that suffer according to God's will do?

h. What happens when the chief shepherd appears?

i. What does God do to the proud? How about the humble?

3. Psalms 119:81-96
    a. What acrostic is used in the one hundred, nineteenth Psalm? Why doesn't it sound like an acrostic to us?

    b. In what did the Psalmist put his hope?

    c. Did the Psalmist forget God's decrees?

    d. How does the Psalmist ask God to preserve his life?

    e. In verse eighty nine, what does the Psalmist say about the Lord's word?

    f. How long before the Psalmist would forget the Lord's precepts?

4. Proverbs 28:15-16
    a. To what is a wicked man ruling over helpless people, likened?

    b. What happens to the one that hates ill-gotten gain?

1. Daniel 4:1-37
    a. To whom was King Nebuchadnezzar writing this letter?

    b. What was he going to tell them about in this letter?

    c. Where was Nebuchadnezzar when he received this vision?

    d. What happened when he asked the astrologers and diviners what his vision meant?

    e. Who came into the presence of the king? What did Nebuchadnezzar ask him to do? Did he do it?

    f. In the dream, who was represented by the mighty tree? How was he described?

    g. What did, "Seven times pass by for him" mean?

    h. What did, "Cut down the tree and trim off its branches; strip off its leaves and scatter its fruit. Let the animals flee from under it and the birds from its branches." mean?

    i. What did "But let the stump and its roots, bound with iron and bronze, remain in the ground, in the grass of the field." mean?

    j. What did Daniel advise the king to do?

    k. What happened to the king twelve months later? What attitude did the king have that was wrong?

    l. What did the voice from heaven tell the king?

    m. How long did it take before these words were fulfilled?

    n. What did King Nebuchadnezzar do at the end of the prophesied time?

    o. What happened to the king's sanity? What about his honor and splendor?

    p. In verse thirty seven, what did the king do to the king of heaven?

2. II Peter 1:1-21
    a. Who is this letter from?

    b. To who is this letter addressed?

c. How were they to receive grace and peace?

d. What did Jesus Christ's divine power give them?

e. What seven things were they to make every effort to add to their faith? What is promised, if the believers posses these qualities in increasing measure?

f. Did Peter and company follow cleverly invented stories?

g. Did prophecies come about by the will of men?

3. Psalms 119:97-112
a. What kind of a Poem is psalms one hundred nineteen?

b. What did the Psalmist say about God's law? When did he meditate on God's law?

c. What did the Psalmist gain from meditating on God's statutes?

d. What was said about the sweetness of God's word?

e. What was the Psalmist's feelings about wrong paths?

f. What was a light to his path and a lamp to his feet?

g. What oath did the Psalmist take?

h. What did the wicked do to the Psalmist? Did that cause the Psalmist to stray from God's precepts?

i. On what was his heart set?

4. Proverbs 28:17-18
a. How long will a man tormented by guilt of murder be a fugitive?

b. What is said about a man whose walk is blameless? What about the man whose walk is perverse?

STUDY QUESTIONS FOR NOVEMBER 28

1. Daniel 5:1-31
   a. What goblets did Belshazzar order brought to him?

   b. Who drank from these goblets?

   c. What were they doing as they drank from these goblets?

   d. What appeared to them?

   e. Describe the kings reaction.

   f. Who did the king call?

   g. Were they able to interpret what was written?

   h. What made the king become even more terrified?

   i. What was the queen's advice?

   j. Who was next to be brought before the king?

   k. How did Daniel respond to the king's request?

   l. What mistake did Belshazzar's father (Nebuchadnezzar) make? What did he have to acknowledge before he could come back?

   m. What did Daniel say about Belshazzar?

   n. Who sent the hand that wrote the inscription?

   o. What inscription was written?

   p. What did Daniel say it meant?

   q. What did the king do to Daniel?

   r. How long did it take this prophesy to be fulfilled?

   s. Who took over the kingdom?

   t. How old was the new king?

2. II Peter 2:1-22

a.   In the end of chapter one, Peter talks about true prophesy, what is he warning them about in chapter two verses one through three?

b.   How were the false teachers going to bring in heresies?

c.   What were they bringing on themselves?

d.   "Their _____ has long been _____ over them, and their _____ has not been _____." II Peter chapter two verse three b

e.   What point is Peter making verses four through ten?

f.   What were the false prophets not afraid to do? What did the angels not do in the presence of the Lord?

g.   How will the false prophets be paid back?

h.   Who loved the wages of wickedness?

i.   To what is a man a slave?

j.   How is the false prophet like the dog in the proverb?

3.   Psalms 119:113-128
      a.   What does the Psalmist hate? What does he love? In what does he put his hope?

      b.   What will happen when God upholds him? For what would he always have regard?

      c.   Who does God reject? Who does he discard like dross?

      d.   How does the Psalmist ask to be dealt with by God?

      e.   What does the Psalmist love more than gold? Why?

4.   Proverbs 28:19,20
      a.   What will happen to the one that works his land?

      b.   What happens to the one that chases fantasies?

      c.   What happens to the faithful man? What happens to the one eager to get rich?

STUDY QUESTIONS FOR NOVEMBER 29

1.   Daniel 6:1-28
      a.   How many satraps did Darius appoint? How many administrators did he appoint?

      b.   What did Darius plan to do with Daniel?

      c.   What did the satraps and administrators try to find in Daniel? What kind of a trap did they set for Daniel?

      d.   Did the king do what they asked?

      e.   What did Daniel do when he learned that the decree had been published? Was this a change from his normal actions?

      f.   What did the satraps and administrators do next?

      g.   What was the reaction of the king when he found out what had been done?

      h.   What did the king say to Daniel? What was placed over the mouth of the den?

      i.   How did the king sleep that night? What did he do at the first light of dawn? What did he call out to Daniel?

      j.   What was Daniel's answer?

      k.   How many wounds were found on Daniel when they lifted him out?

      l.   What did the king command to be done to the ones that falsely accused Daniel?

      m.   What did king Darius write to all the peoples, nations and men of every language throughout the land?

      n.   What four things did Darius say about God's existence?

      o.   What four things did he say that God did?

      p.   What is said about Daniel during the reign of Darius and Cyrus the Persian?

2.   II Peter 3:1-18
      a.   Why did Peter write these two letters? What did Peter want them to recall?

      b.   What was the first thing that they must understand? What would these people say?

c.   What did they deliberately forget?

d.   What one thing did Peter tell the people not to forget?

e.   How will the day of the Lord come?

f.   What will happen to the heavens? How will the elements be destroyed?

g.   What question does Peter ask in the first part of verse eleven? What was the answer?

h.   In keeping with the promise, to what were they looking forward?

i.   How were they to grow? To whom was to be glory?

3.   Psalms 119:129-152
        a.   What does the Psalmist say is wonderful?

        b.   For what was the Psalmist longing?

        c.   How did the Psalmist want his footsteps to be ordered?

        d.   Who is righteous? What about his laws?

        e.   In verse one hundred forty-three, what came upon the Psalmist? What was his delight?

        f.   In verse one hundred fifty-two, what did the Psalmist learn long ago?

4.   Proverbs 28:21-22
        a.   What is not good?

        b.   For what will a man do wrong?

        c.   What is a stingy man eager to do? Of what is he unaware?

1.   Daniel 7:1-28
      a.   When did David have the dream talked about in this chapter?

      b.   In his dream, what were the four winds of heaven doing?

      c.   How did Daniel describe each of the four beasts that he saw in his dream?

      d.   How many horns did the fourth beast originally have? What happened while Daniel was thinking about these horns?

      e.   How was the clothing of the ancient of days described? How about his hair?

      f.   What did he say about his throne?

      g.   How many attended him? How many stood before him?

      h.   How long did Daniel continue to look?

      i.   What happened to the other beasts?

      j.   In Daniel's vision at night, what did he see? What did this person do? What was this person given?

      k.   What did all the peoples, nations and men of every language do?

      l.   What was the meaning of the four great beasts?

      m.   What explanation was given of the fourth beast that was different from the rest? What did the ten horns represent? How about the horn that appeared later?

      n.   How long would the saints be handed over to the last king?

      o.   To whom will the sovereignty, power and greatness of the kingdoms be given?

      p.   Who will be the ruler of this kingdom?

2.   I John 1:1-10
      a.   What were they proclaiming concerning the word of life?

      b.   What was said about the life?

      c.   Why were they writing this?

d. Where did they hear the message? What was the message that they heard?

e. What is said about the one that claims to have fellowship with Christ yet walks in darkness?

f. What happens to the one that walks in the light as Christ is in the light?

g. What is said about the one that claims to be without sin? What if they confess their sins?

3. Psalms 119:153-176
a. What chapter is the longest chapter in the bible? What is distinctive about the way that Psalms one hundred nineteen was written?

b. What did the Psalmist request from the Lord in verse one hundred fifty-three?

c. Why is salvation far from the wicked?

d. How did the Psalmist look on the faithless? Why did he look on them like that?

e. In verse one hundred sixty, what does the Psalmist say about God's words and laws?

f. Why did the Psalmist obey God's statutes?

g. What did the Psalmist long for and in what did he delight?

4. Proverbs 28:23-24
a. What will gain more favor than a flattering tongue?

b. What is said about the man that robs father or mother and says, "It's not wrong"?

STUDY QUESTIONS FOR DECEMBER 1

1. Daniel 8:1-27
   a. When did Daniel see the vision recorded in this chapter?

   b. Where did Daniel see himself in this vision?

   c. What did he see when he looked up?

   d. How does Daniel describe the goat in the vision? From where did this goat come?

   e. What did the goat do to the ram?

   f. What happened to the goat at the height of his power?

   g. What came out of one of the four horns that grew up in place of the large horn that was broken?

   h. How long did it grow and what did it do to the starry host?

   i. What did it set itself to be as great as? What was given to it because of rebellion?

   j. How long was it going to take to for the vision to be fulfilled? What would happen to the sanctuary at the end of this time?

   k. What did the man's voice tell Gabriel to do? What did Daniel do when Gabriel came near? What did the vision concern?

   l. What did the two-horned ram represent?

   m. What did the shaggy goat represent? What about the large horn?

   n. What were the four horns that replaced the horn that was broken off?

   o. What seven things will the stern-faced king do? Will humans destroy him?

   p. In verse twenty-seven, how did Daniel react

2. I John 2:1-17
   a. Why was John writing this letter?

   b. If one does sin, who does he have to speak to the father in his defense?

   c. How did John say that his hearers could know that they know Jesus Christ?

d. Was this a new command that John was writing to them?

e. What does he say about the one that hates his brother?

f. Why did John write to the children? To the fathers? To the young men?

g. What should a believer not love? What is said about the one that does love it?

h. What happens to the world and its desires? What happens to the man who does the will of God?

3. Psalms 120:1-7
   a. What does the Lord do when the Psalmist calls in his distress?

   b. From what does the Psalmist request the Lord to deliver him?

   c. How does the Psalmist picture the discipline of the tongue?

   d. Why did the Psalmist say, "Woe to me"?

   e. Where had the Psalmist lived too long? What happened when the Psalmist, a man of peace spoke?

4. Proverbs 28:25-26
   a. What does a greedy man stir up?

   b. What is promised to the one that trusts in the Lord?

   c. What is said about one who trusts in himself?

   d. What about a man that walks in wisdom?

STUDY QUESTIONS FOR DECEMBER 2

1. Daniel 9:1-11:1
   a. In what year did this narration take place?

   b. How long would the desolation of Jerusalem last?

   c. Name at least four things that Daniel confessed?

   d. Why were the curses and sworn judgements written in the law of Moses poured out on God's people?

   e. What had been done to Jerusalem that had not been done under the whole heaven? Did God's people seek God's favor by turning from their sins and giving attention to truth?

   f. What requests did Daniel make of the Lord in chapter nine verses seventeen through nineteen?

   g. Who came to Daniel while he was still in prayer? What did he say about Daniel's prayer?

   h. How many sevens were decreed for the people?

   i. When was the revelation of chapter ten given to Daniel?

   j. How long did Daniel mourn?

   k. How did he mourn?

   l. How did Daniel describe the man he saw in the vision?

   m. What did his voice sound like?

   n. How many around Daniel saw the vision that Daniel saw? What did the other men do?

   o. What delayed the man that came to Daniel? How long was he delayed?

   p. What did the man tell him after he gave Daniel strength?

   q. What did the man say to Daniel?

2. I John 2:18-3:6
   a. In chapter two verse eighteen, what did John say to his listeners about atichrist?

b. Did the recipients of John's letter know the truth? Why did John write to them?

c. Who is the liar? What does John call such a man?

d. What is said about one that denies or acknowledges the Son?

e. What were they to do with what they had heard from the beginning?

f. In chapter two verse twenty-eight, what did John instruct the dear children to do? Why did he tell the people to do this?

g. What is the reason that the world did not know the children of God?

3. Psalms 121:1-8
    a. What does the Psalmist do with his eyes?

    b. From where does his help come?

    c. Who would not let his foot slip?

    d. What does he say about the one who watches over Israel?

    e. Who is the shade at the hearer's right hand?

    f. What is said about the sun and moon?

    g. What will the Lord watch over? How long will the Lord watch over this?

4. Proverbs 28:27-28
    a. What is said about the one that gives to the poor?

    b. What will the one that closes his eyes to the poor receive?

    c. What do the people do when the wicked rise to power?

1.   Daniel 11:2-35
   a.   How many more kings will appear in Persia?

   b.   Which king will be the richest?

   c.   What will this king do when he has gained power by his wealth?

   d.   How is the next king to appear described? What happens to his kingdom? Will his empire go to his descendants? Will his empire have the power that the king exercised?

   e.   What will happen to the king of the South? What about one of his commanders?

   f.   What will the daughter of the king of the South do? Will her power last?

   g.   Who will attack the forces of the king of the North? What will he seize?

   h.   What does the king of the South do when king of the North raises a large army to fight against him?

   i.   Were the Jews successful when they rebelled against the king of the South?

   j.   What will the invader from the north do? Who will be able to withstand him?

   k.   Who will put an end to the insolence of the Northern king? What will happen to this king?

   l.   What will happen when the richest provinces feel secure?

   m.   Why was the king of the South unable to stand against the king of the North even though he had a large and powerful army?

   n.   What did the two kings do as they sat at the same table?

   o.   How will the king corrupt those who have violated the covenant? What will the people who know their God do to the king?

2.   I John 3:7-24
   a.   What does John ask his listeners not to do?

   b.   What does he say about the man that does what is right?

   c.   What about the man who does what is sinful?

d.   Why did the Son of God appear?

e.   Will the person who is born of God continue to sin? Why?

f.   How does one know who are the children of God and who are the children of the devil?

g.   What was the message they heard from the beginning?

h.   Why did he say, "Don't be like Cain"?

i.   How does one know what love is?

j.   How should love be shown?

k.   How can one know that Jesus lives in him?

3.   Psalms 122:1-9
       a.   With whom did the Psalmist rejoice?

       b.   How was Jerusalem built?

       c.   Why did the tribes go up to Jerusalem?

       d.   Where did the thrones of judgement stand?

       e.   For what were the listeners encouraged to pray?

       f.   What did the Psalmist say about peace?

       g.   What did the Psalmist seek?

4.   Proverbs 29:1
       a.   What will happen to the man that remains stiff-necked after many rebukes?

1. Daniel 11:36-12:13
   a. What three things will the king do?

   b. How long will he be successful?

   c. Will he show regard for the gods of his father?

   d. How would he exalt himself?

   e. Who will engage the king in battle at the time of the end?

   f. The king will invade many countries and sweep through them like what?

   g. What will happen to Edom, Moab and the leaders of Ammon?

   h. What about Egypt?

   i. How did the king react to reports from the east and the north?

   j. Where will he pitch his royal tents?

   k. What was said about the time of distress?

   l. What happened to everyone whose name was found written in the book?

   m. What was Daniel to do with the words of the scroll? Until what time was this to be done?

   n. What did the man in linen answer when asked, how long will it be before these astonishing things are fulfilled?

   o. What answer did Daniel receive when he asked, "My Lord, what will the outcome of this be?"?

   p. What will the wicked continue to be?

   q. Who will understand?

   r. What will happen to Daniel at the end of the days?

2. I John 4:1-21
   a. What did John ask his friends not to believe? Why were they to test the spirits?

b.   How were they to recognize the Spirit of God?

c.   How did the dear children overcome? Who was greater?

d.   Who listens to us? Who does not listen to us?

e.   Who are the friends to love? From where does love come?

f.   How did God show his love to mankind?

g.   How can we know that we live in him? (God)

h.   What does complete love drive out?

i.   What is a person called that says he loves God but hates his brother? What command has God given us?

3.   Psalms 123:1-4
    a.   To whom did the Psalmist lift up his eyes? Where did this person have his throne?

    b.   What two illustrations did the Psalmist use to illustrate that our eyes look to the Lord?

    c.   What request does the Psalmist make two times in succession?

    d.   What did he say was the reason that he made this request?

4.   Proverbs 29:2-4
    a.   What happens when the righteous thrive? What about when the wicked rule?

    b.   What does a man that loves wisdom bring to his father?

    c.   What does the companion of prostitutes do to his wealth?

    d.   How does a king bring stability to a country? What happens when the king is hungry for bribes?

STUDY QUESTIONS FOR DECEMBER 5

1. Hosea 1:1-3:5
    a. Whose son was Hosea?

    b. Under what kings did he prophesy?

    c. What did the Lord tell Hosea to do about a wife?

    d. Why did the Lord tell him to do that?

    e. Why did the Lord tell Hosea to call his first son Jezreel?

    f. What was going to happen to the kingdom of Israel?

    g. Why did God tell Hosea to call his daughter Lo-Ruhamah?

    h. Why was he to call his second son Lo-Ammi?

    i. In spite of not being God's people what were the Israelite going to be like?

    j. What would happen to the people of Judah and the people of Israel?

    k. Why was God not going to show love to her children?

    l. What did the lady do after she chased after her lovers but could not catch them?

    m. What did she do with the silver and gold that was lavished on her?

    n. What was God going to do with the grain and new wine?

    o. What was Israel going to call God instead of my master?

    p. What was God going to do with her vines and fig trees?

    q. What did the Lord tell Hosea to do about his wife?

    r. How much did he pay for his wife?

    s. What happens to Israel after they are with out a king or prince for many days?

2. I John 5:1-21
    a. Who is born of God?

    b. What is the love of God?

c.   What happens to everyone that is born of God?

d.   What are the three that testify of Christ?

e.   Whose testimony is greater, man or God's?

f.   What does anyone that doesn't believe in God make out God to be? Why?

g.   From where does the eternal life come?

h.   What does he that has the Son have?

i.   What confidence does one have in approaching God?

j.   What should a Christian do when he sees his brother sin?

k.   What is all wrongdoing?

l.   What does John say about idols?

3.   Psalms 124:1-8
      a.   What would have happened to Israel if God had not been on their side?

      b.   What about the flood?

      c.   Who was the Psalmist praising?

      d.   What word picture did he give about escaping?

      e.   From where did his help come?

4.   Proverbs 29:5-8
      a.   What is the man that flatters his neighbor doing?

      b.   What concerns a righteous man, what about the wicked man?

      c.   What do mockers do? What do wise men do?

1.   Hosea 4:1-5:15
     a.   Who did Hosea tell to hear the word of the Lord?

     b.   What was missing in the land?

     c.   What was in the land instead?

     d.   What happened to the ones that live in the land? What happened to the beasts of
          the field, the birds of the air and the fish of the sea?

     e.   Who stumbled day and night? Who stumbled with them?

     f.   From what were God's people destroyed?

     g.   For what did the priests exchange their glory? On what did they feed and what
          did they relish?

     h.   Who was the Lord going to punish and repay for their deeds?

     i.   What kind of a spirit was leading them astray?

     j.   In chapter four verse sixteen, what is said about the Israelites?

     k.   What will their sacrifices bring them?

     l.   In chapter five, what did Israel's arrogance do against them?

     m.   What would happen to Israel, Ephraim, and Judah when they go out with their
          flocks and herds to seek the Lord? Why would that happen?

     n.   What were Judah's leaders like? What was God going to do to them?

     o.   On what was Ephraim intent? What did Ephraim do when he saw his sickness?
          Did that help?

     p.   What will these people do in their misery?

2.   II John 1:1-13
     a.   To whom does John address this second letter?

     b.   What three things did John send to the addressees?

     c.   What gave John great joy?

d. Was the command John was writing new? What did John ask them to do?

e. What was the command that they had heard from the beginning?

f. For what were they to watch out?

g. What were they to do if one brought false teaching?

h. What did John want to do instead of writing to them with paper and ink?

3. Psalms 125:1-5
   a. To what are the ones that trust in the Lord, likened?

   b. Why are they likened unto that?

   c. How does the Lord surround his people? How long does he surround them?

   d. What will happen to the scepter of the wicked? What was the reason that would happen?

   e. What does the Psalmist ask for those that do good and those that are upright in heart?

   f. What will the Lord do to those who turn to crooked ways?

   g. What will be on Israel?

4. Proverbs 29:9-11
   a. What happens when a wise man goes to court with a fool?

   b. How do bloodthirsty men regard men of integrity?

   c. What does a fool do? What does a wise man do?

STUDY QUESTIONS FOR DECEMBER 7

1. Hosea 6:1-9:17
    a. What did Hosea encourage the people to do?

    b. Hosea said that God had torn them and injured them but what was God going to do for them?

    c. To what did he liken Gods actions toward them?

    d. What did God desire from the people? What did God see in the house of Israel?

    e. What are the sins of Ephriam and crimes of Samaria that Hosea mentions in the first part of chapter seven?

    f. What did Ephraim fail to realize?

    g. How did the king respond to the wickedness of Ephraim? To what did the princes respond?

    h. What did foreigners do to the strength of Ephaim? Was Epharim aware of it?

    i. Did the people cry out to God from their hearts? What did they do instead?

    j. Why was Hosea to put a trumpet to his lips and an eagle was over the house of the Lord?

    k. What did Israel do with their gold and silver?   What did they reap when they sowed to the wind?

    l. In chapter nine, why was Israel told not rejoice and not to be jubilant like other nations?

    m. Would the sacrifices of Ephraim be pleasing to God? What would these sacrifices be like?

    n. What was going to happen to their treasures of silver?

    o. What was it like when God found Israel?

    p. In chapter nine verse seventeen, why did God reject the people?

2. III John 1:1-14
    a. To whom was John writing? What did John pray for his friend?

319

b.   What was John's greatest joy?

c.   What compliment did John give about his friend?

d.   What did the strangers tell the church about John?

e.   What did John say about Diotrephes?

f.   What was John going to do if he came?

g.   What did he ask his friend to imitate?

h.   What does John say about anyone that does good? What does he say about anyone that does what is evil?

i.   Why did John not want to write with pen and ink?

3.   Psalms 126:1-6
        a.   What were the men like when the Lord brought back the captives to Zion?

        b.   With what were their mouths filled and what was on their tongues?

        c.   What was said among the nations?

        d.   With what were the people filled?

        e.   What did the Psalmist request of the Lord?

        f.   What will happen to the one that sows in tears?

        g.   How will the one that goes out weeping, carrying seed to sow, return?

4.   Proverbs 29:12-14
        a.   What happens when a ruler listens to lies?

        b.   What does an oppressor and a poor man have in common?

        c.   What happens when a king judges the poor with fairness?

STUDY QUESTIONS FOR DECEMBER 8

1.   Hosea 10:1-14:9
     a.   What did Israel do as his fruit increased?

     b.   What is said about the heart of the people?

     c.   How did the lawsuits spring up?

     d.   How long had Israel sinned?

     e.   What would they reap if they sowed righteousness for themselves? What did they reap when they planted wickedness? On what had they depended?

     f.   In chapter eleven, what did Israel do, the more that God called them?

     g.   In verse seven, what were God's people determined to do?

     h.   With what did Ephraim surround God and the house of Israel?

     i.   In chapter twelve, verse two, how was God going to punish Jacob and repay him?

     j.   What did the Lord use to bring Israel up from Egypt?

     k.   In chapter thirteen, what happened when Ephraim spoke? Of what did he become guilty?

     l.   What were the three downward steps of God's people mentioned in chapter thirteen verse six?

     m.   Why did God say that Israel would be destroyed?

     n.   What is Israel encouraged to do in chapter fourteen, verse one and two?

     o.   What promises does God make to Israel chapter fourteen verses five through seven?

     p.   What does the Lord say about his ways? What do the righteous do? What do the rebellious do?

2.   Jude 1:1-25
     a.   How does Jude describe himself?

     b.   To whom was Jude writing?

c. In verse three, what does Jude encourage the people to do?

d. Who slipped in among them? How were they described?

e. Of what three things did Jude remind his hearers?

f. What three things did Jude say these dreamers did?

g. What did Enoch prophesy about the dreamers?

h. What did the apostles of the Lord Jesus foretell about the last days?

i. How does Jude end this book in verses twenty-four and twenty-five?

3. Psalms 127:1-5
   a. What happens if the house is not built by the Lord?

   b. What happens if the Lord doesn't watch over the city?

   c. Who grants sleep to those he loves?

   d. What does the Psalmist say about sons and children?

   e. What are like arrows in the hand of a warrior?

   f. What man is blessed?

   g. Who will not be put to shame?

4. Proverbs 29:1-5
   a. What does the rod of correction do? What happens to a child left to himself?

   b. What happens when the wicked thrive? What will the righteous see?

   c. What two results will one get when he disciplines his son?

STUDY QUESTIONS FOR DECEMBER 9

1. Joel 1:1-3:21
   a. Who is the prophet in this book?

   b. What question did Joel ask the elders? Who were they to tell about these happenings?

   c. Who invaded God's land? How was this entity described?

   d. What did he tell the farmers and the vine growers to do?

   e. List at least four things that Joel told the priest to do.

   f. In chapter two what was to be done with the trumpet? What was this to announce?

   g. How was the mighty army described in chapter two verse two?

   h. What happened to the nations at the sight of the mighty army?

   i. What were the people asked to do in chapter two verse twelve and thirteen?

   j. When the Lord was jealous of his land and took pity on his people, what did the Lord do and how did he reply to them in chapter two, verse nineteen?

   k. What is asked of the people in chapter two verse twenty-three? Why were they to do this?

   l. What would the people know when the Lord did these promised things?

   m. What would happen to the sun and moon before the coming of the great and dreadful day of the Lord?

   n. What was God going to do to the nations at the time he restores the fortuncs of Judah and Jerusalem?

   o. In chapter three verse sixteen, what will the Lord do?

   p. What promise was made to Judah and Jerusalem?

2. Revelations 1:1-20
   a. To which servant did God give his revelation?

   b. Who would be blessed?

c. What blessing does John pronounce on the seven churches?

d. Who will see Christ at his coming?

e. Where was John when he received this revelation?

f. What did the voice instruct John to do with a scroll?

g. List the seven churches.

h. What did John see when he looked around to see the voice that was speaking to him?

i. How was the man dressed?

j. How did John describe this man?

k. What did the man say to John?

l. What were the seven stars? What were the seven lampstands?

3. Psalms 128:1-6
a. Who are blessed?

b. What blessing will the laborer receive?

c. What will his wife be like?

d. What will his sons be like?

e. What three things does the Psalmist wish for his hearers?

f. What does he wish for Israel?

4. Proverbs 29:18
a. What happens when there is no revelation?

b. Who is blessed?

STUDY QUESTIONS FOR DECEMBER 10

1. Amos 1:1-3:15
   a. Where did Amos, a shepherd, live?

   b. When were these words given? Who was king of Judah and who was king of Israel?

   c. What was going to happen to the pastures of the shepherds?

   d. For how many sins of Damascus would the Lord not turn back his anger? Why would God not turn back his anger?

   e. What was God going to do to the walls of Gaza? What was God going to do to the king of Ashdod?

   f. How long was God going to turn his hand against Ekron?

   g. What did Tyre do to bring the wrath of God?

   h. What was the Lord going to do to Tyre?

   i. What did Edom do to displease the Lord?

   j. What did Ammon do? What was his punishment?

   k. What did Moab do? How would she go down?

   l. What did Judah do? How would they be punished?

   m. What six things did Israel do that displeased the Lord?

   n. What happened to even their bravest warriors?

   o. What was God going to do with the altars of Bethel, the winter house, the summer house, the houses adorned with ivory, and the mansions of the house of Jacob?

2. Revelations 2:1-17
   a. To what angel was John asked to write in the first of chapter two?

   b. From whom is this message given?

   c. For what five things was the church in Ephesus commended?

   d. What one thing was held against Ephesus?

e. What three things was the church at Ephsus asked to do?

f. What would happen to them if they failed to repent?

g. What was the next church to be addressed?

h. What did the Lord know about this church?

i. What was his encouragement to the ones that were afraid?

j. What was one that had an ear to do?

k. What was the last church to be addressed in today's reading?

l. Where did these people live?

m. What two things were held against this church? What were they to do?

n. What two things will be given to the one that overcomes?

3. Psalms 129:1-8
    a. What would Israel say?

    b. To what was the Psalmist referring when he said, "Plowmen have plowed my back and made their furrows long?"

    c. Who is righteous?

    d. What did the Psalmist desire to happen to all who hate Zion?

    e. What did he ask that they be like?

    f. May those that pass by not say what?

4. Proverbs 29:19-20
    a. Why can a servant not be corrected by mere words?

    b. What is said about a man that speaks in haste?

1. Amos 4:1-6:14

    a. What did Amos say about these women?

    b. What was going to happen to these women?

    c. What did Amos say to the Israelites?

    d. Did the Israelites return to God when he gave them empty stomachs and lack of bread in every town?

    e. Did God treat all fields the same?

    f. Beside drought, what did God use against their gardens, vineyards, fig and olive trees?

    g. Then did they return to God?

    h. What other things did God do to Israel to get them to turn to him?

    i. In chapter four verse twelve, what did God say that Israel was to do?

    j. What were the Israelite to do to live? What did God say about seeking help from Bethel, Gilgal, and Beersheba?

    k. What two things will happen to the one that tramples on the poor and forces the poor to give him grain?

    l. What will happen when a man seeks good and not evil?

    m. What should a man love? What should a man hate?

    n. In chapter five verses sixteen and seventeen, what did God promise would happen to his people?

    o. What did the Sovereign Lord abhor? What did he detest? What was he going to do?

    p. What did the people turn justice into? What did they turn righteousness into?

    q. What did the Lord God Almighty declare?

2. Revelation 2:18-3:6

    a. To which angel was John now asked to write?

b.   How was the Son of God described in this passage?

c.   What did the Son of God say about the church at Thyatira?

d.   What did he have against the church at Thyatira?

e.   What punishment was Jezebel going to receive? What would happen to the ones that committed adultery with her?

f.   What would the churches know when they see this punishment take place?

g.   What will happen to him who overcomes and does God's will to the end?

h.   What does he tell the one that has an ear to do?

i.   Which church does he talk to next?

j.   What reputation did they have? Did they deserve that reputation? What were they told to do?

k.   Had everyone in Sardis soiled their clothes?

3.   Psalms 130:1-8
       a.   From where did the Psalmist cry?

       b.   What did the Psalmist request from the Lord?

       c.   Where can one find forgiveness?

       d.   Where did the Psalmist put his hope?

       e.   Who will redeem Israel from all their sins?

4.   Proverbs 29:21-22
       a.   What happens if a man pampers his servant from youth?

       b.   What does an angry man do? What does a hot tempered man do?

STUDY QUESTIONS FOR DECEMBER 12

1.   Amos 7:1-9:15
      a.   What did the Sovereign Lord show Amos?

      b.   What did Amos cry out to the Sovereign Lord?

      c.   By what was the Sovereign Lord calling for judgement?

      d.   What was Amos' response?

      e.   What did Amos see in chapter seven verse eight?

      f.   How did the people of Israel measure up to this instrument?

      g.   What did Amaziah say about Amos?

      h.   What did Amaziah tell Amos to do?

      i.   How did Amos answer Amazaiah?

      j.   What did Amos see in chapter eight?

      k.   What was going to happen to the songs of the temple?

      l.   When was the Lord going to make the sun go down?

      m.   How were the religious feasts going to change? How about their singing?

      n.   What was this famine going to be like?

      o.   In chapter nine, where did Amos see the Lord standing?

      p.   How many would escape God?

      q.   Whose eyes are on the sinful kingdom?

      r.   What was going to happen to the reaper? The planter?

      s.   What was God going to do with his exiled people, Israel?

      t.   What were his people going to do to the ruined cities?

2.   Revelation 3:7-22
      a.   What church is addressed now?

b.   Whose words are these?

c.   What did God say about their strength?

d.   What was God going to do to those that were of the synagogue of Satan that claimed to be Jews but they were not?

e.   What was God going to do for this church since they kept his command and endured patiently?

f.   Who was going to be tested?

g.   What was God going to do for the one that overcomes?

h.   What is the one that has an ear to do?

i.   What church is written to next? Whose words are these?

j.   What was the problem of this church?

k.   What was God going to do with them?

l.   What does God do to those that love him?

3.   Psalms 13:1-3
       a.   What did the Psalmist say about his heart?

       b.   What did he say about his eyes?

       c.   What did he do about great matters?

       d.   What did he do about his soul?

       e.   Where should Israel's hope be placed?

       f.   When were they to place this hope?

4.   Proverbs 29:23
       a.   What does a man's pride do to him?

       b.   What does a man with a lowly spirit gain?

1. Obadiah 1:1-21
    a. Who had the vision in this book?

    b. Who was this vision about?

    c. What was the envoy that was sent to the nations told to say?

    d. What was the Lord going to do to Edom? What had their heart done to them?

    e. What did the people of Edom that lived in the heights say to themselves?

    f. What did the Lord declare that he was going to do to them even though they soared like the eagle and made their nest among the stars?

    g. In verse six, what was going to happen to Esau? What would their allies do to them? What about their friends?

    h. "In that day", what was the Lord going to do to the wise men of Edom and the men of understanding in the mountains of Esau?

    i. What would happen to the warriors of Teman?

    j. What would happen to them because of the violence against their brother Jacob? What had they done while strangers carried off Jacob's wealth?

    k. What eight things does Obadiah list that Edom should not do?

    l. What would Edom reap in "the Day of the Lord"?

    m. What were the people of the Negev going to possess? What were the people from the foothills going to possess? What was Benjamin going to possess?

    n. The last verse says that deliverers will go up on Mount Zion to govern the mountains of Esau, but to whom does the kingdom belong?

2. Revelation 4:1-11
    a. What did John see when he looked?

    b. What did the voice he heard sound like? What did the voice say?

    c. What did John see in the heaven while he was in the Spirit?

    d. What kind of appearance did the one that sat on the throne have?

e.   What encircled the throne? What surrounded the throne?

f.   How many creatures were in the center around the throne? With what were they covered?

g.   What was each living creature like? What did all have?

h.   Of what was their Lord and God worthy?

3.   Psalms 132:1-18
    a.   What is the Lord asked to remember about David?

    b.   What kind of a vow did David make to the Lord?

    c.   What did they hear in Ephrathah?

    d.   What oath did the Lord swear to David that he will not revoke?

    e.   Why had the Lord chosen Zion?

    f.   How long would this be the resting place for the Lord?

    g.   With what was the Lord going to bless Zion?

    h.   How was the Lord going to clothe the priests? How was the Lord going to clothe the enemies of David?

4.   Proverbs 29:24-25
    a.   What happens to the accomplice of a thief?

    b.   What will fear of men prove to be? What will happen to the one who trusts in the Lord?

STUDY QUESTIONS FOR DECEMBER 14

1. Jonah 1:1-4:11
   a. Where was Jonah to go? What was he to do?

   b. Where did Jonah go? What did he do? Did he have a smooth voyage?

   c. What questions did the sailors ask Jonah?

   d. What continued to happen to the sea? Now what additional question did the sailors ask Jonah?

   e. What happened to the sea when the sailors threw Jonah into the sea?

   f. What did the Lord provide for Jonah?

   g. What did the Lord command the fish to do when Jonah remembered the Lord and prayed?

   h. What did the word of the Lord say when it came to Jonah the second time?

   i. What did Jonah proclaim the first day that he entered Nineveh?

   j. How did the Ninevites respond? What did the king do?

   k. What did God do when he saw that the people turned from their evil ways?

   l. Was Jonah happy about the great revival that happened? Why did he have that reaction?

   m. What question did the Lord ask Jonah?

   n. What did Jonah do next?

   o. What did God provide for Jonah? Did Jonah like this provision? What happened at dawn the next day? What did Jonah say?

   p. What illustration did God use to show Jonah how he should care about Nineveh?

2. Revelations 5:1-14
   a. What did the Revelator see in the right hand of him who sat on the throne? What was on both sides of this?

   b. What did the loud voice say?

c. Why did the Revelator weep and weep?

d. What did the elder say to the Revelator?

e. What did he see? Where was the person standing? What encircled him?

f. How was he described?

g. What did he do with the scroll?

h. How many angels were there? What did the angels sing in a loud voice?

i. What did the four living creatures say? What did the elders do?

3. Psalms 133:1-3
    a. What did the Psalmist say was good and pleasant?

    b. What did he say this was like?

    c. Whose beard did he mention?

    d. On what else did the oil run down?

    e. What else does the Psalmist liken to brothers living together in unity?

    f. Where does the Lord bestow his blessing?

    g. What is the blessing that the Lord bestows?

4. Proverbs 29:26-27
    a. Where does a man get justice?

    b. Who detests the dishonest?

    c. Who detests the upright?

STUDY QUESTIONS FOR DECEMBER 15

1. Micah 1:1-4:13
    a. During whose reign did the word of the Lord come to Micah?

    b. What did his vision concern?

    c. What happens to the mountains beneath the Lord? What happened to the valleys beneath the Lord? What caused this judgement?

    d. What was the Lord going to make of Samaria?

    e. Where did Samaria gather her gifts?

    f. Who was the beginning of sin to the daughter of Zion? Where were the transgressions of Israel found?

    g. In chapter two, to whom does he say "woe"? Why did they carry out what they planned?

    h. Therefore, what does the Lord say to them?

    i. How did God's people act in chapter two, verses eight and nine?

    j. How did Micah describe the rulers of the house of Israel in chapter three, verses two and three?

    k. To whom were the people going to cry out? Would they be answered? Why?

    l. What was going to happen to the seers? How about the diviners? What would they do?

    m. What was going to happen to Zion, Jerusalem, and the temple because of the leaders, the priests, and the prophets of Israel?

    n. In chapter four, what was going to happen to the mountain of the Lord's temple in the last days?

    o. What is God going to give to the daughter of Zion so that she can break to pieces many nations?

2. Revelation 6:1-17
    a. In this chapter, what did the Revelator see first as he watched?

    b. What color was the first horse? What did the rider hold and what was he given?

c. What was he bent on?

d. What did the second creature say? What was the color of the second horse? What kind of power was given to the rider?

e. What color was the third horse? What was the rider holding? What did the voice that he heard among the four living creatures say?

f. What color was the fourth horse? What was the name of the rider? What was following close behind him?

g. How is the power described that was given to them?

h. What did he see when the fifth seal was broken? What did the souls cry out?

i. What six things took place when the sixth seal was opened?

j. What did the kings, the princes, the generals, the rich, the mighty, and every slave and free man do?

3. Psalms 134:1-3
    a. Who was asked to praise the Lord?

    b. When did these men minister in the house of the lord?

    c. What were they to do in the house of the Lord?

    d. What did the Psalmist ask the Lord, the maker of heaven and earth to do?

4. Proverbs 30:1-4
    a. What four things did the man admit to Ithiel and Ucal?

    b. What did he say about the Holy One?

1.   Micah 5:1-7:20
      a.   To what is the prophecy in Micah chapter five verse two referring?

      b.   How long would Israel be abandoned?

      c.   How far would the greatness of the promised one reach?

      d.   Whom did Micah say would be like a lion among the beasts of the forest, like a young lion among flocks of sheep, which mauls and mangles as it goes and no one can rescue?

      e.   What was God going to do about their witchcraft? What was God going to do about their carved images and sacred stones?

      f.   In chapter six, what had God done for Israel?

      g.   What was the answer to the question that Micah asked, "With what shall I come before the Lord and bow down before the exalted God?"?

      h.   What things are listed in chapter six verses fourteen and fifteen that the people will suffer because of their sins?

      i.   In chapter seven what happened to the godly? How many upright men remained?

      j.   What family relationships have gone astray? Who are a man's enemies?

      k.   How did Micah watch and for whom did he wait? Why did he wait for him?

      l.   Why would the earth become desolate?

      m.   What did God say he would do as in the days that Israel came out of Egypt?

      n.   After Micah says, "Who is a God like you?" what things arc listed that God does for his people?

2.   Revelations 7:1-17
      a.   Where were the four angels standing that John saw? What were they doing?

      b.   What did the fifth angel have? What did he say?

      c.   How many were sealed? How many people were from each tribe?

      d.   How many were in the next great multitude of people that he saw?

e.   What nation did these people come from?

f.   What were they wearing? What were they holding in their hands?

g.   What did John answer when the elder asked him who the people that wore the white robes were and where they came from?

h.   What did the elder have to say about the people in this multitude?

i.   Who would spread his tent over the multitude? What other things will this person do for the multitude?

3.   Psalms 135:1-21
        a.   How does this Psalm begin and end?

        b.   Why should they praise the Lord?

        c.   "I know that our God is greater than" what?

        d.   Who struck down the firstborn of Egypt?

        e.   What were the idols of the nation made of and how were they made?

4.   Proverbs 30:5-6
        a.   What is said about every word of God?

        b.   What is God to those that take refuge in him?

        c.   What happens if one adds to God's word?

STUDY QUESTIONS FOR DECEMBER 17

1. Nahum 1:1-3:19
    a. What does this oracle of Nahum concern?

    b. What does he say about God's anger and power?

    c. What do the mountains do before God?

    d. What does chapter one, verse seven say about the Lord?

    e. What was the Lord going to do to Nineveh?

    f. From where was one who plots evil against the Lord going to come?

    g. What was the Lord going to do for Judah?

    h. What command did the Lord give concerning Nineveh?

    i. In chapter one, verse fifteen what did the Lord tell Judah to do? What promise did he make?

    j. How were the soldiers, warriors, and the chariots that come against Nineveh described?

    k. What did he say that Nineveh was like?

    l. What was going to happen to the voices of Nineveh's messengers?

    m. In chapter three verse seven what would the ones that see Nineveh do?

    n. What were Nineveh's fortresses like?

    o. What was said about her troops? What about the gates of the land?

    p. To what extent did they increase the number of their merchants?

    q. To what did he liken the guards?

    r. What were people that hear about Nineveh going to do?

2. Revelations 8:1-13
    a. What happened when he opened the seventh seal?

    b. What was given to the seven angels?

c.   What was the angel with the golden censer given?

d.   What went up from the angel's hand?

e.   What happened when the angel hurled the golden censer on the earth?

f.   What was burned up when the first angel sounded his trumpet?

g.   What happened to the sea when the second angel sounded his trumpet?

h.   What was the name of the star that fell from the sky when the third angel sounded his trumpet?

i.   How much of the waters turned bitter?

j.   What happened when the fourth trumpet sounded?

k.   What did the eagle call out?

3.   Psalms 136:1-26
     a.   In this chapter, how many time is the phrase, "His love endures forever", used?

     b.   Why should one give praise to God?

     c.   Who alone does great wonders?

     d.   Who struck down the first born of Egypt and brought Israel out from among them.

     e.   Who remembered them in their low estate? To whom were they to give thanks?

4.   Proverbs 30:7-9
     a.   What two things are requested of God?

     b.   What might happen if God gave him too much?

1. Habakkuk 1:1-3:19
   a. What prophet received this oracle?

   b. What four questions does the prophet ask the Lord?

   c. In chapter one verse five what does the Lord tell the prophet to do?

   d. What was God going to do with the Babylonians? How were the Babylonians described?

   e. In chapter one verse thirteen, what does the prophet say about God? What two questions does he ask God?

   f. In the first part of chapter two, what did the prophet say he was going to do?

   g. What did God tell him to do?

   h. How will the righteous live?

   i. In chapter two the word "woe" is used five times, what are the five times?

   j. Where is the Lord? What does the world need to do before him?

   k. Where was the prophet when he prayed the prayer of chapter three?

   l. What does he say about God's glory and his splendor?

   m. What did God do to the leader of the land of wickedness when his warriors stormed out to scatter Judah?

   n. What did the prophet's heart and lips do as he observed God's wrath poured out?

   o. What was the prophet going to do even though the fig tree did not bud and there are no grapes on the vine?

   p. Who was the prophet's strength? Like what did the Lord make the prophet's feet?

2. Revelation 9:1-21
   a. What did John see when the fifth angel sounded his trumpet?

   b. What happened when the he opened the abyss?

   c. What happened to the sun and sky when the abyss was opened?

d.   What did the locusts attack?

e.   Did the locusts have power to kill humans?

f.   Who did the locusts have as a king over them?

g.   After the first woe is past, how many are to come?

h.   How much of mankind did the four angels kill?

i.   Did the rest of mankind that were not killed repent?

3.   Psalms 137:1-9
a.   What did the Psalmist do beside the rivers of Babylon? What were they remembering?

b.   What did their tormentors demand?

c.   What question did he ask concerning the songs of the Lord in a foreign land?

d.   What did the Psalmist say should happen to him if he forgot Jerusalem and if he did not consider Jerusalem his highest joy?

e.   What did he ask the Lord to remember?

f.   To what was the daughter of Babylon doomed?

g.   What was the attitude of the one who repays the daughters of Babylon?

4.   Proverbs 30:10
a.   What is said about slandering a servant?

b.   What did he say would happen to the slanderer?

STUDY QUESTIONS FOR DECEMBER 19

1. Zephaniah 1:1 - 3:20
    a. Who was king of Judah when Zephaniah received the word of the Lord?

    b. What was God going to sweep away from the face of the earth?

    c. What will the wicked have left?

    d. Who was God going to stretch out his hand against?

    e. Why were the people to be silent before the Lord?

    f. What was God going to do on the day of the Lord's sacrifice?

    g. Why would God punish all who avoid stepping on the threshold?

    h. What was going to happen to the merchants of the city?

    i. How does Zephaniah describe the punishment that will come on the people chapter one verses seventeen and eighteen?

    j. What did he instruct the humble to do?

    k. Did God pay attention to the insults of Moab and the taunts of the Ammonites? How was God going to punish them?

    l. What did God promise his people in regard to Moab and the Ammonites?

    m. In chapter two verse fifteen, what did Nineveh think of herself? What was God's judgement on her?

    n. What has God done to nations?

    o. What was God going to do to the lips of the people? Why was he going to do that? What was God's promise to Israel?

    p. "The _____ your _____ is with you, he is _____ to save." Zephaniah chapter three verse seventeen

2. Revelation 10:1 - 11
    a. How does John describe the angel he saw?
        i. Robed -
        ii. Above his head -
        iii. Face -

  iv. Legs -
  v. Holding -
  vi. Planted his right foot -
  vii. Left foot on -
  viii. He gave a -
  ix. When he shouted -

 b. Why did he refrain from writing?

 c. By whom did the angel swear?

 d. What did the angel say?

 e. What did the voice instruct John to do?

 f. What did the angel tell John to do with the scroll?

 g. How did the scroll taste? What happened after he ate it?

 h. Then what was John told?

3. Psalms 138:1 - 8
 a. How was the Psalmist going to praise the Lord?

 b. How was he going to bow down?

 c. What happened when the Psalmist called on God?

 d. What was his desire for the kings of the earth when they hear God's words

 e. What does the Lord do to the lowly? What about the proud?

 f. What does the Lord do with his hand for the Psalmist?

 g. How long does the love of God endure?

4. Proverbs 30:11-14
 a. How is the self righteous person described?

1. Haggai 1:1-2:23
    a. When did the first word of the Lord in Haggai come?

    b. To whom was this word of the Lord sent?

    c. What did the people say? What did the word of the Lord say about this?

    d. What did the Lord tell the people to do?

    e. What happened when the people planted much, ate, drank, put on clothes, and earned wages?

    f. What did the Lord tell them to do with the timbers from the mountain?

    g. What happened when they expected much? What happened with what they brought home? Why was this happening to them? For what did the Lord call?

    h. Did Zerubbabel, the high priest, and the whole remnant obey the Lord? From the time the message was given, how long did it take the people to respond?

    i. What three questions does the word of the Lord that came on the twenty-first day of the seventh month, ask the people?

    j. What did the Lord say he would do in a "little while"?

    k. How would the glory of the present house compare with the former house? What would the Lord grant in this place?

    l. What two questions was the prophet, Haggai to ask the priests?

    m. What did the Lord say through the prophet Haggai about the people and this nation?

    n. In chapter two verse twenty-three, what was going to happen to Zerubbabel?

2. Revelation 11:1-19
    a. What was John given?

    b. What was he to do with it? Who was he to count?

    c. What was excluded? Why was it excluded?

    d. Who gave power to the two witnesses? How long were they to prophesy? How were they clothed?

e.   What happened to anyone that tried to harm the witnesses?

f.   What three things did these witnesses have power to do?

g.   What happened to the witnesses when they finished their testimony? What happened after three and a half days?

h.   What did the voice from heaven say to them? What happened at that very hour?

i.   What did the twenty-four elders do? What was seen in God's temple in heaven? Then what came?

3.   Psalm 139:1-24
a.   In the first six verses of this chapter, list the things that the Lord knows about the Psalmist. How did the Psalmist feel about this knowledge?

b.   What places did the Psalmist try to hide from God but found that he was there?

c.   How did the Psalmist describe how he was made in verses thirteen through sixteen?

d.   What did the Psalmist consider precious? What did the Psalmist say about God's enemies?

e.   In the last two verses of this chapter, what six things does the Psalmist ask of the Lord?

4.   Proverbs 30:15-16
a.   What do the two daughters of the leech cry?

b.   What three things are never satisfied?

STUDY QUESTIONS FOR DECEMBER 21

1. Zechariah 1:1-21
    a. Who was Zechariah's grandfather?

    b. With whom was the Lord very angry?

    c. What did the Lord tell Zechariah to tell the people?

    d. Had the forefathers listened to the earlier prophets when they said, "Turn from your evil ways and your evil practices."?

    e. What three questions did the Lord ask the people through Zechariah?

    f. How did the people respond to Zechariah's message?

    g. What happened on the twenty-fourth day of the eleventh month, the month of Shebat, in the second year of Darius?

    h. What three color horses did Zechariah see in his night vision?

    i. What question did Zechariah ask?

    j. What answer did the angel give?

    k. What did the man standing among the myrtle trees say?

    l. What did they find when they went throughout the earth?

    m. What did the angel of the Lord ask the Lord?

    n. How did the Lord speak to the angel?

    o. How was the Lord going to return to Jerusalem? What would be stretched out over Jerusalem?

    p. What does the Lord say about his towns and Zion and Jerusalem?

    q. What were the four horns? What were the craftsmen going to do?

2. Revelations 12:1-13a
    a. What great and wondrous sign appeared in heaven?

    b. What other sign appeared in heaven? What did his tail do?

347

c. Why did he stand in front of the woman who was about to give birth?

d. Where did the woman go? Who prepared a place for her? How long will she be there?

e. Who was fighting in the war in heaven?

f. What happened to the great dragon and his angels?

g. Why is the devil filled with fury?

h. What did the dragon do when he saw that he had been hurled to the earth?

i. What was the woman given that she might fly to the place prepared for her?

j. What did the dragon do when he became enraged with the woman?

3. Psalms 140:1-13
   a. What two things does the Psalmist ask for in the first two verses?

   b. How does the Psalmist describe the tongues of violent men and what is on their lips?

   c. What did the proud men do to the Psalmist?

   d. In verse eight, what two things does the Psalmist ask that the Lord not do? Why did he ask that?

   e. In verse twelve, what does the Psalmist know about the Lord?

4. Proverbs 30:17
   a. What will happen to the eye that mocks a father and scorns obedience to a mother?

STUDY QUESTIONS FOR DECEMBER 22

1. Zechariah 2:1-3:10
   a. What did Zachariah see?

   b. What did Zachariah ask?

   c. What did the man say?

   d. Why was Jerusalem going to be without walls? Who was to become a wall of fire around Jerusalem?

   e. Where had the Lord scattered his people?

   f. To whom was the Lord calling?

   g. Who was the Lord sending against the nations that had plundered them?

   h. Who was the apple of the Lord's eye?

   i. To whom was the Lord going to raise his hand? How was he going to raise his hand?

   j. What did he ask the daughters of Zion to do. Why did he ask them to do that?

   k. Who did Zechariah see standing before the angel of the Lord?

   l. How was he dressed?

   m. What did the angel say to do with his clothes?

   n. With what were they going to replace his clothes? What did they put on his head?

   o. What did the angel say to him?

   p. What charge did the angel give to him?

   q. What was the Lord going to do in a single day?

   r. "In that day," what would each one do?

2. Revelation 13:1b-3:10
   a. How is the first beast in this chapter described?

   b. Who gave the beast his power and his throne and great authority?

c. What happened to the wound that seemed to be fatal?

d. Who followed the beast? Who did they worship?

e. How long did this beast utter proud words and blasphemes?

f. What was this beast given power to do?

g. How was the next beast described?

h. What kind of miracles did this beast perform? How did he use this power?

i. What did he force everyone to do?

j. What is man's number?

3. Psalms 141:1-10
   a. What does the Psalmist desire that his prayer be like?

   b. What does the Psalmist ask that the lifting of his hands be like?

   c. What did he want God to do for his mouth, his lips and his heart?

   d. When the Psalmist says, "Let me not eat their delicacies," to whom does "their" refer?

   e. What was the Psalmist's prayer against?

   f. On whom were the eyes of the Psalmist fixed?

4. Proverbs 30:18-20
   a. What four things does the author find amazing and that he does not understand?

   b. What does the adulteress say?

1.   Zechariah 4:1-5:11
      a.   What did the angel do when he returned?

      b.   What question did the angel ask Zechariah?

      c.   What did Zechariah answer the angel?

      d.   What question did Zechariah ask the angel?

      e.   What did the angel say these things were?

      f.   What was the mighty mountain going to become before Zerubbabal?

      g.   What was going to happen to the captives?

      h.   What promise was made about Zerubbabel? What would the people know when this promise came to pass?

      i.   When will the men rejoice?

      j.   What were the seven lights?

      k.   What did the angel say were the two olive trees?

      l.   What did Zechariah see next? What was the size of what he saw?

      m.   What was written on the object that he saw?

      n.   Where will the Lord Almighty send it?

      o.   What will it do to the house?

      p.   What did the angel say to Zechariah? What was Zechariah's question? What was the angel's answer to this question?

      q.   What was in the basket when the lid was raised?

      r.   What did this represent? What did the angel do to it?

      s.   Where were they taking the basket?

2.   Revelations 14:1-20
      a.   Who did John see in verse one? Where was he standing?

b.   What was written on the foreheads of the one hundred forty-four thousand?

c.   How did John describe the sound he heard from heaven?

d.   What kind of a song did the one hundred forty-four thousand sing before the four living creatures and the elders? Who could learn the song?

e.   How did the one hundred forty-four thousand act? From where were they purchased?

f.   What did the next angel have? What did the angel say to the people?

g.   What did an angel say about Babylon?

h.   What will happen to the one that worships the beast and his image?

i.   What did the voice from heaven tell John to write?

j.   What does the last angel in this chapter do with the sickle?

3.   Psalms 142:1-7
        a.   To whom did the Psalmist cry?

        b.   To whom did the Psalmist pour out his complaint?

        c.   Who knew the Psalmist's ways?

        d.   Who hid a snare for the Psalmist?

        e.   To whom did the Psalmist cry?

        f.   What request did the Psalmist make in verse six? Why did he make this request?

4.   Proverbs 30:21-23
        a.   Under what four things can the earth not bear up?

STUDY QUESTIONS FOR DECEMBER 25

1. Zechariah 8:1-23
   a. Who is the word of the Lord talking about in this chapter?

   b. How did the Lord feel about her?

   c. Where was the Lord going to dwell?

   d. What will Jerusalem be called? What will the mountain of the Lord Almighty be called?

   e. Who would sit in the streets of Jerusalem with cane in hand? With what would the city streets be filled?

   f. What did the Lord Almighty say in verse six?

   g. From where was the Lord Almighty going to save his people? What was he going to do for his people?

   h. Why did the Lord say that they should let their hands be strong?

   i. Why could no one go about their business safely? What had God done that caused this to happen?

   j. What did the Lord declare that he was going to do differently now?

   k. What was Judah and Israel going to be now instead an object of cursing among the nations?

   l. What two things did the Lord tell them to do? What two things did the Lord tell them not to do? Why should they do and not do these things?

   m. How were the fasts going to change?

   n. What were they to love?

   o. Why were many peoples and powerful nations going to come to Jerusalem?

   p. In verse twenty-three, why did the Lord Almighty say that in those days ten men from all languages and nations will take hold of one Jew by the hem of his robe and say, "Let us go with you,"?

2. Revelations 16:1-21
   a. What did the loud voice from the temple tell the seven angels to do?

b.   What happened when the first angel poured out his bowl on the land?

c.   What happened when the second angel poured out his bowl on the sea?

d.   What happened with the third angel? What did the angel in charge of the waters say?

e.   What happened when the fourth bowl was poured out? Did the people repent and glorify God?

f.   How did men respond to the punishment of the fifth bowl?

g.   What happened to the river Euphrates? What did the spirits that came out of the mouth of the dragon, the mouth of the beast and the mouth of the false prophet, look like?

h.   In verse eighteen, what four things happened from the pouring out of the seventh bowl?

i.   What happened to the every island, the mountains, and the sky?

3.   Psalms 144:1-15
      a.   What did the Psalmist say his Lord did for his hands and his fingers?

      b.   What did the Psalmist say God was to him.

      c.   What was the Psalmist's question of the Lord, the Son of Man?

      d.   The Psalmist said man is like a breath, what did he say his days were like?

      e.   What seven requests did the Psalmist make of the Lord?

      f.   What did the Psalmist promise to do with the ten-stringed lyre?

      g.   From whom did the Psalmist ask to be delivered and rescued?

      h.   Of what did he say their mouths were full?

      i.   With what will their barns be filled?

      j.   What people were blessed

4.   Proverbs 30:29-31
      a.   What four things move with a stately manner?

STUDY QUESTIONS FOR DECEMBER 26

1. Zechariah 9:1-17
    a. In this chapter, who is the word of the Lord against?

    b. On what four cities will the word of the Lord rest?

    c. Who built herself a stronghold and heaped up silver like dust and gold like the dirt of the streets?

    d. What was going to happen to their possessions?

    e. How would she be consumed?

    f. What will Ashkelon do? Gaza? Ekron?

    g. Who will occupy Ashdod?

    h. Against whom was God going to defend his house?

    i. When will an oppressor overrun God's people again?

    j. Why should the daughter of Zion rejoice and shout?

    k. How far will God's rule extend?

    l. What will the blood of the covenant accomplish?

    m. Who will appear over the sons of Zion? What will his arrow do?

    n. Who will shield them?

    o. In verse fifteen, what will the sons of Zion do?

    p. Who is going to save them on that day?

    q. Where and how will they sparkle?

    r. What remark did Zechariah make about the sons of Zion in verse seventeen?

    s. What will make the young men thrive?

    t. What will make the young women thrive?

2. Revelation 17:1-18

a.   How many angels were there?

b.   How many angels came to him in this passage?

c.   What title was written on the forehead of the woman sitting on a scarlet beast in the desert?

d.   On whose blood was this woman drunk?

e.   What was Zechariah's reaction to seeing this woman drunk on blood?

f.   What does the seven heads of the beast represent?

g.   What did the ten horns represent?

h.   To whom do the kings give their power and authority?

i.   Could the beast overcome the lamb?

j.   What did the waters, where the prostitute sat, represent?

k.   What did the woman represent?

3.   Psalms 145: 1-21
a.   Who was the Psalmist going to exalt?

b.   How long will he praise God's name? How often will he praise God?

c.   Who can fathom God's greatness?

d.   How is the Lord described in verses eight and nine?

e.   What will praise God in verse ten?

f.   How long will God's kingdom last?

g.   Which creatures were to praise God's holy name for ever and ever?

4.   Proverbs 30:32
a.   What should one do if he has played the fool and exalted himself or planned evil?

STUDY QUESTIONS FOR DECEMBER 27

1.   Zechariah 10:1-11:17
        a.   For what does Zechariah tell the people to ask God?

        b.   Who makes the storm clouds and gives showers of rain to men?

        c.   What do idols speak? What do the diviners see? What about the dreams that they tell?

        d.   Because of this, what do the people do?

        e.   What four things will come from Judah?

        f.   What was the Lord going to do for the house of Judah and the house of Joseph?

        g.   What will the Ephraimites become like?

        h.   From where was the Lord going to bring the Ephraimites back and from where would he gather them? Where was he going to bring them?

        i.   What was going to happen to Assyria's pride and Egypt's scepter?

        j.   What was Lebananon told to do? Why were they told to do this?

        k.   Why was the pine tree told to wail? What about the oaks of Bashan?

        l.   What happened to the pasture lands of the shepherds? What about the lush thicket of Jordan?

        m.   To whom was the Lord going to hand over everyone?

        n.   How did the flock react to the Lord? What did the Lord say he would no longer be to the people?

        o.   To what is the thirty pieces of silver referring in chapter eleven verse twelve through verse thirteen?

        p.   What is said about the worthless shepherd?

2.   Revelation 18:1-24
        a.   What did John see coming down from heaven? How was the earth illuminated?

        b.   What was fallen? What had she become? What had the nations drunk?

  c. What did the kings of the earth do with her? What about the merchants of the earth?

  d. What did the voice from heaven tell God's people to do? Why did the voice tell them to do that?

  e. What will the kings do when they see her burning?

  f. How were all the nations led astray? What was found in her?

3. Psalms 146:1-10
  a. How long was the Psalmist going to praise the Lord? How long would he sing praises to his God?

  b. In whom should people not put their trust? Why should they not trust in them?

  c. Who is blessed? Who is the maker of heaven and earth? Who remains faithful?

  d. What does the Lord do for the oppressed? What about the hungry? What does the Lord do for the prisoners?

  e. What does he do for the blind?

  f. What does he do for the ones that are bowed down?

  g. What does he do for the alien? What about the fatherless and the widow?

  h. What does the Lord do to the ways of the wicked?

4. Proverbs 30:33
  a. What does churning milk produce?

  b. What does twisting the nose produce? What does stirring up anger produce?

1.   Zechariah 12:1-13:9
      a.   What does the word of the Lord concern in this reading?

      b.   In describing the Lord, what three things does Zechariah say that the Lord does?

      c.   What does the Lord declare that he is going to make Jerusalem?

      d.   Who was going to gather against Jerusalem?

      e.   What will happen to the ones that try to move Jerusalem?

      f.   What was God going to do with the horses and riders of the nations coming against Jerusalem and Judah?

      g.   What will the leaders of Judah say in their hearts?

      h.   What was God going to set out to do to the nations that attack Jerusalem?

      i.   What was God going to pour out on the house of David and the inhabitants of Jerusalem?

      j.   In chapter twelve verse ten, what does God say about the house of David looking on God? To whom does this section refer?

      k.   What will the opened fountain do to the house of David and the inhabitants of Jerusalem?

      l.   What was the Lord going to do to the names of the idols in the land?

      m.   What was the Lord gong to do to both the prophets and the spirit of impurity?

      n.   What happens to the sheep when the shepherd is struck with the sword?

      o.   In the whole land, how many will be struck down and perish? How many will be left in it?

2.   Revelation 19:1-21
      a.   After this, what did he hear?

      b.   What did the twenty-four elders and the four living creatures do? What did they cry?

      c.   What did the voice that came from the throne say?

d.   What was given to the bride of the lamb to wear?

e.   Who did the angel say were blessed?

f.   When the angel said this, what did John do? What did the angel say to John?

g.   What was said about the rider of the white horse?

h.   What was written on his robe and his thigh?

i.   What happened to the beast and the false prophet?

3.   Psalms 147:1-20
       a.   What does the Psalmist tell the people to do?

       b.   What does the Lord do for Jerusalem and the exiles of Israel?

       c.   What is the limit of the Lord's understanding?

       d.   Who supplies the earth with rain and makes the grass grow on the hills?

       e.   In what does the Lord delight?

       f.   What five reasons does the Psalmist give that the people should extol the Lord and praise their God?

       g.   What did the Lord do for Israel that he did not do for any other nation?

4.   Proverbs 31:1-7
       a.   From where did these sayings come?

       b.   On what did the mother tell her son not to spend his strength?

1.   Zechariah 14:1-21

      a.   What was going to happen to Jerusalem when God gathers the nations?

      b.   After that what was God going to do to those same nations?

      c.   Where will God's feet stand on that day?

      d.   What will happen to the mountain where he is standing?

      e.   Where were the people to flee?

      f.   Who will come at that time?

      g.   What is said about light, cold, frost, daytime, and nighttime?

      h.   What would flow from Jerusalem and where would it flow? In what seasons would it flow?

      i.   Who will be king over the whole earth?

      j.   When the whole land becomes like Arabah, what will happen to Jerusalem?

      k.   What will happen to the flesh, eyes and the tongues of the ones that fought against Jerusalem?

      l.   By what will the men be stricken on that day?

      m.   What will happen to the wealth of all the surrounding nations?

      n.   What will happen to the horses, mules, camels, and donkeys?

      o.   What will the survivors from all the nations that have attacked Jerusalem do year after year?

      p.   On that day, what will be inscribed on the bells of the horses and cooking pots in the Lord's house?

2.   Revelation 20:20:1-15

      a.   Where did the John see the angel? What did the angel have?

      b.   What did the angel do with the dragon? How long was he bound?

      c.   Why was he bound for this amount of time? What is to happen to him after that period of time?

      d.   Who were seated on the thrones that John saw?

      e.   Who did John see? What happened to them?

      f.   Who are the blessed and holy? What has no power over them?

      g.   What happened to the ones that marched across the earth and surrounded the camp of God's people?

      h.   What happens at the great white throne?

      i.   What happened if anyone's name was not found written in the book of life?

3.   Psalms 148:1-14
      a.   How does this Psalm start and end?

      b.   From what two places does the Psalmist say that one should praise the Lord?

      c.   In verses two through five, what seven things should praise the Lord?

      d.   Who set the heavens in place?

      e.   What things from the earth were to praise the Lord?

      f.   Why should they praise the Lord?

      g.   Whose splendor is above the earth and the heavens?

4.   Proverbs 31:8-9
      a.   For whom should one speak up?

STUDY QUESTIONS FOR DECEMBER 30

1.   Malachi 1:1-2:17
      a.   Who delivered this oracle of God?

      b.   What did God say about his relationship with Israel?

      c.   What does the Lord say about Jacob and Esau?

      d.   What did the Lord say that he would do even if Edom rebuilt?

      e.   What would the people say when they saw it with their own eyes?

      f.   What did God answer when the people asked, "How have we shown contempt for
            your name?" How about when they asked, "H ow have we defiled you?"

      g.   When the people were bringing crippled animals and animals with diseases to be
            sacrificed, what did God suggest that they do to the governor?

      h.   Was God pleased with the people? What did God say he would do about their
            sacrifices?

      i.   Where would God's name be great?

      j.   Who is cursed?

      k.   What did the Lord say about his name among the nations?

      l.   What admonition was for the priests?

      m.   Who was the Lord going to rebuke because of the priests?

      n.   Who was the Lord talking about when he said, "My covenant was with him, a
            covenant of life and peace, and I gave them to him;"

      o.   In chapter two, verse sixteen, what two things does the Lord God of Israel hate?

      p.   How had the people wearied the Lord?

2.   Revelations 21:1-27
      a.   What did John see?

      b.   What happened to the first heaven and the first earth?

      c.   What did John say about the Holy City?

d.   What was God going to do about the tears of his people? What about death and mourning?

e.   What happens to the cowardly, unbelieving, the vile, the murderers, the sexually immoral, those who practice magic arts, the idolaters and all liars?

f.   How was the great street of the city paved? Why did the city not have a moon or sun?

3.   Psalms 149:1-9
      a.   How does this Psalm start and end?

      b.   What were the people to sing to the Lord?

      c.   In what was Israel to rejoice?

      d.   How were God's people to praise him?

      e.   Why were they to praise God?

      f.   In what were the saints to rejoice?

      g.   What was the glory of all God's saints?

4.   Proverbs 31:10-24
      a.   What is the worth of a wife with noble character?

      b.   What does this type of wife bring her husband?

      c.   What does she do for her family?

      d.   What does she do about a field?

      e.   What does she do for the poor and the needy?

      f.   What does she do with linen garments?

STUDY QUESTIONS FOR DECEMBER 31

1.   Malachi 3:1 - 4:6
     a.   Who was God going to send? What was this person going to do?

     b.   Who will come suddenly to his temple?

     c.   To what is this person likened?

     d.   What will he do to the Levites?

     e.   How will the Lord's men bring offerings?

     f.   Will the offerings of Judah and Jerusalem be acceptable?

     g.   Why was the Lord going to come near the people? Who would he be quick to testify against?

     h.   What will happen if Judah returns to the Lord? How did men rob God?

     i.   How much of the tithe were they to bring into the storehouse?

     j.   In what does God ask men to test him?

     k.   What does God promise those that tithe in chapter three verse ten?

     l.   What were the people saying about God in chapter three verse fourteen?

     m.   What kind of remembrance was made of those who feared the Lord and honored his name?

     n.   Who would be the Lord's when he makes up his treasured possessions? What distinction would the people see?

     o.   In chapter four verse one, how is the day described that is coming?

     p.   What promise is given to the ones that revere the name of the Lord?

     q.   What will the prophet Eelijah do for the hearts of the fathers and the hearts of the children?

2.   Revelation 22:1-21
     a.   What did the angel show John in verse one?

     b.   Where did the river flow?

c. What stood on each side of the river?

d. What were the leaves of the tree for?

e. What is said about the one that keeps the words of the prophecy of this book?

f. Who saw and heard these things?

g. Who did John fall down and worship? What did the angel say?

h. What was he to do about the sealing up the words of the prophecy of this book?

i. What is told to John in verses twelve and thirteen?

j. Who sent the angel to give John the testimony for the churches?

k. What will happen to the one that adds to or takes away from the prophecy of this book?

3. Psalms 150:1-6
   a. Who is to be praised?

   b. Where is God to be praised?

   c. What were five ways that the Lord was to be praised?

4. Proverbs 31:25-31
   a. To whom are these scriptures referring?

   b. With what does she speak?

   c. What do the children of this woman do? What does her husband do?

   d. What kind of a woman is praised?

Answers can be downloaded at harrishousepublishing.com/melvin.

www.ingramcontent.com/pod-product-compliance
Lightning Source LLC
La Vergne TN
LVHW081332060426
835513LV00014B/1255